SAGE was founded in 1965 by Sara Miller McCune to support the dissemination of usable knowledge by publishing innovative and high-quality research and teaching content. Today, we publish over 900 journals, including those of more than 400 learned societies, more than 800 new books per year, and a growing range of library products including archives, data, case studies, reports, and video. SAGE remains majority-owned by our founder, and after Sara's lifetime will become owned by a charitable trust that secures our continued independence.

Los Angeles | London | New Delhi | Singapore | Washington DC | Melbourne

RETHINKING
PLURALISM, SECULARISM
AND TOLERANCE

RETHINKING PLURALISM, SECULARISM AND TOLERANCE

Anxieties of Coexistence

NEERA CHANDHOKE

Los Angeles | London | New Delhi
Singapore | Washington DC | Melbourne

First published in 2019 by

SAGE Publications India Pvt Ltd
B1/I-1 Mohan Cooperative Industrial Area
Mathura Road, New Delhi 110 044, India
www.sagepub.in

SAGE Publications Inc
2455 Teller Road
Thousand Oaks, California 91320, USA

SAGE Publications Ltd
1 Oliver's Yard, 55 City Road
London EC1Y 1SP, United Kingdom

SAGE Publications Asia-Pacific Pte Ltd
18 Cross Street #10-10/11/12
China Square Central
Singapore 048423

Published by Vivek Mehra for SAGE Publications India Pvt Ltd, typeset in 10.5/13 pts Adobe Caslon Pro by Zaza Eunice, Hosur, Tamil Nadu, India.

Library of Congress Cataloging-in-Publication Data

Name: Chandhoke, Neera, author.
Title: Rethinking pluralism, secularism and tolerance: anxieties of
  coexistence/by Neera Chandhoke.
Description: Thousand Oaks: SAGE Publications India Pvt Ltd, [2019] |
  Includes bibliographical references and index.
Identifiers: LCCN 2018043680 | ISBN 9789353281984 (print (hb)) | ISBN
  9789353281991 (e-pub) | ISBN 9789353282004 (e-book)
Subjects: LCSH: Minorities—Civil rights—India. | Secularism—India. |
  Religion and state—India. | Religion and politics—India. | Religious
  pluralism—India. | India—Ethnic relations.
Classification: LCC JQ220.M5 C53 2019 | DDC 323.154—dc23 LC record available at https://lccn.
loc.gov/2018043680

ISBN: 978-93-532-8198-4 (HB)

SAGE Team: Rajesh Dey, Alekha Chandra Jena and Ritu Chopra

For I have neither wit, nor words, nor worth,

Action, nor utterance, nor the power of speech,

To stir men's blood. I only speak right on.

I tell you that which you yourselves do know.

—Mark Anthony in William Shakespeare,
Julius Caesar Act III, scene II

Thank you for choosing a SAGE product!
If you have any comment, observation or feedback,
I would like to personally hear from you.

Please write to me at **contactceo@sagepub.in**

Vivek Mehra, Managing Director and CEO, SAGE India.

Bulk Sales

SAGE India offers special discounts
for purchase of books in bulk.
We also make available special imprints
and excerpts from our books on demand.

For orders and enquiries, write to us at

Marketing Department
SAGE Publications India Pvt Ltd
B1/I-1, Mohan Cooperative Industrial Area
Mathura Road, Post Bag 7
New Delhi 110044, India

E-mail us at **marketing@sagepub.in**

Subscribe to our mailing list
Write to **marketing@sagepub.in**

This book is also available as an e-book.

Contents

Foreword

This is a timely study undertaken, in the author's words 'in an environment of deep desolation at insistent and deliberate violations of secularism, tolerance and democracy'. It sets out to clarify and reconceptualise the idea of secularism.

Professor Neera Chandhoke has written a good deal on the principles and values that influence the civic and political discourse in contemporary Indian society. She is a powerful advocate of civil society initiatives and draws upon a life-long experience of academic and public debates on terms that have been used and abused in these discussions. Above all, her perceptions are backed up by some diligent field work in situations that tested them in practice.

The four ideas that form the core of the book—*Pluralism, Secularism, Tolerance* and *Coexistence*—need to be examined to determine their nature ontologically and to ascertain whether they represent *a fact* (true or false) or *an idea* or *a value* (desirable or otherwise). Such a framework propels us to regard the first as an existential reality emanating from acknowledged diversity and heterogeneity of our society, the second as a desirable and unavoidable value, the third a drifting condition on a receding horizon that can be both a reality and a value, and the fourth as expressive of the tensions that the process generates.

These concepts are not mere abstractions and need to be posited in space and time. In an earlier essay, Chandhoke had argued that the debate should be shifted from secularism per se to the antecedent moral principles from which secularism derives its specific meaning; she accordingly asserted that it has to be relocated in its constitutive context of equality, democracy, rights and freedom.

The historical context lends relevance to it. On the morrow of Independence, it was perceived that the greatest danger to unity and integration emanating from 'casteism', 'communalism', 'linguism' and 'regionalism' and these were, as Granville Austin put it, frequently compounded and named 'communalism', and thus 'secularism' became its antidote.

Chandhoke takes a wider view and initiates her quest with the purpose for which the State exists as an institution of society. Justice is the first virtue of social institutions and all citizens therefore have to be treated equally, protected equally and ensured freedom from discrimination. This necessitates civility and harmony, leading to fraternity. Thus, pluralism in practice in a religiously diverse society like ours compels its acceptance as a normative virtue and propels it in the direction of non-discriminatory practices premised on calibrated equidistance to ensure equality and freedom of religion. Such an approach necessitates not merely tolerance and avoidance of bigotry but conscious cultivation of acceptance as a civic virtue.

The author has rightly concluded that secularism is not a stand-alone concept and is intrinsically linked to democracy since a secular deficit in a plural society results in denial of the democratic right to equality and equal share in its benefits. It would also help reverse the trend indicated in the 2017 Global Democracy Index.

New Delhi

M. Hamid Ansari
Former Vice President of India

Preface

This is, perhaps, not the best moment to resurrect a defence of secularism. Since 2014, India has an extreme right-wing party in power at the centre—the Bharatiya Janata Party (BJP). The party's ideological backbone, the Rashtriya Swayamsevak Sangh (RSS), and other assorted fringe outfits belonging to the larger Hindutva brigade have been granted an opportunity to carry out their a little less than a century-old project of creating and sustaining a nation exclusively of and for the Hindu community, almost by divine right. Although the geographical boundaries of India contain a multiplicity of belief systems, and the Hindu community is decentred and plural in nature, the cadres of the extreme right concentrate on drumming up old bigotries and unearthing ancient antipathies to unify an otherwise plural and decentred Hindu community, and pit it once again against the Muslim community.

Their rhetoric that focuses on primeval hostilities, forces memories of the oppression of Mughal rule, and of the way the Mughal rulers destroyed temples, may be largely executed for electoral gains. But it has permeated everyday lives of people in the workplace and in residential areas. We see with fear and trepidation the making of another partition—this time of minds and hearts. We witness with anxiety the growing rift in solidarity and sympathy between our fellow citizens. In the process, one of the norms that has been quickly abandoned is that of secularism. Or perhaps the abandonment of secularism has opened the gates to communal rhetoric and hate-filled actions.

In any case, the ascent to power of a cadre that flourishes the trident like a deadly weapon, is militant to a fault and has legitimised the verbal and physical bashing of our own people merely because they are born into a Muslim household is cause for dismay and intense anxiety among democrats. The number of provocative incidents such as lynchings, hate speech, threats and coercion has mounted alarmingly.

What happened to the grand Nehruvian dream of unity in diversity, the value of a plural society, the necessity for minority rights and the dire need for secularism and tolerance? What on earth has happened to the determination of the leaders of the freedom struggle that the State will not be aligned to any religion, let alone the majority religion? Their vision of a multi-religious India, where no one would be discriminated against and no one would be advantaged merely because he/she was born into 'this' or 'that' religious community, lies in tatters. It is in the environment of deep desolation at insistent and deliberate violations of secularism, tolerance and democracy that I attempt to clarify, reconceptualise and defend secularism. I do so by suggesting that the principle is an integral part of the democratic imaginary. To infringe the basics of secularism is to infringe the fundamentals of democracy.

Admittedly, it may not be the best of times to defend both the norm and its attendant principle of tolerance. Tolerance has disappeared from the political scene as lynch mobs, self-appointed censors, repression of dissent, vigilantism and murderous crowds try to hammer a plural nation into conformity with slogans of one language, one religion, one people and one cuisine. The language of secularism has practically vanished from the political horizon of Indian politics. Whatever remains of secularism is subjected to contemptuous remarks, some ribaldry and offensive dismissal by cadres and supporters of the religious right. The concept is, in their depressingly vulgar and crude language, no longer 'pseudo-secularism', but 'sickluralism'. The verbal distortion of the term is simply not amusing, nor is it particularly interesting. The abuse of secularism is a symptom of constricted political imaginations and a deplorable lack of vision of how a plural society can be held together. The dismissal of both norms has led to the closing of the Indian mind and truncated creativities. The rot runs deep.

On second thoughts, it is precisely in these troubled times that the virtue of the norm of secularism needs to be rediscovered, reworked and reiterated. This is what the argument in this work tries to do. The wider objective of the book is to explore how people who belong to different religious persuasions can live together with a certain degree of civility. Civility demands more than the institutionalisation of democracy and the abstract notions of rights and equality. It necessitates an attitude of respect towards each other. The project also calls for a State policy that treats all religious communities equally and discriminates against none. This is in consonance with democracy. Above all, it stresses the need to respect differences and rights of minorities. This is in consonance with equality. After all, people should be able to choose which religion they wish to follow, which language they wish to speak, which way of life they wish to adopt, who they want to love and marry, how their children should be brought up and what they intend to eat, read, watch and listen to. This is the least democracy promises us. People have the right to be who they are. They have a right to choose what they want to be in a democratic society.

Democracy needs to be buttressed. We need the State to champion secular policies and civil society to defend tolerance. The argument explores the relevance of secularism and its conceptual twin tolerance for our plural society. I make no apology for focusing on the obligations that the majority community holds towards vulnerable sections of our own people, not only towards the Muslim community but also towards the Christian community. This work dwells more on the former than the latter, but the argument applies to the Christian community as well, a community that has been subjected to the most unspeakable crimes that humanity has known. The Hindu credo, however, has been built around the imagined or even the real oppression of the Muslim rulers in the past for more than a hundred years. Therefore, the focus of the work is on the injustice done to our minorities.

Well-meaning critics allege that both the theory and practice of secularism are unsuited for India, because the concept that distinguishes between the secular and the sacred was born in the specific historical experience of Western Europe. They forget that concepts in different historical circumstances shape up differently. In India, secularism was adopted as one of the basic principles of a democratic polity in the early 20th century by leaders of the freedom struggle, precisely because society had been wracked by communal riots. It might have been a Western import, but, like other Western imports, secularism has acquired meanings that are the specific outcome of political and social life in India. As Rajeev Bhargava[1] in a different but related argument has shown, Indian secularism is distinctive.

[1] Bhargava, 'The Distinctiveness of Indian Secularism', 99–120.

In the fifth chapter, I suggest that the concept of secularism was adopted in India in very different circumstances. Notably, the leadership of the freedom movement adopted secularism not despite, but because religion had been irremediably catapulted into the public sphere as identity, nationalism and a nation-making project. This was politically significant because the trail of ugly communal riots between the Hindus and the Muslims at the turn of the 20th century had wrecked the carefully maintained balance between different religious communities in the country.

I have, in this work, drawn upon the findings of two field-based research projects that I and my team at the University of Delhi had conducted some years ago. The first project on Ahmedabad formed part of the larger comparative programme on 'Conflict and Institutional Change' directed by James Putzel of the London School of Economics and Political Science. My thanks to Praveen Priyadarshi, Neha Khanna and Silky Tyagi for some great research help. The second project on Malerkotla formed part of a wider project on 'Dialogue on Democracy and Pluralism in South Asia' directed by Niraja Gopal Jayal of the Centre for the Study of Law and Governance at Jawaharlal Nehru University, New Delhi. I express my gratitude to Ravi Ranjan who proved a formidable one-man research team.

In the first chapter, I introduce the complexities of pluralism and clarify the meaning of the concept of secularism. The argument in the second chapter details the background against which secularism acquires relevance and some urgency for India. I focus on communalism which forms the backdrop of secularism. The third chapter explores the European debate on secularism. The fourth chapter delves into history to discover how and why religious identities were politicised and polarised in times of colonialism. The fifth chapter, as suggested above, tracks the historical development of secularism in India. The sixth chapter elaborates the theme of minority rights. The seventh chapter discusses tolerance in the context of Supreme Court judgements that equate secularism and tolerance. The eighth chapter wraps up the argument.

The Indian Council of Social Science Research (ICSSR) granted me some funds for research on this theme. I wish to express my gratitude to Professor Sukhadeo Thorat, the previous chairman of the ICSSR, for the research grant. My profound thanks to Dr Sridharan, the director of the University of Pennsylvania Institute for the Advanced Studies of India (UPIASI). He readily accepted my request to locate the project in the centre. The staff members of UPIASI were extremely helpful in administering the project, particularly since the funding proved partial. Thanks to Charusheel Tripathi for help in the research.

I express my gratitude also to Partho Dutta for guiding me through the intellectual thicket of the Bengal Renaissance. Writing this chapter was very enjoyable, even though Aakash Rathore warned me about the hazards of writing hotly contested intellectual history. I spoke on the theme of 'Revisiting Secularism' at conferences organised by the Centre for the Study of Law and Governance, Jawaharlal Nehru University, at the conference organised by G. Ajay at the Centre for Political Studies, Jawaharlal Nehru University, at a conference organised by Nandini Deo, University of Lehigh, Pennsylvania, at a conference on post-coloniality convened by Gurminder Bhambhra of the University of Sussex in a charming manor in Sweden, at the Presidency University in Kolkata, at a meeting at National Academy of Legal Studies and Research in Hyderabad, a memorial lecture at the University of Pune organised by Mangesh Kulkarni and at other meetings. My thanks to the participants of these seminars for their valuable feedback.

Thanks as always to Rama, Manju and Renu for their friendship and solidarity, and consistently warm and enjoyable company. My gratitude to Niraja G. Jayal. I am privileged to enjoy her confidence and friendship over the years. This book is for the four of my closest friends. Thanks to Karan for his sustained support and encouragement. My gratitude to Omita Goel and Sunanda Ghosh for their help in getting this manuscript to SAGE and for enthusing me to complete the project. I am delighted that SAGE is publishing this work; it is homecoming for me, because my first book on civil society was brought out by this prestigious publishing house. Thanks to Manisha Matthews and Rajesh Dey at SAGE for their help and guidance.

My thanks as ever to the smiling young men and women who run the library of the India International Centre in New Delhi. A special word of thanks to Kanchan Nagpal. She helped me to access, otherwise inaccessible, material online. And I managed to develop the art of reading online, though I must confess that I would rather read a book that I can hold lovingly in my hands and cherish. My heartfelt gratitude to my two children and their children, little Abir and littler Ivaan. They make life worth living.

CHAPTER 1

Pluralism and Secularism

What then are we to do? What shall we aim at and what road should we travel by? It is of the foremost importance that we should not lose ourselves in the passion and prejudice of the moment.... Greatness comes from vision, the tolerance of the spirit, compassion and an even temper which is not ruffled by ill fortune or good fortune.[1]

'How can we', asked the Buddhist philosopher Jayant Bhatt (CE 800–950) in his *Nyayamanjari*, discover a new fact or truth in philosophy? One should consider only our novelty in rephrasing the older truths expounded by the ancients in modern terminology.[2] Let us try to rephrase this invaluable suggestion in the following way. The questions that political theorists ask of the human condition are eternal. The answers to these questions—what makes for a good society, what is justice, what is the nature of and the limits on a State, and what is distinctive about the human condition—fetch answers that are necessarily bound by reasons of time and space. Even as they address political predicaments, political theorists build on older truths to generate new answers suitable for their age. In the process, they

---

[1] Nehru, 'The Tolerance of the Spirit', 323–324.
[2] Opening citation in Bimal Krishna Matilal, *Epistemology, Logic, and Grammar*.

rearticulate ancient truths for every era in vocabularies, which makes sense for that age.

In recent years, the vocation of political theory in India has turned significantly to the past and to ancient texts to recover a tradition that is distinctively Indian. They have taken on a formidable task, because, unlike Buddhism and Jainism, Brahmanical and metaphysical texts are more concerned with substantive conceptions of the good, or how individuals can lead a good life, than what we consider to be specifically political. In the Western tradition, the academic division of labour is fairly clear. Philosophers debate on the good life, and political philosophers tell them and the world that a good life can only be led in a good society. The ancient Greek philosopher Aristotle's *zoon politikon* or political man spent his life reflecting and deliberating on building a political community in which the male, propertied, Athenian-born citizen could realise his basic nature. That is, political philosophy was an essential precondition for an individual to live a good life.

Part of the problem in reading historical texts in India is that the distinction between the religious and the secular (in the sense of non-religious) philosophical aspects of texts was blurred by the colonial intervention in the late 18th century. The philosopher Sharad Deshpande suggests that the Orientalist bias against non-Western forms of knowledge and rationality resulted in the neglect of vibrant traditions of philosophical reflections in diverse fields of human experience that existed in India. More significantly, Deshpande argues that philosophical engagements against the *Naiyayikas* and the *Vedantins* or among the *Mimansakas* was seen as part of the Hindu religious discourse. The view that philosophy in India was embedded in the religious discourse found its legitimacy in Max Muller's view that philosophy and religion in the country are inseparable.[3]

Yet, it is possible to discern the origins of a theory of the powers of and the duties of the monarch in ancient Indian texts. A number of texts put forth a concept of a social contract among people. This

[3] Deshpande, 'Introduction', 6–7.

established the institution of kingship and elaborated the limits on kingly power. Take the text the *Santi Parva*, the 12th book of the epic Mahabharata. After the Great War, the patriarch Bhishma tutors Yudhishthira, the new monarch of Hastinapur, on the responsibilities of the ruler. Yudhishthira convulsed with grief at the massive loss of lives, including that of his brother Karna, his sons and his nephews during the war, agonises whether it is worthwhile to take up the reins of kingship. What he wonders is the point of power: if the path to this goal is drenched with the blood of his own people? 'Indeed', he ruminates, 'The whole Earth has been subjugated by me…. This heavy grief, however, is always sitting in my heart, viz., that through covetousness I have caused this dreadful carnage of kinsmen'.[4]

He is advised to seek the advice of the patriarch of the clan, Bhishma, a skilled exponent and an even more accomplished practitioner of the art of statesmanship, who since the Great War has been lying on a bed of vertically planted arrows, waiting for an appropriate time to order his own death. Yudhishthira approaching the great hero and his paternal great-uncle with some trepidation utters, 'Persons conversant with duty and morality say that kingly duties constitute the highest science of duties…. Do thou, therefore, O king, discourse on those duties'.[5] Bhishma's discourse on the duties of the righteous ruler, or on *Rajdharma*, is known as the *Santi Parva*, a text that belongs to the genre of the tutelage literature. His discourse on statesmanship wends a leisurely path through advice on statecraft, and knowledge of geography, metaphysics, the cosmos, mythology, genealogy, history, and Sankhya and Yoga philosophies, to finally arrive at the question of what the ruler owes his people.

In section LIX of the *Santi Parva*, Yudhishthira asks Bhishma about the origins of kingship and the symbol of power 'the *danda*' or the sceptre. The answer to this question is familiar to all students of political theory—the deterioration of the original habitat of human beings that is the state of nature and their willingness to sign the metaphorical social contract that rescues them from a state of profound

---

[4] *The Mahabharata of Krishna-Dwaipayana Vyasa*, 1–2.
[5] Ibid., Section LVI, 113.

instability. The vocabulary and the imaginary of the theory in the Indian text are, however, different from that of Western political thought. The origins of sovereignty, according to Bhishma, begin with the degeneration of human beings and their inability and unwillingness to abide by the laws of *dharma*. 'At first there was no sovereignty, no king, no chastisement, and no chastiser. All men used to protect each other righteously'. But after some time, they began to find this task impossible because their perceptions were clouded by lust, driven by avarice and motivated by covetousness. The natural consequence of the decline of civility was the loss of virtue:

> And because men sought to obtain objects, which they did not possess, another passion called lust (of acquisition) got hold of them. When they became subject to lust, another passion, named anger, soon soiled them. Once subject to wrath, they lost all consideration of what should be done and what should not.... Righteousness was, in the process, lost.[6]

The pre-political state of nature was not asocial, what it lacked was a ruler who could mediate and arbitrate conflict situations according to righteous laws.

In another space, and at a time much later in history (the 17th century), the English theorist John Locke was to similarly speak of the need for a State that could interpret and implement the law of nature. The *Santi Parva* not only anticipated John Locke but also his predecessor Thomas Hobbes in the 16th century. Beset by greed, men in the pre-political State began to devour each other, a classic case of the big fish devouring small fishes—the theory of *matsyanyaya*. Overcome by fear, and wracked by uncertainty, a few inhabitants of the state of nature assembled and, via divine intervention, made certain compacts to regulate relationships with each other. Very soon they realised that without a king who wielded the symbol of sovereignty and chastisement, the sceptre, they would be destroyed. For Covenants without swords, as Hobbes was to write later, are mere words.

---

[6] Ibid., 122.

The gods, says Bhishma to Yudhishthira in his discourse on the righteous rule, created the institution of kingship for one main objective: the protection of the people. 'If there were no king on earth for wielding the rod of chastisement, the strong would then have preyed on the weak after the manner of fishes in the water'.[7] In return, our inhabitants of the pre-political State committed to give the ruler a 50th part of their animals and precious metals, and a 10th part of their grain, promised to offer him beautiful maidens who had reached the age of marriage, and also render to him a procession of accomplished men skilled in the use of weapons.[8] This commitment holds as long as the ruler, Bhishma tells Yudhishthira, rules in accordance with *dharma*.

At first glance, the concept of *dharma* is not very helpful, because *dharma*, which can best be understood as righteous conduct, applies as much to the individual as it does to society, and as much to inter-social relations as to the foundations of law and governance. In the Mahabharata, suggests Chaturvedi Badrinath who has translated and interpreted the epic, concepts are not defined, because definitions are by their nature arbitrary. A concept is elaborated, understood and manifested in terms of its attributes or *lakshanas*.[9] If we extrapolate from the generic concept of *dharma*, the attributes of kingly *dharma* are as follows.

The first property of *Rajdharma*, *prabhavaya*, is that of nurturing, cherishing, providing more amply, endowing more richly, prospering, increasing and enhancing—in short, providing for the well-being and flourishing of the subjects. The second property of *Rajdharma* is *dhaarna*, or holding together, supporting, sustaining and bringing together all human beings. This particular aspect of *Rajdharma* emanates from the philosophy of non-dualism or *Advaita*. According to this branch of Indian philosophy, human beings are neither separate from the divine nor from each other.

The other is a part of me as much as I am a part of her. It follows that if I hurt someone, I hurt myself, and I violate my own integrity.

---

[7] Ibid., Section LXVII, 146.
[8] Ibid., 146.
[9] Badrinath, *The Mahabharata*, 418.

In contrast to individualism, the Indian political philosophy tradition endorses a social and relational concept of the self. Not only is the construction of divisions between human beings, or the forging of notions of 'us' and 'them' highly arbitrary, but also it is completely unnecessary. In order to complete ourselves as human beings, we have to recognise our connectedness with each other. This *Rajdharma* must be ensured. In political terms, the concept of *dhaarna* implies that a righteous king cannot sunder non-dualism by making artificial divisions between those who belong to it and those who do not.

The third property of *Rajdharma* is that of non-violence or ahimsa.[10] The monarch has to protect the people from violence. In Indian philosophy, the notion of violence is closely connected to ignorance about our own nature, and of our relationship to others and to the world. Enlightenment dissipates violence and enables us to choose between our propensity to violence and non-violence. Non-violence, therefore, cannot be seen as cowardice. When they choose non-violence over violence, human beings make ethical choices. In the aftermath of the Great War that caused suffering on an unprecedented scale, the *Santi Parva* places great importance on non-violence as the highest *dharma* and as the highest truth.

These three injunctions of *Rajdharma* are part of a larger mission of the ruler. The king has to protect all creatures, even if he is personally inclined to dislike them. Simply put, his rule has to be impartial. He is not expected to make any distinction whatsoever between his subjects. He protects them from external impediments such as threats of violence, but he also provides the preconditions of material flourishing:

> As the mother, disregarding those objects that are most cherished by her, seeks the good of her child alone, even so, without doubt, should kings conduct themselves (towards their subjects). The king that is righteous … should always behave in such a manner as to avoid what is dear to him, for the sake of doing that which would benefit his people.[11]

[10] Ibid., 419–20.
[11] *The Mahabharata of Krishna-Dwaipayana Vyasa*, Section LVI, 116.

More significantly, if the purpose of the State is to protect the small fish from the big fish, the ruler must certainly not turn into a big fish that devours everything in sight. On the contrary, power is meant to protect the weak. The king who follows the path of *dharma* is the creator, whereas a sinful king is the destroyer. The ruler should beware of exploiting the weak, for the eyes of the latter can scorch the earth:

> In a race scorched by the eyes of the weak, no children take birth. Such eyes burn the race to its very roots.... Weakness is more powerful than even the greatest Power, for that Power which is scorched by Weakness becomes totally exterminated. If a person, who has been humiliated or struck, fails, while shrieking for assistance, to obtain a protector, divine chastisement overtakes the king and brings about his destruction. ... the divine rod of chastisement falls upon the king. If it practices injustice, a great destruction comes upon the state.[12]

The responsibility of the ruler towards his subjects is clear: he has to be neutral towards all communities. It is only then that he can establish justice. The proposition that every ruler must follow certain limits on power, and that obligations to subjects pose one of the most powerful constraints on the exercise of power, has come down to us as a part of sage political wisdom, relevant for all days and ages.

Recasting the Question of Living Together

The belief that the State has to protect the interests of all citizens and discriminate against none on morally arbitrary ground, such as birth into a community, lies at the centre of theories that try to negotiate the problems of plural societies. Most, if not all societies, are far more diverse and differentiated today than they were in ancient and perhaps in hypothetical time. The difference is that now citizens in a democracy can claim non-discrimination or its stronger version, equality, from the State as a matter of right. Older wisdom on the limits of the State is thereby addressed, renegotiated and embodied

[12] Ibid., Section XCI, 199–200.

in new meaning systems. In other words, the question 'What is it that the ruler does when he rules?' fetches a different answer in a different time. The rights of citizens place limits on the power of the monarch.

It is, however, also true that every age throws up new questions that are relevant for a society. One of the most intractable problems that stalks India since the beginning of the 20th century is how people who belong to different religious persuasions, worship different gods in their own way and subscribe to comprehensive conceptions of the good can live together in considerable civility if not harmony. We have still not found an answer to this question. Our society continues to be rocked by incredible brutality towards the so-called lower castes, the minority Muslim community, women, sexual minorities and dissenters.

In any case, it is not easy to formulate an answer to the question of how people can live together in some degree of civility for a rather significant reason. The proposition that a complex society like India contains within its spatial and symbolic boundaries, different cultural communities and is by that fact plural is, by now, a part of everyday understanding. That society would not be plural otherwise. Enthusiastic advocates of pluralism should, however, pay attention to the intricacies of the concept.

For one, the disparity between beliefs in such a society may be negotiable. Consider the difference between meat eaters and vegetarians or that between teetotallers and those who believe that a bucolic existence is preferable to a life without alcohol. We call these differences 'thin' not because they do not matter for their adherents, but because, given the right conditions and some formidable capacity for persuasive argument, people can, perhaps, be led to change their attitudes. A meat eater can, possibly, be coaxed that not eating meat is just a reliable route to a healthy life. An alcoholic can be told of the dangers that a bucolic existence hold, for example, liver disease and diminished responsibility. The common adjudicator in this instance is health. We may, therefore, discover some meeting ground in the foreseeable future, given the right conditions, and some ready capacity for persuasion. It is, of course, possible that the wheel may turn, and the persuader might be converted to meat eating and to alcohol. But let us leave this contingency for discussion at another time and place.

Some societies, India is a good example of such a society, are marked by 'deep' differences between world views. For example, religion provides a comprehensive worldview to its followers, ranging from rituals, ceremonies to the routines of quotidian existence. Axiomatically, different world views are bound to be diverse, reflecting the philosophical foundations of the religion, its objectives and specifications of the route that leads to the divine. It is this deep plurality that has come to obsess and perplex political theorists across the world. Two, the proposition that a society is plural insofar as its members worship different gods, hold different conceptions of what the good life is and/or speak different languages is an empirical proposition. It is a description of how things are and not how things should be in a society. There is absolutely nothing in this descriptive proposition that allows us to move on automatically or smoothly to the normative proposition that each of these conceptions of the good is of worth, that they deserve respect or indeed that pluralism is of value.

Take the possibility that religious groups, even if they are tied to members of other groups by economic bonds, may keep to themselves and regard others as the unknown and perhaps the unknowable. We, the members of X group, can believe, have our own reasons for doing things that we want to, and the members of the Y group have their own reasons for doing things that they want to. These reasons, they can believe, have to do with their internal self-understandings, their shared language, traditions and histories. These internal understandings can neither be comprehended nor appreciated by people who have not been born into a religion, moulded by the values of that religion and by discrete narratives of belonging. That is members belonging to a distinct religious community can view other groups in different ways, and none of these may be of any significance for social life. We accept other groups but assume that our lives are not touched by them in any way.

The second choice is that we do not accept others but still do not do anything about our attitudes that range from passive tolerance to inert dislike. The third option is that we accept the presence of different religious groups as legitimate. Members of each group by virtue of being citizens of this country, we can believe, have the right to their own beliefs within the ambit of the law. And the fourth choice is that citizens fervently believe that all of us, despite our deep differences, can try to move together towards a shimmering horizon of a life lived in civility, based on solidarity and mutual respect.

The first two sorts of attitudes inhibit the creation of a shared conversation which can bring people together across boundaries. Axiomatically, these attitudes pre-empt the making of a political community, which has some potential for deliberating and discussing what a good society is and how it can be brought into being. They constrain the development of sentiments of civility, harmony and amity. The third attitude to pluralism is frankly passive. It is only the fourth attitude that can help us move along the path of history by living together civilly. But to take this route, we have to transit from empirical to normative pluralism.

Moments of Transition

Why should we make the transition? There are, arguably three, and possibly more reasons why reflective Indian citizens should begin to ask the following basic question: why should different communities of belief, or religious communities, value pluralism? The first reason is instrumental. In our country, citizens who have not broken any law or injured anyone can be, and have been, subjected to great indignity and violence, ranging from verbal and online abuse and coercion, to public lynching. They are condemned to die painfully, often on the road, and often on the sidewalk, because their community of birth has been stigmatised and typed as the 'inferior', as the 'enemy' or as the 'other' with whom there can be neither truck nor transaction.

Every fundamental right guaranteed by the Constitution of India proves incapable of protecting citizens from harm, if the group of which they are a member has been subjected to perverse stereotyping and labelled as 'threatening' or as the 'polluted'. Unless a society learns to value and respect different ways of life and different religions, members of vulnerable communities will be, always, subjected to hate speech and acts that maim and diminish dignity. The right of a group to respect, and its right to exist with dignity and with the assurance that its practices and its beliefs are protected from aggression, is an essential prerequisite for individual rights. This is what our history tells us. Unless we learn to respect the right of vulnerable religious minorities, our fellow citizens are at risk. In the history of the world, we must remember that genocide has accompanied the typing of a community in vicious ways. Can a civilisation as great as India afford to be silent in the face of discrimination on the ground of religion? Can a democratic India afford the indulgence of not thinking what the preconditions of fundamental rights to life, liberty, equality and justice are?

The second reason for moving from empirical to normative pluralism is based on the presumption that individuals are social beings. They realise their nature through membership of different associations in civil society. These associations can range from bird watching clubs, to book reading groups, to literary societies, to theatre-going groups, to cricket clubs, to civil liberties unions that keep watch on acts of omission and commission of the government and to film fan clubs. Yet, undeniably, we are intimately attached to the community we are born into. We sometimes have little control over affiliations that seem to have penetrated our genes.

Let me insert a caveat at precisely this point of the argument. Some people identify strongly with their community, others identify weakly, and still others move on and adopt the meaning systems of another community. But most of the time, most of us, are intimately attached to the community of birth. For it is from here that we learn the first alphabet of a language that teaches us how to live with people who are like us and those who are not like us. The alphabet of this language simply allows us to make sense of ourselves, our worlds and of our relationships with others. That is why political theorists describe the community of birth as a constitutive community. The knowledge systems of a constitutive community affect our understanding of what it means to be human, and how we can coexist in a society with amity. It follows that an individual should be ensured secure access to his/her community. Neither the State nor society should harm my community, because by harming my constitutive community through perverse imaging and acts of violence, you harm me—a citizen of India. Human beings without community are lesser human beings, homeless and wanderers searching for belongingness on a road that has no signboards.

The third reason for recognising the importance of pluralism is that the meaning systems of different cultures expand and enrich our grasp of complexities, and dilemmas of, the human condition. A mono-cultural society or a society that allows only one system of belief to flourish is, by definition, soulless and bare. Stripped of the excitement of learning new languages, acquaintance with new values, familiarity with new cuisines, literature, music, art, sculpture and ways of conceiving the world, monochromatic societies are dull, predictable and tedious. Life in a plural society, on the other hand, promises adventure and novel ways of understanding ourselves and our worlds. Where would, after all, Bollywood films, which fuel romantic imaginations of the young and old, be without love poetry written in Urdu by Gulzar or Javed Akhtar? The valuation of plurality or diversity is an unambiguous good, because the awareness of difference expands our horizons, deepens sensibilities, cultivates empathy and enhances solidarity. Living in a plural society allows us to launch out a new journey and a new adventure every day.

For these reasons and more, the gap between the two propositions on pluralism, one empirical and the other normative, needs to be theoretically bridged through pluralism. The norm of pluralism holds that there is no one truth or absolute value that explains the world or serves as the originating point of different belief systems. The concept of pluralism challenges dominant beliefs and value systems. Normative pluralism is a value, but it is a value with a difference. Like other normative concepts such as equality, freedom and rights, it captures the significance of something important. But unlike other values, pluralism is a *precondition* for the existence of a plurality of norms and principles. It is, therefore, a *second-order* value insofar as it tells us that all belief systems are of equal significance, or that X is as significant as Y. Its task as a second-order value is to equalise these belief systems.

Pluralism encourages us to arrange these systems on a horizontal axis, thereby prohibiting any vertical arrangement of religion as higher or lower, superior or inferior. Of course, these belief systems must fall within the ambit of what is democratically permissible. We can hardly place a religious cult where the so-called god-man exploits female devotees on the same level as sophisticated religions that deepen the cognitive capacities of their members.

As a second-order value, pluralism seeks to re-order an already organised world. If our world has been semantically organised to privilege a certain concept of nation and nationalism, pluralism tells us that there are other equally valid ways of organising a political community, cosmopolitanism for instance. If one language acquires dominance in society, the concept of pluralism teaches us that other languages also deserve the pride of place in the linguistic domain. And above all, pluralism teaches us to maintain equal respect for all belief systems. In short, the notion of pluralism abjures the idea that there is a uniquely true set of beliefs and a uniquely right set of moral standards, against which we can measure the validity or the morality of other values. Above all, pluralism teaches us to maintain equal respect for all belief systems, and thus performs both a pedagogic and a political role. Finally, pluralism abjures the idea that there is a uniquely true set of beliefs and a uniquely right set of moral standards, against which we can measure the validity or the morality of other values. The transition from empirical or descriptive pluralism to normative pluralism is best accomplished when we adopt secularism as a norm. Secularism ensures equality or even its weaker form non-discrimination in a plural society.

What Is Secularism?

Words are tricky things, and we can never be sure/certain/confident/ assured that we have used the right word to express/convey what we wanted to say. An interesting exchange between Alice and Humpty Dumpty in Lewis Carrols' *Through the Looking Glass* might illustrate the point. 'I don't know what you mean by "glory"?' said Alice to Humpty Dumpty. The latter smiled contemptuously, 'Of course you don't-till I tell you. I meant there's a nice knock-down argument for you!' 'But "glory" doesn't mean "a nice down argument,"' Alice objected. 'When I use a word' Humpty Dumpty said scornfully, 'It means just what I choose it to mean-neither more nor less'. 'The question is', said Alice, 'whether you can make words mean so many different things'. 'The question is', said Humpty Dumpty, 'which is to be master-that's all'. Lewis Carroll, a mathematician and logician, excelled in the subtle art of satire and word play. Coded in this exchange between Alice and Humpty Dumpty, which appears a piece of delightful literary nonsense at first sight, is a message. The search for unequivocal meaning, Carroll seems to tell us, is doomed. A word can carry different implications depending on the context. Let us, following this suggestion, explore briefly the many meanings of secularism.

Although the terms secular, secularisation and secularism are, in many cases, spoken of in one breath, or used interchangeably, the meanings of these terms are different, distinctive, but often overlapping. We need to distinguish *secularisation* as a social process, which involves the relegation of religious belief and practices to the private sphere, and *secularism* as a principle of state policy. In most discussions, the two meanings are conflated. This has given rise to the expectation that the secularisation of society is a necessary precondition for secularism as a political norm.

The term secular stands in for the non-religious. It can be used purely descriptively, to illustrate, say, non-religious practices or beliefs. For example, it is possible to distinguish education based on modern, rational, 'scientific' and, therefore, secular pedagogies, from instruction on how to read a religious text. We should recollect that the notion of the 'secular' is a peculiarly modern concept. It denotes critical engagement with ideas, systems of thought and beliefs. In history, the moment believers began to diagnose, evaluate and critique religious doctrines, practices and the awesome power of the clergy, or the moment they metaphorically 'stood back' and judged beliefs they and their ancestors had followed unthinkingly; this process was given a name—secular. The term 'secular' is a property of political modernity, insofar as it denotes an attitude of critical rationality towards even religion.

European societies were secularised with the onset of modernity in the 18th century insofar as the public sphere was emptied out of religion and religion banished to the private domain. The term 'secularism' was, however, first coined by the British freethinker George Jacob Holyoake in 1851. The freethinkers were ideologically connected with the emerging socialist movement, and Holyoake drew his inspiration from prominent freethinkers, such as Richard Carlile, Richard Owen and Thomas Paine. For Holyoake, religion provides no answer to the eternal problems of poverty and ill-being. What does the poverty-stricken artisan, he asks rhetorically, have to do with Christianity that tells him *not* to resist evil? Religion 'brands him with inherited guilt' and 'fetters him by an arbitrary faith'. It menaces the poor with eternal damnation.[13] Can we, queries Holyoake with an oratorical flourish, do without religion? Can we substitute secularism, 'the practical philosophy of the people', for a discredited religion?

Secularism for Holyoake embodies scientific rationality that was privileged by the Enlightenment. The concept combats superstition, and dispenses with Christianity, or anything that stands in the way of truth and progress. It allows us to think for ourselves and legitimises the right to difference of opinion and the right to subject all views to criticism. These mental processes of reflection are essential for intellectual enquiry.[14] But secularism, Holyoake hastens to clarify, is not atheism. The concept is not defined in opposition to, or as a negation of, religion. It is an alternative way of understanding and dealing with matters of the world.

Towards the end of the 19th century, the term secularism had become an integral part of political vocabularies in England, not only through the labours of Holyoake but also as a mode of political rhetoric adopted by liberals over the content of primary education, and the proper limits of religious instruction in the school system. In this sense, secularism can be conceived of as an embodiment of reason, and of the spirit of science, progress and modernity. It offers a distinctive perspective on life; it is not the binary opposite of religion.

[13] Holyoake, 'Secularism', 3.
[14] Ibid., 4.

In effect, the term secular is not synonymous with atheism, nor does it stand in opposition to religion. Atheists are non-believers; secular people can be religious, but also hold that their conversations with God are a personal matter and that the religion should not be used to discriminate between citizens or mixed up with politics. Secularisation is a social process that entails the privatisation of religion. Secularism, in the sense attributed to it by Holyoake, is synonymous with reason and a scientific outlook.

The home of this concept is Europe, but secularism acquired new dimensions in the historical context of India, particularly because the principle was adopted not in the context of the secularisation of society but in the context of the politicisation of religion in the public sphere, of this more anon. The politicisation of religion led to the construction of a unified identity, the harnessing of this identity to nationalism and later competitive nationalism, and the Partition of India in 1947.

It was precisely communal tension and violence between the Hindus and Muslims that were addressed by the leaders of the freedom struggle when they began to speak of secularism along with minority rights in the second decade of the 20th century. They attempted to ensure the Muslim minority that its interests would be safeguarded in a democratic India. They warned the Hindu majority that the power bestowed by numbers is not reason enough to monopolise power. The majority principle is workable, but it is not morally correct, nor is it politically prudent.

The mission of the leaders of the freedom struggle did not succeed completely because the country was partitioned. But it did not fail or even falter because post-Independence India remained committed to secularism and to the rights of minorities. The message that went out strongly is that the majority would not be given an advantage despite its numerical strength, and the minorities would not be disadvantaged even though they did not possess such strength. The minorities would be protected against the majority. The State would be neutral towards all religious communities.

India was partitioned in 1947 on the ostensible grounds of religion, but the problem remains, stalking our collective life as it were.

Communal riots have pitted ineradicable scars on the body of the polity since Independence. According to the 2017 Global Democracy Index compiled by the Economist Intelligence Unit, India has slipped from the 32nd to the 42nd place in 2017. The world's largest democracy is flawed. The report states that this is due to the rise of conservative religious ideologies, *in an otherwise* secular country, and an increase in vigilantism, violence against minorities, particularly Muslims, and dissenting voices. The media is but partially free, and journalists are at risk from the government, military, non-State actors and radical groups. The threat of violence has had a chilling effect on media coverage. India has become a more dangerous place for journalists, especially in the central state of Chhattisgarh and the northern state of Jammu and Kashmir. The local authorities have restricted freedom of the press, closed down several newspapers and heavily controlled mobile Internet services. Several journalists were murdered in India in 2017 and 2018. India is a flawed democracy concluded the report.[15]

The conclusions of the report are not misplaced. India has been marked by the rise of vigilante's who maim, murder and wound in the name of the religion. The sorry saga of immense violence against the Muslim community was initiated with the killing of Akhlaq Saifi in Dadri district in Uttar Pradesh shortly after the Bharatiya Janata Party (BJP) had taken over power in 2014. On the evening of 28 September 2015, a mob of fanatical Hindus armed with lathis (a long thick stick, especially one used as a weapon) and other lethal weapons stormed into his house and lynched a 50-year-old Akhlaq to death. They did so on the mere suspicion that he had butchered a calf that had gone missing, consumed its flesh and stored the rest in his fridge. Akhlaq's son Danish was beaten up, and reportedly his grandmother was assaulted. Mob violence was presaged by incendiary speeches delivered by leaders of the right-wing party over a loudspeaker in a temple. A First Information Report was filed against 10 people who were complicit in

---

[15] https://www.livemint.com/Politics/India-slips-to-42nd-place-on-EIU-Democracy-Index-US-at-21st.html (accessed on 26 May 2018).

the lynching, but it made no mention of beef as a cause for violence. Till today, none of the accused has been punished.[16]

In February 2018, the BJP hardliner and the Member of Parliament Vinay Katiyar went further and stated that Muslims should not even be living in this country; they should go to Pakistan or Bangladesh. The Muslims, he said, partitioned the country, they were given a separate territory and, therefore, they should go there. What business do they have here?[17] Katiyar who had founded the youth wing of the Vishva Hindu Parishad, the Bajrang Dal, merely enunciated what many members of the BJP saw as the unfinished job of the Partition. They, in effect, call for complete ethnic cleansing. The signs are ominous; not only are these poisonous statements against the spirit of secularism, but also they violate the democratic Constitution of India and the rights it grants citizens.

If communalism has got a fresh lease of life by what many have called the culture of impunity, the need for secularism, which enables us to evaluate and judge a practice and ideology as worthy or unworthy, and which becomes the touchstone for democracy, is more not less. We cannot abandon secularism when minorities are in danger and legitimise the communal divide which goes deep as the next chapter establishes. We need to address and perhaps renegotiate the concept. This is an essential precondition for democracy.

[16] Agarwal, 'The Dadri Truth'.
[17] https://timesofindia.indiatimes.com/india/muslims-should-not-even-be-living-in-this-country-should-go-topakistan-bangladesh-says-bjp-mp-vinay-katiyar/article (accessed on 26 May 2018).

CHAPTER 2

The Political Context
Communalism

But in the gross and scope of my opinion, this bodes some strange eruption to our state.[1]

Ahmedabad (1969), Belchi (1978), Delhi (1984), Bombay riots (1993), Bathan Tola (1996), Laxman Bathe (1997), Gujarat (2002), Kherlainji (2006), Dharmapuri (2012) and Muzaffarnagar (2013)—these are not only names given to towns and villages on the map of our country. They are signposts that direct our attention to the sordid biography of communal and caste violence in India. History will tell a blood-soaked story of shameful incidents in post-colonial India and of inhuman acts performed by one human being on another for reasons outside the latter's control, birth into a vulnerable religious or a caste community, for instance.

There was a time when many Indians believed that murderous riots between religious communities constituted exceptions to normal ways of being. As disconnected occurrences, bloody assaults, in the main between Hindus and Muslims, were nothing more than random episodes of chaos and breakdowns. Many of us felt that during riots, the

[1] Horatio in Shakespeare, 'The Tragedy of Hamlet Prince of Denmark', Act I, Scene 1, 653.

codes of civility, which otherwise earmark, or at least should earmark, the practices of everyday life are suspended, and that the norms and boundaries that govern social transactions are, in the process, transgressed. We would have had very good reasons for our beliefs. Some very insightful work in historical interpretation has told us that the riot constitutes a departure from the norm. Elias Canetti focusing on destructive collective behaviour during the 1789 French Revolution in his *Crowds and Power* suggests that such behaviour transgresses generally established and universally valid distances and boundaries. It destroys a hierarchy that is no longer recognised.[2]

There was a political moment when we thought that riots constitute episodic and spasmodic events. However, this breakdown in social codes cannot be permanent; they are put into abeyance for the time being. These codes are restored when normalcy returns to the body politic. Riots have a short time span, and when the psychic high that is generated during the course of the riot is spent, people return to coexisting with each other, and boundaries are restored to their rightful place. Riots, we could have said, somewhat comfortably at one point in our history, take place in a no-man's-land where neither the past nor the future is of any importance. They occur in a time warp that mindlessly and meaninglessly constitutes a present—a present that is caught up in an admittedly vicious but, nevertheless, terminable spiral of violence. This was a reassuring thought; for then, we could with some ease dismiss the riot as a contingent event, which is marked by unreasonable crowd behaviour. On such occasions, individual participants simply descend into irrationality and momentary insanity.

Moments Constituting Communal Violence: The Procession

Take the strange case of the religious procession. On 28 March 2018, extremist Hindu right wingers took out a procession on the occasion of Ram Navami in Bihar Sharif in the state of Bihar. Even as the number of participants in the procession swelled, and even as

[2] Canetti, *Crowds and Power*, 19.

participants began to brandish weapons from sticks to the trident and mouth obscenities against minorities, the procession diverted its route and entered Muslim mohallas. The natural result was a communal riot. On the same day, four persons died in clashes between the two communities in the Raniganj–Asansol Belt in the Paschim Bardhaman district in West Bengal. The casualties would have been higher but the Imam of a mosque in Asansol, who had lost his young son in the clashes, declared that if anyone from his community retaliated in kind, he would leave the town. This voice of sanity and humanity amidst the madness caused by a religious procession calmed down inflamed passions and averted further disasters. We doff our metaphorical hats to him.

In Rajasthan, a religious procession included a float glorifying Shambhu Lal Raigar, who is currently in prison for hacking an innocent Muslim, and cynically videotaping his death to the tune of his own anti-Muslim slogans. After the festival, communal tension spread to more districts of the state. Communal violence followed the defeat of the ruling coalition between Janata Dal United and the BJP in the recent by-elections in the state. Across swathes of North India, held a report in *The Hindu*, a reputed newspaper, daily interactions between the majority and minority communities have been rendered fraught with the probability of violence. The increasingly assertive Ram Navami and other processions are drawing new fault lines.[3]

The incident is not new to Indian history. Taking out of a procession on religious days has been, since the late 19th century, used as a strategy to cement identity and flex muscles. Historians tell us that in that period Muslims and Hindus lived in harmony and very often took part in each other's religious processions in the Presidency of Bombay. In 1893, a patch of a dark cloud appeared on the sky of Bombay. Bitter communal riots in the aftermath of 1892 reforms introduced by the colonial government caused death and suffering. The riot, writes the Maharashtrian leader Bal Gangadhar Tilak's biographer, Ram Gopal, upset the communal equilibrium of Poona (nowadays Pune).

---

[3] http://www.thehindu.com/opinion/editorial/exposing-fault-lines-the-violence-over-ram-navami-processions (accessed on 26 May 2018).

Hindus flocked to Tilak and implored him that, as a fearless leader of Maharashtra, he should take up the cause of their protection with the colonial government.

The riot prompted Tilak to think of regenerating, what he considered to be, the lost pride of Hindus. This could be accomplished by the revival of festivals that had died out after the end of the Peshwa regime in Maharashtra, such as the Ganapati and Shivaji festivals. The transformation of a festival from a personal to a collective celebration led over time to the consolidation of identity around the pole of Hindu Gods and icons, the creation of competitive nationalism and anti-colonial sentiments. Five Ganapati statues were set up in Pune and funds were collected for celebrations. The 10-day festival was marked by the delivery of fiery lectures and playing of patriotic music. Tilak wrote in his newspaper the *Kesari* that the Ganapati festival was comparable to the Olympian and Pythian festivals of the Greeks.[4]

The tone of the proceedings was alarmingly belligerent. The pageants staged during the festival comprised choirs of young men dressed in the uniform of Shivaji's soldiers who had fought Mughal rulers. Music, poems, lectures and songs were directed as much towards the colonial government as towards the Muslim rulers in the past. The consequences could have been foretold. In 1894, a procession to commemorate the festival defied the orders of the district magistrate not to take the procession past a mosque and triggered off a communal riot.

By the opening years of the 20th century the festival spread to different parts of Western India. A hitherto private ritual for the worship of the God Ganesh had been turned into a site for revolutionary songs and dissemination of literature. Fiery anti-colonial speeches were greeted with rousing acclaim. The coalescing of a political community around a Hindu God was created and recreated through the staging of plays, stories of liberation from demons and revolutionary music. Memories of historical political figures like Chhatrapati Shivaji, who had fought the Mughal Empire, were celebrated almost in the same way as the festival of God Ganapati was celebrated. In Eastern

---

[4] Gopal, *Lokmanya Tilak*, 82–88.

India, the worship of the Goddess Durga in Bengal and the practice of *Kurbani* or animal sacrifice in Islam were turned into public displays, and resultantly into political constituencies that lined up behind competitive national projects.

So easily, as we have repeatedly seen, a ritual associated with a public religion can slide into the eruption of communal violence in a shockingly short period of time. It is almost as if violence against the other community, and often human sacrifice, is an extension of religious celebrations. Processions that wend their way to the place of worship do not always take the shortest possible route, they intentionally enter the residential or even the workplace spaces of the other community. These incursions provide opportunities to entrepreneurs and organisers of violence to mobilise crowds, wreak havoc on the other community, burn, maim and kill.

The psychiatrist Sudhir Kakar in his *Colors of Violence* writes that among various precipitating incidents, two occur with such regularity in reports of riots that they may fairly be called archetypes. One of them has to do with rumours of killing of the cow and the other relates to disputes over religious processions. The former cause is specific to India, but riots over religious processions are common in the history of religious violence. Both causes are seen as legitimate reasons for the flare-up of violence. The former leads to a procession. In the latter case, the procession is in itself a precipitating incident. A procession, argues Kakar, is necessary for the creation of a physical group or a group represented in the bodies of its members rather than in their minds. This shift from individual minds to a collective body is essential for a group to become an instrument of actual violence.

The sensory experience of belonging to a relatively abstract entity, for example fellow Hindus, touches a very different chord of the self than the one touched by being a member of a physical group such as a tightly packed congregation in a Hindu temple. The self-experience of the former is determined more by concrete bodily communication and physical sensations in the press of other bodies.[5] The individual

[5] Kakar, *Colors of Violence*, 56–57.

gets wrapped up in the crowd is continuously and sensually pounded through all avenues that his body can afford.

This argument conforms to the findings of some very insightful work in historical interpretation that has told us that the riot constitutes a departure from the norm.

Kakar insists that the religious procession produces the most physical of all groups. Mere presence in a crowd that has produced and responded to hysteria over imagined or real slights, or provocative statements, dissolves the boundaries between our and other corporeal selves in that period of time. Kakar, always the psychologist of mass violence, has insightfully pointed out the psychological processes that overwhelm individuals who take part in a procession.

There is more. When the procession takes a route that has not been agreed upon by the urban authorities and enters neighbourhoods and workplaces largely occupied by the other community, strategists plan deliberately that the boundaries between urban spaces inhabited by different communities are wiped out. Taking of detours from the sanctioned route sends a message to the other community—that of the destruction of physical boundaries represented by frontiers between different segments of the neighbourhood and workplaces. The procession marks out and appropriates the space as one's own. Usually, the violence embodied in the procession, members of which carry sharp weapons and shout slogans of hate, is followed by looting of shops, sacking of places of worship, burning of sacred books and desecration of everything held holy by the other community. This has been the experience of India till today. Processions organised by Hindus around religious festivals as well as national ones have invariably targeted the Muslim minority. Often reprisals follow. Angry responses to provocative slogans lead to mayhem and bloodshed.

This is not to suggest that the riot and the chaos that follow are spontaneous. A definite link is created between slogan mongering, affirmations of the collective self, accusations targeted against other communities and the outbreak of violence. The spark is provided by agents of violence who provide deadly weapons to the crowd, instigate inflammatory slogans, design deviations in routes and often mark shops, factories or households run or inhabited by the other community as ready for destruction. The festival quickly turns into a political rally and then into violence, thereby providing multiple opportunities for leaders to produce and reproduce an aggressive 'nationalist' constituency.

Background Violence

The problem is that if we think of riots in this fashion, we type them as abnormalities or as departures from the norm as if they have nothing to do with history as well as the present, with social and political representations that are the stuff of everyday life or with the tensions which arise out of the project of living together—tensions that permeate neighbourhoods and workplaces, rituals and public spaces. It is precisely here that we need to pause, reflect and wonder: Do riots really signify isolated instances in human history that are abstracted both from the past and the present?

Most interpretations of communalism in India tend to be polarised between the primordial school, which argues that religious animosities are integral to processes of boundary making of communities, and the instrumentalist school that argues that violence among communities is prompted by political leaders, land sharks and other sorts of entrepreneurs who feed off human tragedies, from the makers and distributors of arms, to those who loot shops and homes, hearths and workplaces. Other scholars tend to interpret communal violence as a by-product of an alienating modernity and as resistance to the imposition of an alien form of political organisation, namely democracy. And yet other scholars argue that social dislocations of globalisation and neo-liberalism have led to anomie and an increase in communal violence. Alienation, breakdown of communities, unemployment and consumerism are seen as proximate causes for distorting relations between communities.

We should have understood from history that religious processions cannot be understood only as a resource or as a strategy for the mobilisation of a constituency and the building up of a larger movement. If a political movement is successful in tapping deep structures of sentiment in a society, arguably these sentiments must already be there, lurking under the skin of a shallow modernity that is expected to usher in a secular age. After all, religion cannot be harnessed to the cause of political mobilisation until it has some grip on people's minds and psyches. Religious hatred towards the other community is integral to the making of a community, to the construction of boundaries and to processes of self-identification with the wider community and distancing from others.

Yet, this neat formulation—customised prejudice translates into murderous assaults on members of the other community—gives sufficient cause for unease. People may or may not be inclined towards religiosity, and yet they might hesitate to dine and socialise with, let alone marry members of another community. But this does not mean that they ritually inflict harm on the bodies of other people. We can believe that others have their own reasons for thinking and doing what they think and do, and we have different reasons for thinking and doing what we wish to do. These are some of the modalities by which groups in society identify themselves and distinguish themselves from others. For these reasons, they construct symbolic and often spatial barriers between themselves and others.

Yet, at precisely this point of the argument, we must pause. Note that the bracketing-off of identities is a sociological phenomenon. Despite these social barriers, forms of cooperation can and do arise in the workplace, in social and political organisations, in and through movements and through associational life. When these bracketed identities are transformed as weapons in pursuit of a symbolic or material gain, a sociological phenomenon translates into a political movement that lays claims upon the body politic. The politicisation of identities invariably leads to open and ruthless competition for all sorts of power, often at the cost of human lives.

What is important is that the translation of, often, hidden animosities into violence involves a trigger. This trigger is provided by organisations that belong to cadres of the religious right in all communities, and/or entrepreneurs and merchants of hate who excel in excavating, often, hidden sentiments of resentment against other communities and in playing up incidents that otherwise can be passed off as minor. These entrepreneurs do not belong to any specific community, they have no loyalty and they are most often than not mercenaries up for sale to the highest bidder. The trigger stokes and evokes hellfires of hatred, devastating violence and eternal damnation. In India communal organisations, such as the Muslim League, the Hindu Mahasabha and later the Rashtriya Swayamsevak Sangh, popularly known as the RSS, triggered off the brutalisation of social and political identities, creation of divides, exacerbation of hitherto muted schisms and the creation of new ones.

When political parties organically linked to these organisations come to power, hate-filled agendas fetch both covert sanction and overt support from ministers and party functionaries. It is not surprising that incidents of communal violence dot the headlines of daily newspapers since the BJP came into power at the Centre in 2014. These incidents range from public lynching and killings of Muslim citizens on flimsy grounds, nefarious campaigns such as 'love jehad' which targets young people who wish to marry or even fall in love across religious divides, bans on sale of cows and consumption of beef, rewriting of history textbooks to present Muslims as oppressors, the construction of binary opposites such as the good Hindu versus the bad Muslim, to a denial of representation to the Muslim community.

In sum, the conversion of (a) 'religion as faith' into 'religion as politics' and (b) 'religion as politics' into 'communal violence' as the lowest common denominator that binds humanity together is not inevitable. Intentional human action is a catalyst to achieve the transition from religion as a social category to religion as a political one. And when politicised religious identities compete for the same spatial and material resources, members relentlessly inscribe inerasable injuries on others and on the body of the polity. This is the sad lesson of India's history. This is the tragedy visited upon its plural society. In sum, we cannot argue that Indians are inherently communal, nor can we argue that citizens of the country go around killing Muslims who are identified as the enemy with whom there can be neither truck nor transaction. The transition from communal sentiments or background violence to violence involves a trigger. This is the precise lesson we learn from the history of Ahmedabad.

Communalism in Ahmedabad

The city of Ahmedabad, which lies on the banks of the Sabarmati River in Western India, is located in one of the most urbanised and industrialised parts of the state of Gujarat. Ahmedabad is a major and the largest city of Gujarat state and the seventh largest urban agglomeration in the country. According to the 2011 census, the Muslim community constitutes 13.51 per cent of the population. Ahmedabad is a highly globalised city. In the wake of the collapse of the textile industry in the mid-1980s, the city has diversified its industrial base, and established financial and services sectors. The city has attracted foreign direct investment in various sectors, mainly in infrastructure and real estate development. The spatial effects of globalisation are also more than evident. What used to be working class tenements have been converted into malls, restaurants and cinema houses, and old disused textile mills have been converted into office blocks. Historically, Ahmedabad is an important city, and it continues to be so at present for a variety of reasons.

It is possible to tell many stories of the city. One story can be constructed out of the rise and decline of the textile industry, of the rise and decline of one of the largest industrial working classes in India and of the informalisation of labour that followed the dissolution of the working class. We could tell a second story—that of a distinct experiment in trade unionism. Gandhi, who was to inspire and inaugurate a radically different form of trade unionism in the city, and who inaugurated the Majdoor Mahajan Sangh, or the Textile Labour Association (TLA), condensed into this trade union his entire philosophy—that of trust and partnership and that of cooperation rather than conflict. We could tell a third story that centres on the way the city has successfully negotiated two major economic transitions: from a trade-oriented economy to an industrial economy and from an industrial to a post-industrial economy. We could tell a fourth story of how Ahmedabad was constituted as the crucible of nation-building in the country with the establishment of the Sabarmati Ashram by Gandhi, and with the founding of institutions of national importance such as the Gujarat Vidyapith, the Navjivan Trust, the prestigious Indian Institute of Management and the equally prestigious National Institute of Design.

We could as well tell a fifth story of the city, how and why it became the site for Gandhi's experiments in truth, of his efforts in making people belonging to different castes and religious persuasions live together and how the city was the starting point of his famous Salt Satyagraha, which constituted a high point of the struggle for freedom. Erikson argued that the city is in the first place the Manchester of India.[6] Ahmedabad, goes on Erikson to suggest, is a true city. It breathed, if one may say so, the logic of mercantile life, for its industry had grown from native crafts to small enterprises and to a large industry by an uninterrupted process so consistent that it could truly be said to have a corporate identity. This gave it a character, both solid and limited, both strong and ingrown, both alive and isolated, by which it has been able to household through the centuries a remarkable energy.[7]

Gandhi chose Ahmedabad, wrote Erikson, because he himself spoke Gujarati, and, in the city, Gujarati was the official language. It had always been spoken, studied and cultivated. Gandhi chose Ahmedabad because it was an ancient centre of handloom weaving, because it had become the seat of the most modern mechanism of spinning and weaving, and because the weaving tradition was deeply embedded in a system which made guilds, caste and religion intimately interdependent. Gandhi was to call for a rapid modernisation of awareness and aspirations and yet also acknowledge those aspects of the ancient social structure which alone could provide irreplaceable elements of a traditional identity.... Gandhi could do no better than to

---

[6] Erikson, *Gandhi's Truth*, 258.
[7] Ibid.

settle in a modern place that had preserved some ancient structure, so that from there he could travel and study.[8] However, after the 1920s, that is the period when he resided in the city, Gandhi never went back to Ahmedabad.

All these stories are not only fascinating in their own right, but they also provide solid ground for social science research. However, there is one other and a rather dark story that can be narrated about Ahmedabad of how and why the city has led the country in the scale and the number of communal riots between the Hindu and Muslim communities up until 2002. The first riot in the city occurred in 1946 on the eve of Independence of India and on the eve of the Partition of the country. The first serious communal riot occurred in 1969. In this riot, above 660 people were killed, and property worth 40 million rupees was destroyed. The next major riot took place in 1985. However, minor riots occurred in 1971, 1972, 1973, 1977, 1980, 1981 and 1982. After the 1985 riot, minor riots erupted in 1986, 1987, 1989, 1990 and 1992. In 1993, another major riot occurred followed by minor riots in 1994 and 1996. In 1999, a major riot was followed by minor riots in 2000 and 2001. The 2002 case was different, not only because violence was wreaked upon the head of the Muslims by right-wing Hindus, but also because the state government controlled by the BJP made little attempt to protect the lives of its own people, the Muslim citizens of the state and of the country.

The 2002 case of communal violence is distinctive from earlier occasions for at least three reasons. First, the employment of violence was completely one sided. Rather than wait for the rule of law to take its course after the Godhra incident, when Muslim mobs stormed a train compartment returning from Ayodhya, and visited harm upon the heads of the travellers, mobs led by the Sangh Parivar proceeded to administer brutal vigilante justice. The carefully executed and precisely designed pogrom had, it became obvious, meticulously planned and orchestrated by the Bajrang Dal, the Vishva Hindu Parishad and the RSS. Second, although the role of some government ministers and bureaucrats is still under investigation, and others have been cleared

---

[8] Ibid., 260–261.

by various special investigation agencies and courts, it is clear that the state government refrained from *either* preventing Hindu mobs from implementing their macabre designs or from protecting Muslim citizens. Third, whereas earlier riots had more or less taken place in old Ahmedabad, particularly the walled city and the industrial areas, this time the entire city was affected. Almost 1,000 people, mainly Muslims, were viciously murdered, and about 7,000 Muslims were displaced from their homes.

The irony is that Ahmedabad was the site of Gandhi's experiments in truth and non-violence. But these lessons, it appears, were half-heartedly internalised in the collective psyche. In 1919, reports of Gandhiji's detention by the colonial government swept the city, and mobs set fire to the jail, the Telegraph office and the Collector's Office. The Gandhian lesson of non-violence, it seemed, was soon forgotten. But at the same time Gandhians walked the streets to counsel patience and reassure the workers. Regrettably, no Gandhian has walked the streets during the frightening communal riots that had become a recurrent feature of the city. In 2002, when Muslims fleeing murderous mobs tried to seek refuge in the Sabarmati Ashram, which had been established by Gandhi as a project in inter-caste and inter-communal harmony, reportedly the Ashram closed its doors in order to protect its property. The substantial Jain community in the city is wedded to the doctrine of non-violence. But this tradition has not found root in civil society. The community has kept silent in the face of tremendous brutality wreaked against the Muslim community. Numerous holy men who head huge numbers of religious orders, each of which preaches the imperative of coming to peace with the world and with oneself, also kept quiet. And if some civil society organisations kept mum in the face of massive transgression of basic civil rights of the people, and the complicity of state officials and the police in the violence unleashed on Muslims, Hindu right-wing groups were actively involved in the violence. It follows that groups dedicated to democracy, and to battling fascist groups, were rendered helpless.

Recurrent riots in the history of the city have erupted against the background of a communal divide among Muslims and Hindus, both in the workplace and in residential areas. These background conditions that bred communal sentiments have been tapped to facilitate the transition to violence. Both communities have been guilty of transgressing the social codes of living together. Notably, however, after the horrific 2002 violence against the minority community, the Muslims have kept quiet. It is almost as if they have been bludgeoned into submissiveness. Ahmedabad has always been a divided city. However, today it is a city in which the minority has been rendered faceless through ghettoisation and through banishment to the periphery of the city. Their status has declined from citizen to subject.

Ahmedabad in History

The area which came to be known as Ahmedabad controlled the key routes of trade with the North, the East, the West and the South of the country. It was also located in a cotton-growing belt, fact which motivated Sultan Ahmad Shah of the Gujarat Sultanate to establish a city close to where two earlier trading centres, namely Asaval and Karnavati, stood.[9] With the disintegration of the Delhi Sultanate in 1394, in 1403, the Governor of Gujarat declared its independence from the Delhi Sultans. This became the Gujarat Sultanate. The city, which was founded by Ahmad Shah's grandfather, came to be known as Ahmadshahi. In 1411, a walled city was constructed; this was given the name Ahmedabad.

The walled city, built on the eastern bank of the Sabarmati river, 50 miles from the mouth of the river and 173 feet above the mean sea level, replaced Karnavati as a major trading centre and as an important city of the region of Gujarat. The old walled city covered an area of two square miles and was enclosed within walls that were completed in 1487. The second wall with 10 gates was constructed by the Mughals. After 1532, settlements began to proliferate within the walled area. Subsequently, the city expanded spatially to include *puras* (suburbs) outside the walled city.

[9] Raychaudhuri, 'Colonialism, Indigenous Elites', 679; Yagnik and Sheth, *The Shaping of Modern Gujarat*, 9.

Ahmed Shah encouraged merchants, weavers and skilled crafts-men to settle in Ahmedabad so that the city could develop as a flourishing trading and weaving centre. For a hundred years, the city grew in wealth and splendour. This period of growth of Ahmedabad was followed by 60 years of decay. The reason was the decline of the Gujarat Sultanate, and the passing of trade into the hands of the Portuguese. Ahmedabad recovered some if its reputation and prosperity in 1572, after it became a part of the Mughal Empire, and the seat of the Mughal Viceroy of Gujarat. However, as the Mughal Empire began to disintegrate in the 18th century, the city declined once again, mainly because of political instability. The city was ruled jointly by the Muslims and Marathas from 1738 to 1753. In 1757, it came completely in the hands of the Maratha kings. Till 1817, when it was annexed by the East India Company,[10] it has been recorded that the city was almost deserted and was in a deplorable state. Ahmedabad once again began to revive under the control of the East India Company and was transformed into a modern city.

The rise of Ahmedabad as a centre of trade and commerce bred several significant consequences. One, since overseas trade offered lucrative opportunities for economic advancement, a number of Hindu traders converted to Islam, because ritualised Hinduism prohibited overseas travel. This added to the population of the Muslim community, which had settled in Gujarat in the early 7th century. Two, from the beginning, different religious communities occupied differ-ent slots in the weaving and trade-based division of labour. Up to the end of Mughal rule, the officers of the court and skilled weavers were Muslims. The financiers and traders were generally Hindus and Jain, except for the Bohra Muslims, who traded in silk and other goods. The wealth of Ahmedabad was, therefore, controlled by the Hindus and Jains, especially by the old and established family firms. These families possessed hereditary monopoly over trading transactions. The well-established and highly respected Sarafi families, often called 'bankers' (though they used their own capital rather than deposits to finance transactions), dealt in *hundis* (cheques for payments over distances),

---

[10] Gillion, *Ahmedabad*, 14.

changed coins, acted as the pay masters of the army, as financiers to princes and merchants, provided insurance, served as trustees for religious and charitable purposes, and sometimes engaged in commercial activities on their own account. With the decline of Mughal rule and the passing of the city into the hands of the Hindu Marathas, the Muslims were deprived of their status as court officials, but members of the community continued in the skilled profession of weaving. The only section of the Muslim community, which retained wealth, was the Bohra community. Control over trade, financial transactions and wealth, generally remained in the hands of the Hindus and the Jains.

By the late 1800s, Ahmedabad had become a major centre of the textile industry in India, employing one of the largest industrial work forces in the country. The textile industry provided economic incentives and opportunities to all people living in the city, and beyond. Yet not all these opportunities were available to different communities. Whereas some castes in the Hindu hierarchy were able to take quick advantage of the openings provided by the new industry in terms of the ownership of factories, employment in profitable jobs, involvement in the ancillary sector, distribution and finance, Muslims lost out. The *Gazetteer* of the Bombay Presidency reported in 1913 that the Muslim community, largely non-literate, was simply not in a position to take advantage of proffered opportunities.[11] Gillion writes that the Muslims remained humble weavers or gentlemen pensioners living in pride and semi-poverty. They trailed behind the Hindus in government service (except the army), in the professions, in commerce and in industry.[12] The establishment of the textile industry could not alter the situation, because, like land ownership, the structure of employment and profit was deeply embedded in a hierarchical caste and an exclusionary religious social milieu. The majority of members of the Muslim community began to work as labour in the industry.

Within the industry, tasks were allocated on the basis of caste and religion. The workers in the spinning department were mainly Dalits.

---

[11] *Gazetteer of the Bombay Presidency, 1913*, vol. 1V-B, Ahmedabad, Bombay, 25.
[12] Gillion, *Ahmedabad*, 89.

The weaving department consisted, amongst others, of Muslims, because their traditional occupation had been that of handloom weaving. The division of labour on the basis of caste and religion was reflected in the organisation of the trade unions, such as the Majdoor Mahajan Sangh or the TLA. The trade union was organised on the Gandhian principle of compromise rather than that of confrontation, of arbitration and conciliation rather than that of strikes, and that of instilling a culture of social work among the poor.

The irony is that though workers accepted arbitration instead of confrontation, and partnership with capital instead of class consciousness, they failed to internalise the philosophy of Gandhi—that of non-violence. Although members of the trade union played a significant role in quelling political passions during Partition in 1947, matters were different after that period. In the 1969 communal riot, workers clashed in the industrial localities, but the TLA did not mediate. In 1981–1982 and 1985–1986, waves of riots broke out against the extension of protective discrimination for the lower castes to other backward castes. Although the measures would have helped workers who belonged to these castes, the TLA again did not intervene to protect its own members.[13] Leaders of the TLA neither walked the streets to restore sanity, nor did they back their own backward caste workers.

Part of the reason for this indifference has to do with the structure of the union. From the very beginning, the TLA was an umbrella organisation that brought together eight separate craft and occupation-based unions within the industry. Therefore, workers became members through their own occupation unions. And since occupational slots within the textile industry were based on caste and religion, workers joined the TLA as a member of a caste or a religious group. Identities were thus *reinforced* rather than *mediated* by their class identity as workers. The consequences of the segmented workplace were rather serious. Because Muslim workers were largely based in departments that had few workers from other religious groups, they set up a separate organisation. They not only felt excluded from trade union politics, but also felt that the Gandhian union was under the

[13] Shah, 'Communal Riots in Gujarat'.

influence of the mill owners. They felt more at home in their own organisation than in the dominant Hindu TLA.[14]

More importantly, the union leadership repeatedly failed in extending support to Muslim workers. In 1937, mill owners cut the wages of weavers by 25 per cent, but the TLA, which was associated with the Congress, maintained a studied silence. The Lal Vavta Mill Kamgar Union established by the Communists assumed leadership, and about 50,000, mainly Muslim workers, went on a strike that continued for three weeks. The Congress government proceeded to ban all meetings and processions, and arrested several communist and socialist leaders and workers. When the Congress and the mill owners failed to control the strike, Gulzari Lal Nanda, the Majdoor Mahajan leader who was in charge of the labour portfolio of the government, brokered a settlement. The wage cut was thereafter reduced by 7 per cent. Dinkar Mehta, one of the leaders of the striking workers and a pioneer of the Communist party in the state, wrote in his biography:

> Almost all the workers of the weaving sections participated in this strike and a sizeable number among them were Muslim. We realised through experience that although Muslim workers had respect and sympathy for Lal Vavta, their political consciousness had not broken out of the confines of the Muslim League. This ambivalent attitude persisted among Muslim workers for a long time.[15]

After the strike, some textile mill owners discharged a large number of Muslim workers, and thousands lost their jobs. Neither the ministry nor the Majdoor Mahajan leaders took steps to reinstate the workers. On the other hand, the Muslim League leadership condemned the action of the mill owners and held the Congress ministry responsible for the prevailing situation of Muslim workers. It is not, therefore, surprising that the Muslim workers turned to the Muslim League.[16] The League had a big presence in the city where it had established a volunteer corps. Members of the Khaksar Movement, who were mainly Muslim artisans, underwent military training in uniform, and

---

[14] Breman, *The Making and the Unmaking of a Working Class*, 75.
[15] Yagnik and Sheth, *The Shaping of Modern Gujarat*, 218.
[16] Ibid., 219.

they considered themselves the 'Army of Islam'. The Movement mobilised the Muslim community effectively, and when Muhammed Ali Jinnah visited Ahmedabad in 1940, a 35,000 strong crowd consisting mostly of Muslim workers assembled to hear him speak.

Clearly, the trade union could not bring together various communities in a shared project that defined the common interests of the workers. Nor did the structure of this trade union manage to transform the social context of hierarchy and exclusion in the city, even at the point when the textile industry attracted a major part of the workforce in the city. The TLA concludes Masihi remained a conservative union working on Gandhian lines. The whole approach of the union tended to strengthen narrow loyalties of the workers, at the cost of solidarity of the working class.[17]

Although the Gandhian union pursued a policy of positive discrimination with respect to Harijans (children of God), concludes Ian Breman, it displayed a certain reticence towards Muslims. This was reinforced by a tendency among Muslims themselves not to join the TLA. As a result, this religious minority was in a vulnerable position. This vulnerability was reinforced when their interests were not represented adequately.[18]

The final pronouncement on the nature and the consequences of trade union politics was made by the 1929 Royal Commission on Labour, which observed that 'in Ahmedabad the [textile] workers, excluding the Musalman weavers, are organised in a group of craft unions'.[19] A significant precondition for a democratic civil society, that workplace and union politics might forge unity among people divided by religion simply went missing.

The Ghetto

The other aspect of the making of a divided Ahmedabad is the specific nature of the built environment. Distinct housing clusters

---

[17] Cited in Breman, *The Making and the Unmaking of a Working Class*, 133.
[18] Ibid., 133–34.
[19] Cited in Holmstorm, *Industry and Inequality*, 65.

were constructed on the basis of religion, and in the case of Hindus, on the basis of caste. Within the congested walled city, residential, commercial and religious spaces were not separated from each other. Ahmedabad resembled both a traditional Hindu town and a typical Islamic city.[20] However, the residential pattern of the city was characterised by two distinct kinds of housing types for the Hindus and the Muslims. The Hindus lived in a cluster known as the *pol*[21] and the Muslims in *mohallas*. The word *pol* is derived from the Sanskrit word *pratoli*, which means entrance to an enclosed area. This entrance or gate was generally known by the name of the community living in the enclosed area. Even as *pols* and *mohallas* marked the clustering of the city population predominantly on religious lines, *pols* themselves were organised on the grounds of what caste the inhabitant or the prospective inhabitant belonged to.

Right up to the late 19th century, owners of the *pols* would sell land within the area to people of their own caste. In 1872, there were 356 *pols* in Ahmedabad, and some of them exist till today.[22] Within the *pols* were situated a quadrangle, a temple, wells and common toilets. To some extent, residential property in the *pol* was held in common. The residents of the *pol* maintained the area by collecting funds through fines, sale of house property and gifts.[23]

As far back as 1714, violence between the Hindus and Muslims accelerated the process of separate living. Communal violence was precipitated by the festival of Holi which, earmarking the advent of Spring, involves the throwing of colour on other persons. One historian narrates the origins of what is possibly the first communal riot in Ahmedabad through the lens of historical records:

At the doors of his [Madan Gopal's] house, Hari Ram was indulging himself in enthusiastically playing Holi with a group of sarafs

[20] Raychaudhuri, 'Colonialism, Indigenous Elites', 680.
[21] *Pol* (pronounced 'pole') is a housing cluster which comprises many families of a particular group, linked by caste, profession or religion but not invariably.
[22] Notable in the present day *pols* are Mhurat Pol, Mandvi-ni-Pol and Lakha Patel-ni-Po.
[23] Doshi, *Traditional Neighbourhood*, 74.

and companion … pouring colour, smearing gulal in a bacchanalian manner … as is their custom. Perchance, a Muslim happened to pass through that street and fell in with them. Taking hold of him, they showered colour, gulal, and dust, and abuses on him…. He, considering the situation, got away by some means and, in that very condition, took some people and went to intimate to his holiness … Muhammed Ali.

The complaint to Muhammed Ali, who was a sermon giver and who was consequently seized by 'regard for the honour of Islam and the cause of the true faith', bore somewhat expected results. Ali went to the mosque, met people of his own sect and, subsequently, Muslims 'arrived in groups and bands from every nook and corner shouting "faith, faith"'.[24] A general concourse and assemblage of Muslims resorted to riot and lawlessness, murder and plunder. The crowd ransacked and burnt shops in the cloth market and vandalised the property of the sarafs. It then turned to the house of Madan Gopal and other Hindu households. The fight between the barricaded households and the crowd continued for two days and was only dampened when the Governor sent troops to quell the confrontation. But meanwhile, people had been wounded or killed from both sides. The Ahmedabad riot of 1714, notes Haider, was the only incident of its kind in the recorded history of the city from 1411 AD to 1761. It was confined to a particular locality, and the cause of the riot could be traced to professional commercial rivalry.[25] More importantly, the local administration stepped in to calm the situation and terminated the violence.

Although the riot was contained by the Muslim administration in two days, it seems to have intensified not only the trend of separate housing for the two religious communities, but also the construction of barricades between these clusters for purposes of defence. The *pols*, which comprised a labyrinth of high wooden houses, streets too narrow for wheeled traffic, and cul-de-sacs, would have only one or at the most two entrances (apart from secret ones), one main street with crooked lanes branching on either side, and walls and gates that

---

[24] Haider, 'A "Holi Riot" of 1714', 129.
[25] Gillion, *Ahmedabad*, 144.

were barred at night. In short, these *pols* had limited connectivity to the outside world, and particularly to the spaces in which the Muslims lived. Whereas within the walled city, the *pol* and the *mohalla* bred some interaction among the community, these spatial forms also served to pre-empt social interaction with the members of the other community living in their own spaces. Residential segregation bred both suspicion and hatred, and till 2002, most of the communal conflicts have occurred in the old city.

The Making of a Modern Town

Ahmedabad came under British rule in 1817 when the colonial power concluded a treaty with the Peshwa of Poona and the Gaikwad of Baroda. When John Andrew Dunlop, the first British Collector, took possession of Ahmedabad on 30 November 1817, the city presented a sad sight. Walls had broken down, deserted buildings were filled with debris and vegetable growth, houses went unrepaired, and bands of criminals and wild animals roamed unhindered within the walls at night or even in the daytime. One of Dunlop's first requests to the administration was for more police, and more muskets, to deal with all kinds of marauders, both men and animals.[26] But after setting the city to order, Dunlop developed a wider objective—that of reviving Ahmedabad as a centre of trade, weaving and handicrafts.

Compared to other cities in colonial India, Ahmedabad was developed through indigenous endeavours. The first mill that came up in 1858 was established by a Nagar Brahmin Ranchhodlal Chhotalal. These mills were located outside the walled city in the eastern part of the city. The revival of business and manufacturing activity in the city, the introduction of railways that connected the city with markets in the rest of India, the development of ports that allowed textiles to be shipped to Europe, particularly during the time of the American civil war and general intensification of trade created favourable conditions for the growth of the textile industry. By the late 1800s, Ahmedabad had become the centre of the textile industry in India. Between 1914

[26] Ibid., 42.

and 1920, the number of spindles in the city increased by 12.09 per cent, looms by 17.79 per cent and the workforce by 23 per cent.[27] By 1930, the number of textile mills reached 64, and by 1935, the city had 84 mills. Ahmedabad came to be known as the 'Manchester of India'. By the middle of the 20th century, about 80 per cent of the population of the city was dependent on the textile industry for its living. The booming textile industry attracted migrants, and the population of the city swelled.

In the eastern part of the city, working people lived in group housing tenements or chawls built by the mill owners. In these chawls, upper-caste Hindus lived in discrete clusters, whereas the so-called low-caste Hindus and the Muslims lived in other residential clusters. Outsiders were prevented from entering the chawls through the raising of rents and stringent conditions of sale.

By the middle of the 20th century, congestion caused by the juxtaposition of textile mills, chawls, narrow streets and market places in the industrial belt and in the walled city motivated some of the wealthier inhabitants to migrate across the river to the western part of the city. But the practices of residential segregation in the *pol* and in segregated chawl were reproduced in a new form. In the newly developed western part of the city largely formed by outmigration from the old city, housing societies bought land, subdivided it, and developed residential accommodation for families. Because housing societies were formed by like-minded individuals belonging mainly to a distinct religious and caste group, it was relatively easy for them to exclude people from other communities and even other castes. In short, exclusions of residential clusters in the old city were reproduced in the new city, with most housing societies determining who should, or should not, live there. Ahmedabad indeed has the reputation of containing the largest number of housing societies. But contrary to classical theories of capitalism, according to which land becomes a mere commodity in capitalist societies, in Ahmedabad, land was closely connected to the social, that is, religious and caste status.

---

[27] Raychaudhuri, 'Colonialism, Indigenous Elites', 684.

Although these housing societies provided shelters for both Muslim and Hindu communities, a majority of the Muslim community, which belonged to the working class, continued to live in the old city, in areas that rapidly became slums. Some of these areas are Dariapur, Kalupur, Gomtipur, Behrampur, Bapunagar, Jamalpur and Shahpur. Our research has shown that it is precisely in these areas that the worst communal riots have taken place. Narrow streets, congestion and clusters of Muslim families living together have facilitated the targeting of an entire cluster of houses.

The First Phase of Ghettoisation

The first intra-city migration was the product of choice. The second stream of migration from one part of the city to the other was by force of circumstance. By the late 1960s, Muslim families were compelled to leave their homes and places of work. The virulence and the scale of the 1969 riot were to earmark the onset of ghettoisation. This was the time when Juhapura came to be a refuge for the victims of violence. Juhapura is one of the largest settlements of the Muslim community, about 300,000 people containing about 46 per cent of the total Muslim community in the Urban Agglomeration.[28] Located on the highway that leads to the capital city Gandhinagar, Juhapura borders the Vejalpur area that is Hindu dominated. The road between the two areas is ritually typed as the border and the settlement as Pakistan. Originally, Juhapura consisted of poor Muslim households, but after the 2002 pogrom, affluent Muslim families have moved into the area. Juhapura falls outside the boundaries of the Municipal Corporation, and most of the land of this area is agricultural land. Therefore, the ghetto lacks infrastructure and services such as health facilities, schools, power supply, roads, drainage, street lighting and transport. Whatever infrastructure has been created in the area, such as micro-credit networks, schools, shops, eating places and mosques, has been built with private funds. Juhapura is not connected to the city by public transport because it is located on the highway. The location

[28] Fieldwork was carried out in Juhapura in July 2006.

of the ghetto has, therefore, deprived people of employment, access to good schools and health facilities.

The Second Phase of Ghettoisation[29]

Although the ghettoisation process began in 1969, Hindus and Muslims still resided in mixed neighbourhoods, and within these neighbourhoods, Muslims and Hindus lived in separate housing clusters that were separated by a fence or a street. By the 1980s, the ghettoisation process intensified, and by the 1990s, only a few mixed neighbourhoods remained.[30] It was these mixed neighbourhoods that were systematically and brutally targeted in the violence of 2002. During the unleashing of the violence, Hindu houses were marked with saffron flags so that they could be protected from violence. The worst affected areas were on both sides of the railway track in Ahmedabad.

The victims of violence were herded into poorly funded and grossly inadequate relief camps mainly set up by Muslim religious organisations. In a short time, these camps were rapidly wound up, and the inhabitants, after being given pathetically inadequate funds as 'compensation'—funds sometimes as low as ₹1,200—were now on their own, thrown onto the mercy of a society that had proved complicit in the carnage, either actively or through studied silence. The state government, recognising neither the plight nor the needs of the victims of communal violence, simply refused to take any action which would help these people to rebuild their shattered lives. At this point, a few civil society organisations, particularly Islamic organisations such as the Tablighi Jamaat, the Jamaat-e-Islami and the Jamiat Ulama-i-Hind, and specifically the Islamic Relief Committee, which is the relief wing of the Jamaat-e-Islami, stepped in to help people relocate and resettle.

---

[29] Much of this section is built upon the findings of fieldwork carried out in these areas in September 2007. An earlier version of this section was published in *The Economic & Political Weekly*. Chandhoke, Priyadarshi, Tyagi, and Khanna, 'The Displaced of Ahmedabad', 10–14.

[30] Yagnik and Sheth, *The Shaping of Modern Gujarat*, 230.

Some land was acquired on the outskirts of the city, and the victims were resettled in four pockets: Juhapura, Ramol, Vatva and Danilimda.

All of these 'colonies' are on the periphery of Ahmedabad and are poorly connected to the city where most of the jobs are generated. The 729 households that have been relocated in 15 such colonies in Ahmedabad have been displaced mainly from eastern Ahmedabad, from areas such as Naroda Patiya, Gomtipur, Dariapur, Saraspur, Bapunagar Jamalpur, Rakhial and other inner-city areas that have repeatedly suffered from periodic outbursts of communal violence since 1969.

But the legal status of the land upon which these shanty towns have been constructed is legally contested, because much of it is agricultural land. This has instilled dread among the residents that they still live in temporary settlements, which can be easily mowed down by the bulldozers of the Ahmedabad Municipal Corporation (AMC). Not only are most resettlement colonies remotely located from the city where jobs are to be found, but also they are far away from schools and health clinics that are an indispensable prerequisite of living a life free of want, ill-health and illiteracy. In sum, these displaced Muslim families are fated to remain outside the reach of all the amenities that the government slogan of 'Vibrant Gujarat' might perchance offer to those who form an integral part of society and the polity. It is clear that for the government which was controlled by the party of the religious right—the BJP and which was re-elected on a narrow majority in the state assembly elections of December 2017—these families just do not form an integral part of Gujarati society and politics. They have been expelled both spatially and socially to the margins of the city.

In these bare, stark, inhospitable areas, civil society organisations helped potential inhabitants to construct rackety one-room tenements, without water supply, without electricity, without access to internal roads, because there were none, and without sanitation and sewerage for families. And it is here, in these barren spaces, that the victims of the communal carnage in Ahmedabad have been settled, and expected to begin their life anew, amidst even more deprivation that they faced in their original habitats.

Many of these families still own some land—where once houses that were burnt down by Hindutva goons stood—in their original habitats. But even as bitter memories of the brutal violence that was inflicted upon them and their families and community haunt collective psyches, people fear to go back to their homes. They prefer to live in these desolate, ugly and rundown one-room tenements, which house as many as five members of a family. But this is not the major problem that confronts refugees. Other and much more serious problems stalk the everyday life of the inhabitants of these settlements. For instance, in the resettlement colony ironically called the 'Citizens Nagar' in Danilimda, families who once lived in the most communally hit area of Ahmedabad, Naroda Patiya, have been resettled. This particular 'citizen's' colony has been built literally in the shadow of a massive mountain. The only problem is that this mountain has been constructed by human beings, out of the garbage collected from every part of Ahmedabad that is dumped here every morning.

The mountain of garbage dominates the collective life of the inhabitants. The stench that emanates from this rubbish dump overwhelms both sense and sensibilities of people who live not only in the colony but also in the surrounding areas. More critically, during the monsoons, the garbage overflows the mountain-sized dump, runs through what passes for roads within the colony and enters homes. The garbage, which is highly toxic, has penetrated the ground water. Because the inhabitants of the colony do not have access to clean drinking water, they are forced to consume this contaminated ground water. This yellow, grimy and filthy water is so polluted that it cannot be but the harbinger of disease. Not surprisingly, gastronomical diseases are rampant in this locality.

Despite repeated representations, the AMC has made no attempt to look for an alternate site for the dumping of the garbage of the city. To make matters worse, residents complain that the AMC often deposits carcasses of dead animals around the colonies, and the revolting odour makes the place simply uninhabitable. The plight of the residents who have been subjected to involuntary displacement does not end there. When the AMC begins to burn the garbage in the dump, the pollutant-ridden smoke, which manages to pervade every pore of the body, leads to all kinds of health problems, particularly respiratory diseases. But the AMC, which is responsible for providing services to citizens, has refused to take notice of the deplorable condition of this colony or of the appalling lives that the victims who live there lead.

Built as they were in a hurry, these so-called houses are in dreadful condition; water seeps into the rooms during the monsoons and rubbish flows along what passes for internal roads. These houses have low roofs, no ventilation, and have been provided with temporary and unsafe electrical wiring. The land these houses are built on is generally low lying, and, therefore, water logging is common. The situation is worsened by the fact that there is absolutely no drainage system, no pavements or street lighting in the nominal colony. Vulnerable and insecure as the families already are, the highly uncongenial and sorry surroundings in which they are forced to live lead to deep feelings of helplessness and alienation. These feelings are exacerbated by the fact that no aid from the government to make these colonies habitable—to build schools and health clinics or to provide transportation facility to the city where people can work—is forthcoming.

Similar problems attend other resettlement colonies. Since most of these colonies are on the outskirts of the city, they are surrounded by industries spewing pollutants, all of which makes the areas hazardous for human habitation. In Sundaram Nagar in Bapunagar, for example, cotton dust emanating twice a day from the burning of industrial waste makes breathing difficult for the residents. The children and the adults whom we met have developed lung-related diseases.

The residents of most of these resettlement colonies eke out a bare existence without any basic amenities, be it drinking water, sanitation, drainage, health care, education for children or approach roads and modes of transportation. Children have been forced to drop out of school and take to daily wage labour, because it is too expensive to hire rickshaws to take the children to the school. A few colonies have now been given Anganwadi centres, more than five years after they were established, but no schools for children have been provided. Residents of Ekta Nagar complained that they have to pay ₹12 daily to send their children to the nearest school. Since they cannot afford this small sum, children have dropped out of school. Most families are terrified of sending their daughters to school outside the neighbourhood after the sexual violence that Muslim girls had been subjected to in 2002. Resultantly, an entire generation of children of Muslim families, who are less educated than their parents, is growing up in the city. Health care for the victims of the communal violence is equally deplorable. There are barely any health care facilities available for these colonies. There have been instances when due to the absence of health facilities, patients have died on the way to remote hospitals, and babies have often been delivered on the road.

One major consequence of the way in which resettlement has been carried out by private organisations in spatially isolated areas is that people have been forced to abandon their previous vocations and look for alternative employment. Most of them now work in informal and petty jobs, and are known as *chhuttak mazdoors*. Most of the men work as auto and cycle rickshaw pullers, petty vendors and casual workers in nearby neighbourhoods, whereas women work mostly as domestic help. Consequently, there has been a universal decline in income, which has dropped to less than half to what people used to earn before the violence and relocation. The sharp drop in incomes has not only led to extreme pauperisation, but also the ramifications of poverty are seen in a new wave of child labour, and the growth of a generation of illiterate and unskilled youth.

Since the state government continues to be in the denial mode, non-governmental and other civil society organisations have stepped in to support the victims of communal violence. Notably, whereas a small group of such organisations has done a commendable job in resettling victims of communal violence, and it is because of their concerted effort that these people have been able to survive, a majority of civil society organisations have proved indifferent to the cause. The cloud of Hindutva obviously hangs heavily on civil society organisations. Post carnage, the relief work was carried out predominantly with the help of the resources of the Islamic Relief Committee along with few more agencies such as Action Aid. The role played by some of civil society organisations has been highly commendable, and the victims are all praise for them. Organisations such as Aman Biradari and Jan Vikas, for example, have waged a long battle against the indifferent attitude of the state agencies towards the victims of communal violence and the issue of the relocation of these victims. The documentation carried out by some of these organisations has gone a long way in exposing the callous attitude of the state towards victims of violence and in fixing responsibility. It is with the help of these organisations that displaced families have been able to press for their rights and put their demands before the government at the local level. That the plight of these victims has not been subsumed completely in the state-sponsored din about Vibrant Gujarat and the benefits of globalisation is due entirely to these organisations.

However, private initiatives in resettling such massive numbers of the displaced cannot substitute for state action. For one, given the limited resources at the disposal of these agencies, relocation has been partial and insufficient, and falls well short of the requirements of the residents. Neither the poorly constructed houses nor the pathetic state of facilities and services can give the victims a sense of security or a feeling that they are being compensated for a major lapse of justice. Two, since the colonies are a product of initiatives by non-governmental organisations, they are obviously not in accordance with the 'urban plan'. Seventeen years after the communal riot, the victims of communal violence continue to pay for the sins committed by others. The status of these colonies as unplanned or unauthorised gives the civic agency a pretext to deny basic amenities to the inhabitants. Three, the land on which colonies are constructed is privately bought, in most of the cases by the Islamic Relief Committee. This does not help either. According to city authorities, these lands are 'not for residential purposes', and purchase of this land for residential use is not legal. This breeds trepidation and uncertainty among people who have lived amidst fear most of their lives.

The notion of the ghetto codes many messages, none of which carry positive connotations. Consider, for instance, that the term 'ghetto' evokes resonances of not only the clustering together of one community in a constricted and circumscribed spatial location, but also of the stigmatisation of the residents of the area by other inhabitants of the city. Throughout history, ghettos enclose not the favoured but the disfavoured section of the population, as was the case of the Jewish community in Germany and Poland in the inter-war years. Ghettos are normally unmarked by any of the civic amenities and services which are the basic right of citizens in a democracy. Notably the origin of the ghetto lies not in the free choice to live or not to live among one's own community, but in circumstances that are not within the control of the residents, notably fear. Vulnerable groups prefer to live among their own, even if where they have to live is not to their liking. Above all, ghettos are easy to target in times of crisis; therefore, the inhabitants live amidst the perpetual production and reproduction of terror and anxiety.

It follows that the inhabitants of the ghetto are deprived of four sets of basic rights that are the due of every citizen in a democracy such as India: (a) the freedom to move freely and reside wherever one may choose, (b) the right not to be physically harmed or deprived of property without legitimate reasons, (c) the right not be deprived of liberty without due cause and (d) the right to social and economic goods which are the fundamental preconditions of living a life of dignity. In sum, they are denied the right not to be discriminated against and to be treated with equal concern. The spatial marginalisation of the Muslim inhabitants of the city of Ahmedabad, and ghettoisation, is an indication of the denial of basic civil, political, social and economic rights granted by the Indian Constitution. The built environment of the ghetto, to put the point across starkly, can be seen as a geographical manifestation of the exclusion and the disempowerment of an entire section of citizens in a society that claims democratic credentials. It is the product of communalism that has transited to communal violence.

Ahmedabad is today a divided city marked by the spatial marginalisation of the Muslims and their economic, political and social exclusion from city life. A city that has been characterised by different patterns of residential ordering right from its establishment in 1411 is now reorganised on the principle of 'single community areas' where no inter-community mixing is possible.[31] Spatial segregation and resultant ghettoisation mean that the children of one community have

[31] Ray Chaudhary, 'Sabarmati', 698–699.

absolutely no interaction with the children of the other community, no mixed schools, no playgrounds in which children of both communities can play, no extra curricula activities that can form the basis of a future solidarity and no personal friendships that involve visiting each other's homes and inter-dining. In addition, the inhabitants of these areas are subjected to rank and vicious stereotyping and abuses by the majority community.

The ghettoisation of the Muslim community has led to serious consequences. Ghettos narrow the cultural and thereby the political horizons of the inhabitants, close off options and prohibit creative mingling of perspectives. In the process, the idea that cultural communities as living mutable entities are created and transformed through intermingling with other communities is negated. Both Muslims and Hindus have suffered in the process. A culturally plural context provides a vibrant background for assessing and reflecting on one's norms, beliefs and cultures. It follows that interaction with other persons who are like us, or not like us, provides us with a valuable basis of understanding and knowledge, and gives us the capacity to evaluate and rework our own options. When such an opportunity is closed off, this leads to the narrowing of perspectives, constriction of personalities and intolerance. This is applicable both to Hindus and Muslims.

Today, Ahmedabad has few residential colonies with mixed populations and is divided almost completely into Hindu and Muslim inhabited areas. The difference is that whereas Hindus live both in the poverty stricken and in the affluent areas of the city, Muslims live in areas which are not only poverty stricken, deprived of basic amenities, often outside the pale of governance, but also subjected to hateful stereotyping. Involuntary or forced migration to the ghetto is one indication of lack of choices, which arguably is the hallmark of democratic freedom and citizenship rights. The absence of infrastructure in these ghettos in the form of lack of health clinics, educational institutions, provision of clean drinking water, power, proper housing, roads and general environmental degradation is another indication of social and economic rights. In the process, an entire religious minority has been downgraded from citizen to subject.

Ahmedabad provides us with a classic example of an urban area in which members of the majority community have worked together and lived in neighbouring residential areas but at a distance from each other. Separate and unequal living and workplaces have produced and reproduced not only inequality but also hateful communal stereotypes. The road between the Muslim ghetto and Hindu residential areas is called in popular parlance, the border. Muslim residential areas are termed disparagingly as 'little Pakistan'. Industrialisation should have brought solidarity to the working classes divided along religion; on the contrary, it has reproduced communal divisions. This background communalism did not translate into communal riots till 1946, when a number of triggers etched violence onto the public sphere of the city.

Putting 'Minorities in Their Place'

It is more than possible that ignoble motives underpin riots that scar lives and living places, collective memories and individual psyches, for example, the attempt to grab remunerative land or the settling of personal scores. Running like a strong skein through these incidents, however, is another story: that of struggle for power. These incidents of violence are neither random nor abstracted from deeper competition for a monopoly over power in society. They relentlessly pinpoint the deeper causes of violence between communities. Communal violence, simply, throws onto the political horizon the one question that is crucial to democracy—the equal standing of all citizens and their rights to freedom, to religion and to justice. Riots inscribe in blood the following core questions: Who will control society and the state, who will hegemonise symbolic representations of society and who will command the material benefits this society has to offer?

The shameful objective of purveyors of violence, who engineer and direct mass killings, is to redraw the normative map drafted by Indian democracy and the constitution—that of equality of political status irrespective of religion, caste, ethnicity, gender and class. People who wield weapons of violence appear to be in the business of warning others, those others who would dare to subvert social hierarchies that in some sections of our society are considered ordained by the law of nature. Communal violence seeks to create and institutionalise social order based on hierarchy and exclusion, domination and subordination. This form of violence tries to destabilise the new democratic order constructed on the principles of non-discrimination and equality, mutual respect and civility, toleration and secularism as organising principles of the political community.

It is not surprising that over the years, riots have taken a heavy toll on our society. Today, the fond and much-repeated belief that India is a plural and diverse society lies in tatters. The Nehruvian creed of 'unity in diversity' is endangered. It is jeopardised by the so-called cow-protectors and the self-styled representatives of the majority Hindu community who roam freely on the streets always on the lookout for vulnerable Muslim and Dalit citizens of India. The bodies of members of these groups are then imprinted with a vile and destructive brand of politics. It is time we stand back, metaphorically speaking, and consider what kind of a society we have become. We are turning into a distasteful and dreadful majoritarian society. Our political imagination has been crippled by the illusive power of demographic numbers and majoritarianism. We have become insensitive to brutality. We have learned to live with, even if not comfortably, unimaginable vicious acts that target our fellow citizens. The basic principle of justice—that every Indian, irrespective of her caste and community, shall share equally in the burdens and benefits of society—has been infringed repeatedly. Indian democracy is imperilled. Still a majority of us want passionately to live in peace and civility with our fellow citizens. So we ask the following troubled question: How on earth can people who speak different languages, and when language is culture, manage to live together in civility?

The Project of Living Together

It is perhaps undeniable that we can, ultimately, live a life of civility only when we live in a decent society. To reiterate what has been suggested above, philosophy tells us how to lead a good life, and political theory tells us that a good life can only be led in a good society and within a state that reins in and inhibits the ugliness of vulgar human ambitions and fosters solidarity. We have to inhabit a state that ensures dignity and respect to each and every person in order to pursue our plans and our projects. For these, and other reasons, we need to reiterate our commitment to building a good society, unless we wish to be dismissed by history as just another social order that does not value human life, a society where the overpowering impulse to power runs rough shod over all other sentiments.

In any case, in modern India, we simply do not have the luxury of living apart. Indians have to relearn how to live together in civility. There is no alternative. We no longer inhabit a society in which groups and individuals can afford to live in a back-to-back relationship. In a modern competitive economy and polity, people are brought into contact with others who may well be anonymous at other times. They collaborate, they partner each other, but they also compete for the benefits of a competitive market economy and an equally competitive electoral democracy. It is the fabric of this interdependence that right-wing groups, in search of political power, and yet more crude and unabashed power, seek to rent along the lines of religion. Still we have to relearn how to live together in civility, and, for this, we need to recognise the value of secularism, for a majority of Indians have no taste for the credo of hate and the protocols of violence. We have no choice to reiterate and perhaps reinvent ways of living together in a competitive and aspirational society.

This can only be secured when groups of people who belong to different religions, different languages, and different modes of beliefs think about living together because they recognise and respect differences as well as overlapping interests. Secularism is of utmost importance to the human condition, because most of the time, most people do not want quotidian or episodic violence to destabilise their lives and their societies. Their quality of life, relationships, occupations, leisure, hobbies, passions and pursuits, and all activities that make life worth living pale into insignificance and disappear. These cannot be resurrected if the shadow of violence, or even incivility, continues to hover over the horizons of our society. Whereas civility depends, to a large extent, on the way inhabitants of that society think of or approach people who are like them and people who are not like them, the legal framework of the project of living together has to be established by the state. The state must adopt a policy of fairness towards all people. Neutrality towards all religious groups is the responsibility of the democratic state towards the people. We call this 'principle secularism'.

Let us not mistake the matter. India will cede its claim to be a great civilisation if Indians continue to turn inwards towards their own narrow communities, stop being sensitive to the humiliation and the pain of fellow citizens, participate in discrimination against minorities and continue to display with some insensitivity, rank bigotry. The descent into complete incivility has to be stopped in India. It has to be stopped for the sake of India. The moment we conceptualise the project of civility or living together civilly as an alternative to the miasma of fear that hangs over our head today, the concept of secularism as state policy and tolerance as a social principle map themselves onto the claim that India is a great civilisation and has a great future. A society can hardly claim greatness if it preys upon the insecurities of both the minority and, ironically, the majority. A broad and tolerant vision is crucial to the project of civility.

We have little option but to construct civility out of the troubling disorder that attends chaotic and messy political life in India. The two values that might be able to restore civility to the body politic are the political virtues of secularism and the social virtue of tolerance. Although these two virtues have been conflated in our public discourse and in the rulings handed down by the Supreme Court as we shall see, I make a distinction between them in the argument that follows. Secularism runs the argument in this work is a principle of state policy, and tolerance is a principle that holds a diverse and often conflictual society together.

These are not new concepts/values for India, though they seem to have fallen into disuse through sheer neglect. Admittedly, these two concepts cannot match the stormy power of incendiary communalised rhetoric that invokes nightmares of 'religion in danger'. They cannot evoke primordial passions. Nor are they meant to. We have reasons to be thankful for this lack. The politics of anger and retribution is destructive of civility, let alone social harmony; they are best avoidable. Toleration and secularism are 'cool' and cooling concepts that tell us how plural societies should be civilly organised. They tell us how we can live a life of dignity in a society. Let us, again, not mistake the issue or underrate it. To participate in hate speech, or even to listen while fundamentalists rave and rant about minority religions, argue for the divine right of the majority faith to rule and be silent in the face of violence unleashed on bodies and minds, diminishes not only the target, but it also diminishes us as human beings with sensibilities based on mutual respect for fellow citizens and human beings. We become lesser beings, stripped of all the qualities that make us human.

Both secularism and tolerance permit people of different religious persuasions to live together in civility and, perhaps, harmony. It is this property that marks out an inclusive and civil society from an uncivil and odious society based on narrow notions of who belongs and who does not. It is this property that lends to tolerance as a social virtue, and secularism as a political and democratic norm, some charm. This charm is not perceptible at first glance, and it is certainly not visible to a crude political understanding. The appeal of both these concepts is subtle and discreet. We have to look for it. Perhaps only those who appreciate the values of pluralism and civility can discover the key to civil coexistence.

It is time to move towards the aesthetics of the political, to work out what is civil, to see what is worth preserving and to replenish the wasteland our society has been reduced to. It is time to think anew about tolerance and secularism. It is certainly time to turn our faces and attention away from hate speech to civility. It is more than time to re-adopt toleration and secularism as ways of life and politics. And it is definitely time that India redefines itself in imagination and in speech. We ought to remember history. Hateful speeches and actions led to the Partition of India, which decimated lives and devastated livelihoods, and left Northern and Eastern India wracked by brutal memories. Till today, many Indians are wracked by nostalgia for times when all communities worked, lived, celebrated, sang and worshiped together.

Today we are a country in which minds and lives are ghettoised and partitioned. We have lost the ability to accept others not despite, but because of their beliefs. We have to relearn the ethics and aesthetics of civility. For this, we need to recapture the virtue of tolerance and secularism. Tolerance is an ancient virtue, and secularism is a relatively modern one, but even then it was born in India a century ago. Over the time, the principle has become a part of political vocabularies, mainly because it has acquired an Indian face.

CHAPTER 3

Secularism
The Debate

Religion, though it has undoubtedly brought comfort to innumer-able human beings and stabilised society by its values, has checked the tendency to change and progress inherent in human society.[1]

The Political Predicament of Our Age

It has been suggested that the questions that political theorists ask of the human condition are eternal. Some of these questions are as follows: What makes for a good society? How do we realise justice? What is distinctive about the human condition? How do members of a diverse society learn to live together? These questions fetch answers that are necessarily bound by reasons of time and space. Even as they address political predicaments, political theorists build on older truths to generate new answers suitable for their age. In the process, they rearticulate ancient truths for every era in an appropriate vocabulary. It is time, I think, to recast the concept of secularism, an oft used and now abused term, in a new mode and in ways that are appropriate for our current age that has abandoned secularism.

[1] Nehru, *The Discovery of India*, 541–547.

That the BJP has done so is not surprising. The question of how people of a plural and diverse society can learn to live together has simply been dismissed by right-wing organisations. All attempts to put forth an alternative point of view have been dismissed as anti-national or as irrelevant. The Indian National Congress, once the party of Jawaharlal Nehru and Mahatma Gandhi, has given up on secularism and adopted a soft Hindutva. It, sadly, aspires to be a weaker and paler version of the BJP. The only parties who are still committed to secularism are sundry fragments of the Janata Dal (JD). The problem is that we do not know which way the various JDs are going to go, whether they will team up with the BJP or with other like-minded parties to acquire power. Secularism is in danger of being canned either as irrelevant or as unsuited to the deep religiosity of India.

The problem is that secularism has been delegitimised simply because it had become the legitimising motif of many parties at one point of time. The vocabulary remained, but no one seemed to be sure of what the concept meant or what it stood for. Stripped of the historically specific meaning it had acquired in India since the second decade of the 20th century, secularism has been reduced to simulacra. It no longer represents anything in the hands of its friends and foes; that is, it does not represent anything that is of import to the master concept that occupies India, democracy. The last meaningful debate on secularism was held in the 1990s against the spectre of the rise of the BJP in Indian politics, and the destruction of the Babri Masjid in 1992. The only exception has been the work of Rajeev Bhargava who has laboured over the years to expound on the distinctiveness of Indian secularism. In other circles of academia, the search for indigeneity has led scholars away from what they consider imported concepts and towards an authentic Indian political theory. Whether there can be an authentic Indian political theory in a country whose traditions, meaning systems and ways of conceptualising the world have been colonised is another debate, partly addressed in the next chapter.

In sum, this is not, perhaps, the best of time to defend secularism. But it is also not the worst of times to revive the debate in India. The country has paid a heavy price for devaluing the concept. The near exit of secularism from political imaginings, and visions of how a plural and complex society can be held together, is a matter for some regret. We have landed up in a situation where hate speech and incredibly violent acts towards vulnerable sections of our society, the minorities and Dalits, dominate the headlines of morning newspapers. Barbaric and unspeakable acts of violence are the new normal. We are in an age where lynching of vulnerable sections of our own people is videotaped by watching crowds and put on to the social media. These appallingly depraved acts, symptomatic of a society that has ceased to care for its own vulnerable sections, are cause for deep concern. The idea of India as a tolerant and a civil society is under serious attack. Life in India has become fearful and intimidating, as a muscular nationalism is paraded on the streets by self-appointed custodians of a shallow personal and political morality.

They fail to understand that, or perhaps deliberately do not comprehend that by putting aside secularism as superfluous to our political life, India is in great danger of misplacing something that is of great value. The marginalisation of the principle from political debates also happens to be short-sighted. The binary opposite of secularism is not communalism as is popularly believed, but an intolerant and majoritarian government at best, and theocratic government which rules in the name of one religion at worst. Both forms of rule insistently subvert the basic precepts of democratic life, that of freedom, equality, rights and justice. Unless India is prepared to give up on democracy and more importantly on the Constitution, there is need to reiterate and re-inscribe the value of secularism. There is need to discover or rather uncover its discreet charms.

This is not to say that all is well with the concept. Secularism is today caught in a maelstrom of frustrated expectations and hopes belied. It is in crisis, not because it is irrelevant, but because it has been subjected to rank overuse and invested with far too many expectations in the past. The concept has been summoned to perform various and arguably too many functions in our post-colonial society, from national integration to gender justice. In the vocabulary of many an undemocratic political leader, it even stands in for democracy. These leaders may know the 'D' of democracy but are ready to swear in the name of secularism.

Unable to bear the weight of too many political projects and ambitions laden upon it, the overburdened concept of secularism shows signs of imploding. As Needham and Sunder Rajan suggest that secularism is called upon to perform various and arguably too many functions in a post-colonial society: cultural nationalism, minority/community rights, liberal individual rights, identity politics and the politics of gender.[2] Priya Kumar likewise argues that secularism in India has been called upon to resolve thorny social and political issues, the problems of multi-religious and multi-cultural coexistence, the place of minorities within the nation state and communalism. In the vocabulary of many an undemocratic political leader, it even stands in for democracy.[3]

Notably, secularism is not a robust concept like democracy or justice, it is a 'thin' and a limited procedural concept. In Europe, secularism as a principle of state policy rode to prominence on the shoulders of the secularisation of society or the privatisation of religion. In India, we have not, in the main part, distinguished secularisation as a principle of society from secularism as a political norm. We in the Western fashion tend to conflate a sociological process and a political norm. That might be the main reason that stalks the reversals in the biography of this specific concept.

Clarifying Secularism

All is still not lost. I suggest that moments of crisis need not lead to unmitigated despair or abandonment of a concept that is crucial for a multi-religious society. Reversals in the biography of concepts, and the practices associated with them, provide an opportunity to re-examine, rethink and clarify what the concept means, what it stands for and what the political context of the concept is. Such moments can prove productive because re-examination of, reflection on and the reworking of the concept might, well, rescue a beleaguered concept not only from angry and abusive opponents, but also its ardent supporters and

[2] Needham and Rajan, 'Introduction', 12.
[3] Kumar, *Secularism*, 15.

fervent advocates, from its friends as well as enemies. As part of this rethinking, we might succeed in cutting away theoretical flab and dispense with extravagant expectations that overburden the concept of secularism.

The argument in this section of the essay tries to put secularism in its place. For this, we need to recognise that secularism does not stand alone. To reiterate a point made above, in modern Europe, it was propelled into the political domain as a companion concept to secularisation. Now that the secularisation of society has been dismissed as one of the vanities of modernity, and now that religion has made a spectacular comeback into the public domain, not as faith but as sheer politics aspiring to dominate collective life often through violence, political secularism has been abandoned along with secularisation by many of its once ardent proponents. This is nothing short of political disaster, because plural societies can be valued and maintained only on the basis of some norm and some value. The concept of secularism, after all, helps us to build a bridge between empirical and normative pluralism.

We cannot, in sum, discard secularism and its charms howsoever discreet they may be. But we also cannot continue to believe that the concept is dependent on the secularisation of society. Secularism needs a new theoretical home. What other home can modern societies provide, except democracy? The suggestion of this essay is that secularism is a companion concept of democracy. The specific argument is that secularism, as it has been defined in the Indian context, conforms closely to democratic norms of equality. This was the intention of the founders of democracy in India, and this is what secularism should be understood as.

This does not by any means imply that secularism can be collapsed into democracy. We need to distinguish between the two. Indian society is fractured in many ways. Vertically, it is fractured along the axis of caste, class and gender. Horizontally, it is divided along the matrix of different belief systems. Different sorts of analysis are needed to deal with different kinds of inequalities and oppressions. The responsibility of reorganising vertically unequal and unjust communities on the norm of freedom, equality, rights and justice is that of democracy. The normative principle of secularism is intended to ensure equality among religious communities. It is not the job of secularism to re-order unequal gender or caste relations that falls within the provenance of democracy. It is the job of secularism or rather secularists to ensure that the state is not aligned to any one religion, that all religious communities are treated with equal care and consideration, that no community is granted special advantages because it is in a numerical majority and that no religion is discriminated against just because its numbers are smaller than the majority community.

The advantages of secularism are many; among them two stand out as of note. One, secularism extends the principle of equality or even its weaker form non-discrimination, specifically to religious communities. Two, secularism promotes and protects pluralism. On the other hand, if a democratic state openly supports or adopts a religion, the foundations of democracy, especially justice, kneel before power. Democracy is sadly compromised. We should rather think of secularism as a concept that is closely linked with democracy by reasons of shared commitments to basic values such as freedom, equality and justice. In sum, democracy ensures equality between individual citizens, whereas secularism upholds equality between religious communities. It stands on its own ground, located in democracy, but relatively autonomous of the latter.

Notably, we find democracy without secularism in countries that have an official church, even if governments grant and protect the right to religious freedom. But we cannot have secularism without democracy, because the concept is justified by reference to the precepts of democracy, and in particular that of equality. Pre-democratic states, for example, Malerkotla in Punjab, as we shall see, safeguarded civil coexistence between communities through princely fiat or through respect for oral traditions. Modern democratic states need the more tangible, the more concrete and the more democratic concept of secularism. Secularism is a companion concept of democracy. The natural pair of the political norm of secularism is tolerance. But more of that anon. Let us turn briefly to Europe to understand how different the historical background of secularism was.

Secularisation and Secularism: The European Experience

The biography of secularisation in Europe has completed a full circle. Two philosophical moments illustrate the turning of the intellectual wheel. The first moment was exemplified in John Locke's essay on toleration, which is arguably the conceptual twin of secularism. Locke's celebrated *A Letter Concerning Toleration*, written in 1667, and his *Epistola de Tolerentia*, published in 1689,[4] reflected deep concern with religious strife and persecution. Fearing that the English society of his day possessed few resources to survive the onslaught of religious wars, and even fewer resources to enable people to live in peace, Locke proceeded to analyse the origin of political conflict. The origin of discontent, he suggested, lies in the fusion of state and religious power. This resulted in official disregard of other religions and intimidation of minorities. The primary requirement of peace, it follows, is the separation of religion and the church. He wrote:

> I esteem it above all things necessary to distinguish exactly the business of civil government from that of religion, and to settle the just bounds that lie between the one and the other. If this be not done, there can be no end put to the controversies that will always be arising between those that have, or at least pretend to have, on the side, a concernment for the interest of men's soul, and on the other side, a care of the commonwealth.[5]

The argument had a powerful impact on democratic thinking in two ways. One, the separation of the church and the state was understood as an essential precondition for peace among communities. Two, the state should abjure concern with religious belief, devote itself to secular tasks and secure the rights of citizens to liberty, health and property.[6]

---

[4] Locke, 'An Essay Concerning Toleration', 134–59. In 1666, Locke found a patron in the Earl of Shaftesbury, who headed the Whig party in Parliament. The Earl was an enthusiastic defender of toleration as well as of the limited authority of the state. Under the influence of his patron, Locke sought to apply toleration to resolve the issues of this day.

[5] Locke, *A Letter Concerning Toleration*, 67.

[6] Ibid.

This is its proper domain. In any case, suggested John Locke, the two institutions are different. The state is both necessary and inevitable for the welfare of human beings. The only way to escape the uncertainties and inconveniences of the 'state of nature' is to establish a state vide a social contract. The church is a voluntary association; here men gather together for the public worship of God. The church as the institutionalised form of religion is enjoined to promote the personal interests of its members. The task of the state is to protect and preserve the security of life, liberty and property. It is simply not the business of the state to coerce citizens into believing or not believing. It follows that the state cannot force people to give up their religion and follow the dominant one. It also follows that the state should stay away from religion even as it tolerates other beliefs.

Locke's argument for toleration, reflecting as it did the ideas of his patron Earl of Shaftesbury, was pragmatic. He had responded to religious intolerance. We do not tolerate other beliefs only to avoid conflict, averred Locke, but because we know nothing about the conversations human beings have with their God. None of us, he wrote, know why people believe the way they do. To substantiate his argument, Locke distinguished between knowledge based on reason and knowledge that comes from revelation. The former is verifiable, but the latter form of knowledge cannot be empirically proved. None of us possess the competence to judge other human beings and their belief systems. Different religions should be tolerated as long as they do not exert an adverse impact on government and society. 'In speculations and religious worship every man hath a perfect, uncontrollable liberty, which he may freely use, without, or contrary to, the magistrate's command, without any guilt or sin at all'. Locke appeared to have assumed that the believer had tested his faith on the touchstone of rational knowledge.[7]

Once human beings are convinced that their faith is worthwhile, the place, time and manner of worshipping God should be left wellnigh alone.[8] The right to be tolerated was, however, not universal, and

---

[7] Locke, 'An Essay Concerning Toleration', 140.
[8] Ibid., 137.

it is precisely here that we identify the weaknesses of liberal theories of toleration. Locke suggested that Roman Catholics, who owed allegiance to a Pope in far-away Rome, should not be tolerated. The other exception to his principle was atheism. Atheists, he held, cannot be trusted to give reliable evidence in a court room because they do not honour the Bible on which oaths are taken. This is the paradox of liberalism. Liberals believe that the views of other people should be tolerated for many sound reasons, but they cannot tolerate anyone who does not hold quite the same beliefs as they do. There seems to be no point to liberal theories of tolerance; we only tolerate beliefs we believe in, and we have no obligation to tolerate beliefs we do not agree with.

Despite all limitations, Locke's argument on toleration was significant because it embodied the great debates of the Enlightenment, particularly the dispute on the relationship between religion, science and reason. This belief formed the core of the spirit of the Enlightenment. In the 17th and 18th centuries, scholars, policymakers and advisors to princes agreed that the task of intellectuals and political pragmatists was to liberate humankind from the shackles of blind faith, and unquestioning obedience to Christian dogmas. The overbearing domination of the Roman Catholic Church had turned Europeans against their fellow beings. Wars over religion had fragmented society, retarded growth, and fostered superstition and unquestioning obedience. The age of unreason had to be replaced by the age of reason and science, ignorance had to give way to the Enlightenment, and allegiance to sectarian norms had to be substituted by universalism. As we shall see in the next chapter, the Europeans had a very different policy when it came to the colonies. In India, religion was politicised and catapulted into a nascent public sphere. But more on that later.

To return to the argument. Secularisation does not imply that people become atheists or agnostics. Nor do they have to abjure religion and replace the empty space in their psyche with rational and scientific modes of thinking. Human beings are rational and self-evaluating. They can believe, or not believe, faintly or intensely in God. The choice is theirs alone. A reigning ideology codified in, and enforced by the Roman Catholic Church, Christianity was demoted to another domain of belief in Europe. The relevance and importance of religion became dependent on the exercise of free choice and reflection on the relevance of religion for personal belief. In other words, religion was domesticated.

On balance, three sets of historical dynamics led to the secularisation of society in Europe. One was the impulse to power. Monarchs set out to control the domain of religious decision-making, increase the span of their sovereignty by taking over properties, wealth and power of the church, and expand the writ of the state. Two, the Enlightenment generated new epistemic systems, which emphasised scientific modes of knowledge formation and, more importantly, the validation of such knowledge through verifiable methods. The Enlightenment argued for the universality of reason, and the compartmentalisation of individual and collective lives into the public and the private. Three, democratic movements arose in the 18th and 19th centuries to challenge the power of absolute monarchies. These movements demanded as their prime right freedom, not only from monarchical power, but also from the clergy.

In France, for instance, state control over the temporal affairs of the church was initiated in the time of Phillippe de Bell (1268–1314). He relentlessly extended the control of the monarchy over the Gallican Church. In the 18th century, French society was swept by anti-clerical sentiments during the 1789 Revolution. Simon Schama in his magisterial work *Citizens* writes of the opening moves of the French Revolution on 5 October 1789. Hundreds of women fired to anger by hunger invaded the Salle des Menus Plaisirs in Versailles. The moment they saw the Archbishop of Paris in the salon, they began to shout anti-clerical slogans that had become popular in Paris, and accused him of being a prime instigator of the famine plot.[9]

Subsequently, the French Declaration of the Rights of Man guaranteed the right to hold religious beliefs. The assumption was that these beliefs and practices belong to the domestic or the private sphere. The public sphere must be emptied out of religious imageries, symbols and vocabularies. In the period following the revolution, the French

[9] Schama, *Citizens*, 464–465.

government enacted a series of laws to break the hold of the clergy on the state, culture, education, relief works for the poor and pubic rituals. The power of the church was separated from the state, as well as from the civil law that regulated the family and contractual obligations. New legislation appropriated many of the powers that had been hitherto exercised by the church and vested them in the government. Schools were legally compelled to proclaim neutrality towards all religions.

In the second half of the 19th century, French radical liberals along with an emergent Socialist Party, further reduced the authority of the church in poor relief, charity, control over cemeteries and state schools. Catholic leaders responded by setting up private schools and by establishing a Catholic pillar. These institutions established universities, hospitals, youth and adult organisations, trade unions, cultural associations, mass communication, banks and cooperatives. Finally, a Christian political party that promoted and protected the pillar was set up to further the cause. Successive governments in France made every attempt to break the remaining monopoly of the Catholic Church on public affairs. The 1905 French Law on the Separation of the Churches and State codified the uncompromising attitude of the state towards institutionalised religion and separated the domain of the state from that of the church. The law forbade the state from paying the salaries of the clergy and allowed the formation of religious associations to take over religious buildings and properties hitherto owned by the state. The provisions of the 1905 law was accepted by the Protestants and the Jewish community. The law did not, however, apply to Catholics.

In the struggle for control over people and their minds, the Church lost out to the state, and absolute monarchies lost out to democratic movements. These developments, which unfolded over the 18th and 19th centuries, proved decisive for the future of European polities. In the process, religion was relegated to the private domain, and the public sphere was de-sacralised. What we call the secularisation of society was simply the relegation of religion to the private sphere of faith. Religion lost its public role, was transformed into faith and was replaced by the sovereign state as the locus of power. Thereon, the modern state established and maintained the legal framework within which society conducted multiple transactions. One of these rules decreed that the public sphere should be liberated from religious vocabularies and imaginaries. Rational and justifiable political languages found place in the sphere, religious arguments did not. The concept of secularism developed in the background of secularisation or the privatisation of religion. In the European context, it stood for state neutrality towards religious groups.

There is, of course, no one model of secularism that we can find in the Western world. The French concept of secularism as the separation of the church and the state, which has resulted, for example, in a ban on the hijab in schools, is qualitatively different from the English experience of an institutionalised church. Yet France provides funds to main religious groups for service to the public, for example, religious worship and preaching. Norway, Belgium and some state governments in Germany provide subsidies to main religious groups.

The experience of European countries has been quite distinctive from that of the United States. President Thomas Jefferson stated famously that a 'wall of separation' exists between the state and religion. The First Amendment to the United States Constitution has made this clear. The Establishment Clause in the First Amendment stipulates that the Congress shall make no law respecting an establishment of religion or prohibiting the free exercise thereof. The clause prohibits the establishment of a national religion by Congress and establishes that the Congress shall not further the cause of one religion over another. The other aspect of the amendment is that that the government shall guarantee freedom of religion for its citizens. But the American government has found it difficult to distance itself from religious affairs and implement the wall of separation thesis. In 1952, Justice William O. Douglas ruled in Zorach versus Clauson that the First Amendment did not say that in each and every respect, there shall be a separation between the church and the state. And in 1971, in the case of Lemon versus Kurtzman, Warren E. Burger stated that the line of separation is far from being a wall; it is a blurred, indistinct and variable barrier depending on the circumstances.[10] The relationship

---

[10] Sen, *Articles of Faith*, xviii.

between religion and the state is a complex one, and religion fell within the provenance of state governments, but in most cases, we find the state intervening in and regulating practices that relate to religion, in the interests of democracy and justice. The notion that secularism implies a complete distancing of the state from religion is hardly implemented, as we see in this brief report on the practice of secularism in Europe and the United States.

The Second Moment of Secularism

Till about the last decades of the 20th century, the secularisation thesis dominated academic and political thinking on the nature of society and the idea of religion. In 1990, the sociologist Peter Berger famously argued that social and economic developments had crowded out religion from the public sphere and privatised belief systems.[11] A number of scholars were of the opinion that religion was not a given, people could freely choose whether they wanted to live with religion or without religion. The public sphere had place only for rational arguments divested of any religious reference or modes of legitimacy.

This thesis was challenged by the philosopher José Casanova in his 1994 work *Public Religions in the Modern World*. He suggested that in many societies, religion continued to play a significant role in the public sphere, and that religious traditions continue to resist the marginal role charted for them by theorists of modernity. Religious vocabularies might even adopt a new and enhanced public role.[12] The phrase 'public religion', coined by Casanova, directed us to the role and even the importance of religious organisations in the public arena and in the state. This, according to him, did not contradict the primary tenets of democratic theory. The secularisation thesis, he argued, could only be applied to Western European countries, but even here, we see the growing presence of and influence of religion on debates in the public sphere of contestation and affirmation, and

[11] Berger, *The Sacred Canopy*, 127–153.
[12] Casanova, *Public Religions in the Modern World*, 5, 39, 215.

on public policy. Casanova's argument proved prescient. In 1999, Peter Berger was to reverse his original argument and suggested that the world is as furiously religious as it ever was, and in some cases more than ever.[13]

In the last two decades of the 20th century, the second moment in the history of secularism in Europe unfolded against the background of the decline of secularisation thesis. Religion in some societies has made a comeback into civil society: the site for politics of affirmation and contestation. More significantly, religion has returned as aggressive and militant politics, laying political claims on the state and civil society, seeking to either expand or reshape civil society in its image, and providing legitimacy to state-breaking and state-making projects. This is the case in the Arab world, in many parts of Sub-Saharan Africa, in South Asia, but also Europe and the United States. Religious movements are confined not only to various strains of Islam from ISIS (Islamic State of Iraq and Syria) to Boko Haram, but also to Pentecostals and Born Again Christians in Protestant Christianity, Communion and Liberation Opus Dei among Catholics, militant Buddhism in Sri Lanka and Myanmar, and political Hinduism in India.

New religious movements insistently intrude into our individual lives sometimes as promises of redemption, sometimes as vengeance against historical enemies, but always as pure politics that seek to carve out a world governed according to doctrines the leaders of these movements claim are religious. These movements are no longer in the business of saving the soul or showing the path to the divine. They are simply another form of politics in search of endless power. Although the phenomenon has often been described as religious revivalism in opposition to modernity, new religious movements are not opposed to modern science. On the contrary, cadres who proclaim to be in the service of God, kill, maim, torture and perpetrate shocking violence, and use the latest technological inventions to pursue their political projects. Nor are religious identities opposed to other religions or non-religions; many religious wars are conducted between different

[13] Berger, *The Desecularisation of the World.*

strands in one religion. What the current religious revival is opposed to is secularism and pluralism.

It is not surprising that contemporary religious movements are conservative to a fault, centred around the acquisition of raw and brute power, intolerant of dissent and competing interpretations of sacred texts, and rankly undemocratic. Apart from the fact that they seek raw political power under the banner of 'this' or 'that' religion, there is little in these movements/armed gangs that relates to faith as has been understood through the ages. Religion, to put it bluntly, has emerged from the closet to which it had been consigned by Western Enlightenment philosophers, and begun to reshape the public sphere in ways un-thought and unimagined by chroniclers of political modernity, or even religious figures.

The return of religion to the public domain heralds, for many, the onset of the post-secular age. This turn has sparked off reverberations in the academy. For post-modernists, the 'post-secular' is part of a generic rejection of Enlightenment rationality and of the baggage it carries in its wake. The return of religion to public life provides sufficient proof of the incapacities and infirmities of secular reason. Secularism has become redundant. On the other hand, for the eminent German philosopher, Jürgen Habermas, humankind needs to expand understanding to accommodate the challenges of the times, notably the increased visibility of religious practices and affiliations in the public sphere. The task is not to dump secularism because it has been found wanting and adopt religion as it is a popular form of belief, but to understand and reconcile the complexities of the relationship between the two.

After the attack on the Trade Towers in New York in September 2001, in an October 2001 speech titled 'Faith and Knowledge' (on the occasion of the award of the prestigious Frankfurt Peace Prize of the German Publishers and Booksellers Association), Habermas piloted the concept of post-secularism to the centre stage of political theory. 'We', he said, obviously referring to the Anglo-American world, 'are in a post-secular age'. Acknowledging the need to accommodate religious vocabularies into the public sphere, Habermas called for a new dialogue between secular and religious-minded citizens.

Habermas is *the* quintessential scholar of the Enlightenment, and the turn to religion might appear as a disruptive turn in his scholarship. But he had been suggesting since 1992 that religion is a resource for resolving some of the most troublesome ethical problems confronted by human beings, for example, genetic engineering. Expanding his argument in a 2006 essay on 'Religion in the Public Sphere', Habermas suggested that religious actors should possess reciprocal rights in the public domain. Recognition of religious voices, beliefs and opinions in the public sphere, he suggested, will render it more egalitarian and inclusive. More significantly, Habermas, arguing for an expansive use of the American legal philosopher John Rawls' notion of the public use of reason, spoke of the need to establish a uniting bond of civic solidarity through reciprocal 'cognitive adaptation' among secular and religious citizens.[14]

Religious citizens, argued Habermas, must develop a self-reflexive and pluralistic view of modernity, so that truth claims of non-believers are understood as inevitable disagreements to be worked through in rational discourse and not merely rejected out of hand. And secular citizens must develop a non-reductionist and reflexive attitude towards the religious and refrain from passing judgement on religious truths. This is significant because of the power of religious traditions to encourage and foster moral thinking in communal life. This potential makes religious speech a serious candidate for participation in the public sphere. The argument can be translated from the vocabulary of a religious community into a generally accessible language. Thereby, the public sphere becomes more egalitarian. The difference is that citizens will have to work harder to understand and appreciate each other's vocabularies.

A post-secular society adapts, in his opinion, to the fact that religious communities continue to exist in the context of ongoing secularisation. If secular citizens have to adapt to religious arguments, the religious-minded must accept that modern forms of knowledge possess authority. But the state must be secular and neutral. Therefore, institutional thresholds between the 'wild life' of the public sphere and

---

[14] Habermas, 'Religion in the Public Sphere', 1–25.

the formal proceedings within public bodies must be maintained. Only secular voices can pass through, and in the Parliament, the standing rules of procedure must empower the house leaders to expunge religious statements or justifications. Religious claims, vocabularies and arguments must be translated into secular languages the moment the transition is made from the public sphere to policy-making bodies.[15]

The burden Habermas places on secular citizens insofar as they are urged to understand and appreciate religious vocabularies is much less than the burden placed on religious citizens. They are obliged to translate their arguments into secular vocabularies because religious vocabularies are not allowed into domains of law making. That is Habermas sets institutional thresholds between the 'wild life' of the political public sphere and the formal proceedings within political bodies, and allows only secular contributions of pass through. In the Parliament, for example, the standing rules of procedure of the House must empower the House leader to have religious statements or justifications expunged from the minutes.

In admitting religious voices into the public sphere and subjecting them to processes of public justification, Habermas admits that Western societies, which had undergone secularisation, live in a postsecular world that recognises and appreciates the continued existence of religion amidst ongoing secularisation. The level of discourse in the public sphere transcends mere toleration and intensifies communicative action between secular and religious-minded citizens. At the same time, he urges secular citizens to distinguish between faith and validity claims, and separate truth statements that have no direct consequence for public discourse (belief that Jesus is the son of God) from those that do (homosexuality is a sin). In sum, European scholars pronounced a secular age, and they declared the end of this age. Towards this end, they subordinate religion vocabularies, strategies and beliefs to some form of 'reasonable restrictions' or 'reasonable accommodation'. Oddly, philosophers who seek to study the coexistence of religion and nonreligious politics, seldom look at India that has learnt to live with both religion and secularism, not very well but not too badly either. They

---

[15] Ibid., 10.

should study our society; it might dent their complacency a great deal. As the experience of India has shown, the coexistence of religion and non-religious politics is barely amenable to reasonable accommodation. The conflict between the two has sometimes been resolved and sometimes left unresolved. The relationship is troublesome, unpredictable, contingent and chancy. The politics of coexistence between a disparate phenomenon and belief systems is erratic, and it does not lend itself to tidy explanations. It is, indeed, difficult, if not impossible to reconcile different vocabularies, imaginaries, symbols and modes of domination.

More significantly, India adopted secularism not in the context of secularisation or 'religion as faith' but 'religion as politics'. That is the leadership of the mainstream movement, the Indian National Congress, adopted secularism as a companion to the democratic state in a society in which religion had been politicised since the onset of colonialism, and more precisely in the latter part of the 19th century. They had little choice. The colonial intervention in understanding, codifying and politicising religious identities generated sometimes anxious, and sometimes assertive responses by Indian intellectuals and political leaders. Investigations into Hinduism and later Islam, rationalist reformulations and orthodox defences, shaped an emerging public sphere in which religion was debated, discussed and ultimately made the anchor of a competitive nationalist project that led to the Partition of the country. India in sharp contrast to the West did not privatise religion, the religious was politicised even if the colonial power formally declared its intention to stay away from religious practices. It was in this context that leaders of the freedom struggle began to speak of secularism, toleration and minority rights. India proved an exception to the rule established by theorists of secularism that the secularisation of society is an indispensable precondition for secularism.

CHAPTER 4

Colonialism, Nationalism and the Making of Religious Identity

There is cultural subjection only when one's traditional cast of ideas and sentiments is superseded without comparison or competition by a new cast representing an alien culture which possesses one like a ghost. This subjection is slavery of the spirit.[1]

The argument in this section holds that unlike Europe, in India, the political norm of secularism was adopted amidst the deep politicisation of religious identities. The politicisation of religious identities followed investigations into, theorisations of, discussions around and consequent awareness of belonging to a wider community called Hinduism, and later Islam. The development, which was relatively new to Indian politics, bore a significant outcome. Historians tell us that before the late 18th century and the establishment of colonialism, Indians did not, in general, identify themselves as Hindu or Muslim in the religious sense. However, by the turn of the 20th century, they were defining themselves as predominantly in terms of a religious identity.

[1] Bhattacharya, 'Swaraj in Ideas', 101.

In history, the biography of the term Hinduism has been a fluid one, and in pre-colonial India, people tended to identify themselves on different occasions as members of a *jati*, of a caste, of a linguistic group and/or as the residents of a region. Etymologically, Hinduism stems from a Persian term *Hind*, or *Al-hind* in Arabic, first used by the Achaemenid Persians to indicate people who lived beyond the river Indus/Sindu in the region of Hind. References to this term are found in the inscriptions of Darius I and other rulers of ancient Persia from 6 century BCE. The term Hindu was used by Al-Biruni (1030 CE) to refer to Brahmanical Hinduism. Three centuries later, Ziauddin Barani made frequent references to the 'Hindu' in his history of India. However, in his hands, the term Hindu denotes a politico- administrative as well as a religious category.

Harjot Singh Oberoi in his *Constructions of Religious Boundaries* argued that the Vedas, the Ramayana and the Bhagavad Gita, which today are seen by many as the defining religious texts of the Hindus, do not employ the word Hindu.[2] And the historian Romila Thapar pointed out that even in classical texts like the *Dharmashastras*, communities are defined by reference to location, occupation and caste, none of which are necessarily bound together by a common religious identity.[3] Moreover, in the annals of the classical language Sanskrit, Hinduism does not refer to the identity of people who belong to a religious community.[4] Religion was just one of the affiliations Indians subscribed to. By the end of the 19th century, marked, on the one hand, by the introduction of a census that required the respondent to unambiguously state her religion and, on the other hand, by political mobilisation on religious lines, the term Hindu came to be deployed as a social category of self-identification and of identification with a community.

The making of a collective identity was strengthened in the period of high nationalism and competitive nation-making projects that stretched from the late 19th to the first half of the 20th century.

---

[2] Oberoi, *The Construction of Religious Boundaries*.
[3] Thapar, 'Imagined Religious Communities?' 220.
[4] Dalmia and Von Stietencron, 'Introduction', 2; Dalmia, 'Introduction', 1–28.

Affinity with the larger religious community enabled individuals and communities to identify with each other, and thus established the foundations for the nationalist and the anti-colonial struggle. By the first two decades of the 20th century, we saw the eruption of competitive nationalism, the two-nation theory and the demand for a state of ones' own. The nation-making project and competitive nationalism that hinged around a demand of a 'state of ones' own' culminated in the blood-drenched Partition of India.

This development poses one of the puzzles of Indian history. How did the people, who at one point identified themselves as members of a *jati* or of a linguistic group, begin to think of themselves as chiefly Hindu or for that matter overwhelmingly Muslim? In pre-colonial times, it was possible to belong to a linguistic group, as well as to a region, a sub-caste and a religion. People had choices. After the colonial encounter, the freedom to choose one's identity was eclipsed, and collective identities were defined by the religion. The development bred, somewhat, serious consequences for the project of living together.

Notably, there is a considerable difference between religion as a social category and religion as a political identity. Our definition of the individual and collective self, and identification with a religious community is a sociological process. When that community begins to organise itself, and makes demands upon the body politic, we see the politicisation of religion. Religious communities are transformed into political actors laying claim to secular power. It was precisely the politicisation of religious identities that was to reach alarming proportions in the pre-Independence period and the process continues till today. Till today, many Indians are willing to kill and die for their respective belief systems. This is odd, because presumably religion tells us how to live a good life in accordance with the tenets of religious doctrine. Which religion apart from fringe cults tells its members to die for it? It is only religion as politics that demands the sacrifice of lives and sacrifices of other lives, sometimes in the name of protecting the religion and sometime for the cause of protecting the nation.

There is also some occasion for perplexity. Hinduism is more a coalition of plural, diverse and decentred groups than a coherent religion of the book. Decentred traditions do not, in general, facilitate identity politics. In India, however, a great many Hindus, who may otherwise subscribe to dissimilar practices, and are divided along caste hierarchies, tend to line up, often aggressively, behind the banner of a unified and homogenous religion. The identification with the larger community, howsoever episodic and transitory it might be, has neatly fed into the project of the religious right.

In the late 19th century, Hinduism was yoked to the project of the religious right, that of forging not only a religious identity, but an identity that confronted other religious identities as the 'other' or as the 'enemy'. This was countered by the making of an Islamic identity. Conflict between the two identities in the early 20th century was to lead to the Partition of India. In post-Independence India, the religious right tried to take over the state, and it succeeded first in the late 1990s and then in 2014. A loose coalition of, often random and temporary groups, fiercely committed to the project of establishing a Hindu nation, is led by the parliamentary party the BJP. The ideology of the group is formulated, fine-tuned and disseminated by the root cadre of the Hindutva coalition—the RSS—which is, of course, an implacable enemy of pluralism and secularism. Cadres of this tightly knit and regimented organisation spend an inordinate amount of time trying to denounce and destroy both these values, which are arguably integral to democracy.

Today, with the religious right in power, we witness a proliferation of, and overt legitimisation of, ideologies that speak of the right of the majority community to impress the nation and the state with its own brand of symbolism, modes of thinking, customs, conventions, conceptions of politics and even dietary preferences. Yet, the aspiration of the Hindutva brigade—that of imposing a Hindu nation upon a plural society and that of destroying plurality to accomplish the goal— does not cease to mystify. The mind frankly boggles. Historically, Hinduism has accommodated a broad range of divergent beliefs and practices. Some of these continue to resist either neat definitions or coherence. How many traditions, all of which consider themselves

Hindu, can the Hindutva brigade tap and incorporate into its own notion of a unitary religious identity? Is, for instance, the practice of offering red meat and alcohol to the *Akal Bhairon*, an avatar of Lord Shiva, acceptable to this brigade? After all, worshippers at the *lingam* consider themselves Hindu! Yet, the practice simply does not cohere with the project of imposing a Brahmanical vegetarian Hinduism on the diverse population of believers and non-believers alike.

The religious right has devised an easy and illusionary solution to the challenge of religious traditions. It believes in flattening down diversity, unifying discrete practices and homogenising Hinduism. Ironically, the Hindutva brigade does not recollect, or it prefers to ignore that the unification of a plural tradition had already been achieved by colonialism. It has accepted a colonial construct! The right wing in India suffers from poor historical understanding and memory, or so it appears. Perhaps that is why the assortment of sundry Hindutva groups, some of which are lumpen to a fault, has uncritically swallowed the colonial project of defining Hinduism, hook, line and sinker.

The project is, however, deeply flawed, because it were colonial investigations into, and translations of, upper-caste Hindu texts that narrated the religion as highly intellectual, Sanskritised and Brahmanical. This tradition, as will be suggested later in the argument, excluded much more than it included. Certainly, the public doctrine of neo-Vedanta was interpreted differently by different nationalist leaders. What they made of the Vedanta depended on their larger political project, and distinctive notions of politics as an end and as a strategy to attain discrete goals. In the hands of visionary leaders, like Gandhi, this genre of Hinduism is associated with pluralism and toleration. In the acquisitive clutches of the religious right, the political ideology of a Brahmanical Hinduism appears deeply suspicious of deviations, incapable of respecting dissent and highly intolerant. But it serves the agenda of Hindutva, that of building a unified, uncritical and unquestioning Hindu constituency, and ruling in its name.

The attempted homogenisation of Hinduism is dangerous for our plural body politic, contemptuous as the project is of traditions that subvert the standardisation and regulation of what it means to be Hindu. Hinduism has lost its primary status as faith in the hands of these self-appointed representatives of the religion; it has been reduced to a form of politics, hateful slogan-mongering and violence in the name of safeguarding the religion. The political face of Hinduism bears little resemblance to the religious practices of believers. For the first virtue of a Hindu, according to Patanjali's *Yogashastra*, is ahimsa or non-violence. It is precisely non-violence that has been deliberately mislaid during the journey of the religious right from religious identity to power-hoarding politics.

The Homogenisation of Hinduism

The idea that a standardised Hinduism is a product of colonialism was catapulted onto intellectual and political platforms as a puzzle, as a paradox, as a doubt and as a contradiction in the 1980s and 1990s. The debate erupted against the background of an increasingly aggressive Hindutva movement, and the subsequent demolition of the Babri Masjid by cadres of the religious right on 6 December 1992. Scholars in departments of religious studies, anthropology and history, mainly in Western universities, suggested that the glorification of Hinduism was, in essence, the glorification of a conceptual category that was assembled, privileged and theorised by various agents of colonialism. These agents ranged from Indologists, to Christian missionaries, to colonial administrators, to ethnographers and to philologists. Indian advisors were complicit in the interpretation and codification of Hinduism. The project was not steered only by Western scholars and administrators. Brahmins who were familiar with Sanskrit texts of ancient India, and Kayastha scholars who knew both Sanskrit and Persian, helped identify, translate and privilege selected sacred texts, and tutor administrators of the East India Company on what an authentic Hinduism looks like. Resultantly, a differentiated body of religious beliefs and practices was collapsed into a mega-category of a peculiarly upper-caste Hinduism. Some Western scholars were to suggest that there is no religion in India that corresponds to what we understand by the term.

The 1990s debate on the nature of and, indeed, the existence of a category called Hinduism drew lavishly upon an earlier work authored by W. C. Smith in 1962, *The Meaning and End of Religion*. Smith argued that when scholars who belong to one cultural/religious tradition begin to study the religions of another culture that has not experienced these transformations, they tripped on various conceptual obstacles. Religion must be studied on its own terms, through its own categories and not through the theoretical lens of the West. The naming of Hinduism by Europeans, argued Smith, was a mistake; there was no Hinduism in the minds of the Hindus or in empirical reality. The 'richness of what exists, in all its extravagant variety from century to century, from village to village' prevents a clear definition of Hinduism. Hindu religious tradition, which developed historically in the minds and hearts, in institutions, and in literatures and societies, is a growing collection of living realities. It cannot be compressed into any systematic intellectual pattern. Hinduism, he went on to conclude, refers not to an entity; it is a name that the West has given to a prodigiously variegated series of facts. To define Hinduism is to deny the Hindu his right to the freedom and integrity of his faith.[5]

Taking their cue from Smith, scholars focused on the colonial project of flattening out a plural tradition, and casting it in the image of Abrahamic religions. Stietencron suggested that rather than the development of a uniform and centralised religious doctrine and practice that was the characteristic of other religions, in Hinduism, a number of factors promoted fragmentation and regionalisation. None of the traditions of the religion developed an all-India institutional body invested with the power to judge correct exegesis of sacred scriptures except for *Advaita Vedanta*. Divergent interpretations of religion could not be banned, because authority was not vested in a church but in the individual charisma of a teacher. Even dominant *Vaishnavism* and *Saivism* was divided into numerous *sampradayas* or sects, which were further distinguished by regional differentiations in theory and practice. These sects would only come together on occasions when the meaning of a scripture was disputed. The *Vaishnanvas* worship a different god than *Saivas*, they use different holy scriptures in prayer, ritual and mythology, and even their paradise is located in a different

---

[5] Smith, *The Meaning and End of Religion*, 144–149.

mythical world. Why then should we insist, he asked, on a verbal unity of Hinduism?[6]

Religious plurality, he concluded, was characterised by a common cultural heritage, and a common socio-economic and historical background. Otherwise distinct traditions were brought together through intensive intellectual debate. But each of these traditions had an identity of their own. The question he posed was one that should be asked of the Hindutva brigade: Hinduism might give India unity, but does it correspond to reality?

The problem is, of course, that Hinduism has seldom been studied on its own ground, it has been investigated and evaluated through the conceptual lens of Eurocentric *theory*. Many of these scholars preferred to explore and define Hinduism by the Vedantic textual tradition, which is theistic, abstract and marked by the lack of rituals and superstition. This tradition, neatly conformed to European notions of religion, inspired in large part by Protestantism. Consequently, Hinduism, which is composed of plural and often incommensurable traditions, was neatened out and reduced to one strand that cohered closely to the Western notion of what religion is and what it should be.

Romila Thapar chronicles this path. The birth of Hinduism cannot be traced to a distinct point of time, a historically attested founder, or a text associated with the founder, as is the case with Abrahamic religions, she argued. Although various sects perform rituals and engage in practices considered Hindu, not all these sects enact identical rites, beliefs and practices. For example, some sects classified by the census as Hindu offer animal sacrifice and alcohol to the gods, practices which other 'Hindu' sects abhor. The idea that Hinduism is a single set of religious beliefs that can be traced back to the Vedas is the product of a socio-political process—a process of reification that has evolved during the past two centuries, concluded Thapar.[7] It is, in other words, a product of colonialism.

---

[6] Stietencron, 'Religious Configuration in Medieval India', 73.
[7] Thapar, 'Syndicated Hinduism', 57.

Whether Hinduism is or is not a religion has taken up the energy of many a scholar during and after colonialism. It is somewhat surprising that in the 1990s, critics of the colonial construction of Hinduism used the same concept of religion and similar methods to evaluate non-Christian religions as the colonialists did. If a community of faith does not have one sacred text, one founder and one church, was the presumption, it cannot be called a religion. Indisputably, the power of colonialism to constitute traditions, history and culture, and therefore identities has to be taken seriously. Gauri Viswanathan suggests that the inability to view Hinduism on its own terms has shaped the study of comparative religion, whether to prove the superiority of Christianity or to show that Hinduism is part of Christian theology because it is universal. Whether judgements on Hinduism were positive or negative, the same frame persists regardless of whether the attitude was negative or positive.

Whether the colonialists succeeded in flattening a multihued and complex philosophical system and a system of beliefs to one cohesive strand is another story but an important one. It is equally true that till today Hinduism lacks a core or essence, monotheism, a single sacred text and a church that can serve as a unifying symbol. It is best conceived of as T. N. Madan points out a religious tradition, which resists incorporation into the idea of religion as defined by the Abrahamic religions: Judaism, Christianity and Islam. The lack of a single text, or mandatory rituals of performance, or monotheism, does not mean that Hinduism is not a religion as Western scholars tell us, even as they critique colonial efforts to construct a unified religion. It can be thought of as a network of high traditions, localised Gods and practices, webs of mythology coexisting easily with one of the most sophisticated philosophical systems and God men/Gurus, the extent of whose followings challenges the very concept of a unified Hinduism. The idea that a religious community can be decentred, composed of diverse traditions, each of which follows its own faith, its own practices and its own beliefs, has simply not been accepted by Western scholars.[8]

---

[8] Madan, 'Hinduism', xiv–xv.

The debate on whether Hinduism is, or is not, a religion is a fascinating and a complex one, but this particular theme requires another sort of argument. We should note that the debate has hinged around the non-resemblance of Hindu traditions to Western categories of religion. The debate might exaggerate the extent to which Hinduism can, or cannot, be considered a religion, but it signposts the ways a colonised society is understood, or rather misunderstood by scholars of another tradition. In short, it is, as we see, the West that identifies sacred and other texts considered definitive of Indian religion and culture, translates the text and interprets it as definitive of the religion.

The referent point of these debates was religion as faith, or practices of personal salvation, rituals and devotion. But over a short period of time, Hinduism as a mode of faith was transformed into a mode of politics: politics as colonial domination, the politics of discrete identity formation and the politics of nationalist resistance. The epistemological project of defining a non-Christian religion and scholarly projects of interpreting India neatly fed into the system of colonial domination. Indians have had to, since then, view themselves through the frames set by debates amongst the agents of colonialism. These debates not only legitimised colonialism, but they also shaped strategies of national resistance. And they continue to influence policy and politics in an India that has been independent for over 70 years, and help forge the ideology of the religious right.

The Colonial Encounter

Every story has beginning, even if the end is left to the imagination of the reader or to the vicissitudes of history. The story of the politicisation of Hinduism and then Islam (this essay deals more with the making of the majority religious identity, because it is decidedly the majority that is responsible for respecting the spirit of secularism and the rights of minorities) began as an intellectual project. The narrative of Europe's engagement with India goes back to the 17th and 18th centuries. This is the time when European scholars began to take interest in a rich and complex philosophical tradition. Christian missionaries and Indologists proceeded to examine Indian civilisation through studies of art, architecture, philosophy, science and religion. German Romantics, for instance, saw in Hinduism a corrective to the malaise of modernity that had swept Europe in its grasp. Indologists, who engaged in the philological study of South Asian languages, had been for long fascinated with the Sanskrit language, which many saw as the root of European languages. They were enamoured by the philosophical sophistication of the textual traditions of ancient India, particularly the Vedas and Sanskrit hymns.

Orientalists told the world that ancient Indian civilisation was beyond comparison, that the textual tradition of Hinduism and Sanskrit was unsurpassed and that Hindu philosophy and religion were marked, for them, by astonishing philosophical sophistication and richness. By the turn of the 19th century, and the consolidation of colonialism vide, the East India Company, the production of knowledge acquired an extra edge, it was now located in the context of unequal and institutionalised power. The consequences could have been foretold. India with its heterodox traditions, localised power structures, multiple deities, manifold rituals and plural systems of belief was confronted by, and subsequently dominated by, the epistemological power of the Christian West.

It is generally agreed that British colonialism was unlike any other form of rule previously experienced by Indians. Pre-modern rulers might have taxed non-believers, even converted individuals to the religion of the group that was in power, but they seldom tried to regulate the personal lives of their subjects on the scale that modern states seek to do. British colonialism, as a proto-modern state set out to shape and control not only the political and the economic destiny of Indians, but also the way they thought about themselves, the way in which they interpreted their history and the present, and how they conceived of the future. European Indologists or Orientalists, missionaries, administrative officers of the East India Company and intellectuals in prominent European universities began to investigate the culture and the belief system of a people that were brought together under the sway of the British Empire. In the process, European categories of understanding and comprehension were presented as universal and as valid for the human condition, irrespective of specific cultural locations.

In other words, as agents of colonialism set out to decipher a complex civilisation, and unravel the plural and convulsed threads of its dominant religion, Hinduism, they inaugurated a project of cultural and intellectual domination. Not all agents were inspired by the same motives to study India and Hinduism. But as S. N. Mukherjee suggests in his work on the Indologist Sir William Jones, there was an underlying unity to the different missions of understanding India. Men, he argued, came to the country for a variety of reasons, for making money, for adventure and in order to step up the social ladder in England. On balance, a majority were possessed of a missionary zeal to shape the future of the country. Although the subsequent transformation of India was produced by a complex of factors, the ideas, which set politicians in motion to reform the administrative system, left a definite mark upon Indian society.[9]

Among the many enduring marks these colonial agents left imprinted on the collective consciousness of Indians was the homogenisation of a loosely articulated religious tradition—Hinduism. Colonial officials seeking to understand a society they planned to control and govern set about reducing its bewildering complexities to manageable proportions. The first move towards homogenisation was the codification of, to use A. K. Ramanujan's terminology, 'context-dependent'[10] laws into a uniform system. Administrators of the East India Company and colonial courts played an active role in shaping common and personal law. Aided by knowledgeable Indians familiar with the language of law making, Sanskrit as well as Persian, administrators began to select and codify a range of Hindu and Islamic laws. The writ of the colonial hand ran over an impressive range, nothing short of the codification of a plural tradition. In 1786, in a letter to the Viceroy Lord Cornwallis, the administrator and Orientalist William Jones suggested that a project be commissioned to compile a Digest of Hindu and Muslim Laws. Civil law, he advised, should

---

[9] Mukherjee, *Sir William Jones*, 2.
[10] Ramanujan, 'Is There an Indian Way of Thinking?' 41–58.

be in accordance with native practice as enshrined in the 1781 Act of Settlement. The multiplicity of laws had to be thinned down and collated, because Indian law must possess the consistency and the certainty of English law. This would, he hoped, make the task of English judges easier. Copies of the Digest of Laws, he suggested, should be deposited in the proper offices of *Sadr Diwani Adalat* and the Supreme Court. If the British government had to give the natives what Justinian gave to his Greek and Roman subjects, it had to undertake this ambitious agenda.[11]

The difficulty, admitted Jones, is that these laws were written in Sanskrit and Arabic. They can be translated, but the pandits and moulvis who acquainted the colonial power with the relevant law could not be trusted. Jones admits, 'I can no longer bear to be at the mercy of our Pundits, who deal out Hindu law as they please and make it at reasonable rates, when they cannot find it ready made'.[12] Administrators had to learn the language and take on the task themselves.

The codification of an immensely complex system of *sacred texts*, most of which were unfamiliar to the European mind, carried noteworthy consequences. Much of the meaning system of these texts was lost in translation. As the philosopher Ananda Coomaraswamy suggested, translations were carried out by scholars trained in linguistics rather than metaphysics. The educated man of today, he continued, is completely out of touch with intellectual traditions of Christianity that were nearer the Vedic tradition. A European is hardly prepared to study the Vedanta unless he has some knowledge of Plato, Philo, Hermes, Plotinus, the Gospels and, finally, Eckhart who, with the possible exception of Dante, can be regarded by Indians as the greatest of all Europeans.[13] Nevertheless, translations heralded a major step in the consolidation of a loose and plural tradition, and the making of a homogenised Hindu identity. The codification of localised and context-dependent laws into a set of uniform laws has proved one of the lasting legacies of colonialism. The legacy shapes jurisprudence on religious practices till today.

---

[11] Mukherjee, *Sir William Jones*, 130–131.
[12] Ibid., 128–129.
[13] Coomaraswamy, 'Preface', 23.

The second legacy of colonialism that continues to profile waves of political mobilisation and strategies till today is the unification of the plural traditions of Hinduism. Scholars point out that modern notion of religion as a system of beliefs and practices that are rational, metaphysical and private is of recent provenance; it was the product of the Enlightenment. Although the term religion goes back a long way in the history of Christendom, it was this modern, Protestant notion of religion that was universalised as an evaluative and a normative category. In times of colonialism, it was this concept that informed the minds of Western scholars who sought to investigate, classify and interpret different forms of religion in other spaces in the famous comparative religion projects.

The bias in favour of abstract and intensely metaphysical texts is clear in the selection, translation and privileging of texts that were considered representative of Hinduism by Orientalists. Translations of the Vedas, the Upanishads, Manusmriti, the works of Kalidasa, the Bhagavad Gita, the Mahabharata and the Brahma Sutras into European languages were regarded as an interpretive exercise, as providing a window onto Hindu society. The problem is that these texts were abstracted from the social context, as well as from internal debates and discussions, and privileged as the defining feature of Hinduism. They were seen as embodying eternal truths irrespective of the fact that these truths had been contested and challenged throughout the history of ideas by biographies of social movements.

Consequently, colonialists gave importance to a highly metaphysical tradition within Hinduism as constitutive of religion. They failed to consider and incorporate within the canon critical, rationalist philosophies and oppositional movements. Ironically, Indian public intellectuals and nationalists adopted the same tradition. The philosopher Bimal Krishna Matilal reminds us that Western scholars were fascinated by the highly speculative metaphysical system that occupied the overlap between religion and philosophy. And Indian intellectuals, after centuries of foreign domination, were looking for an identity that could help them assert themselves. Some national leaders sought an escape in the mythical aura of Indian spirituality.

As a result, philosophy remained identified with mysticism and was regarded as inseparable from religion.[14]

The Response to Colonial Appropriations

The many tyrannies of colonialism have been well documented, and a veritable publishing industry on this aspect has gained traction. An equally interesting question is the following: Given that India's past had already been appropriated by the coloniser, and the present dismissed as a disintegration of a once great civilisation, how did Indians receive, absorb and negotiate colonial interpretations, critiques and definitions of India's past, philosophy and religion? How did they speak back to colonialism and its many hegemonies and in what vocabularies?

There can be, of course, no one answer to the question of how Indians responded to intellectual colonialism. Some public intellectuals uncritically absorbed the philosophies of the colonial power, some mediated these intellectual resources in innovative ways, others resisted colonial epistemologies and still others, like Gandhi, transformed both Indian and Western thoughts. On balance, Indian intellectuals had to accomplish a double recovery. They had to reclaim their own philosophical traditions to answer the question 'Who are we'. But they also had to retrieve their tradition from the, metaphorically speaking, acquisitive grasp of Western scholars, administrators and missionaries. Was that feasible and doable given the impact of Western scholarship on nationalist sensibilities?

Consider the thesis that the glories of ancient India were followed by a sharp and precipitate decline of India, which continues to hold proponents of the Hindu right in thrall. This thesis was first put forth by Western scholars, for example, the German philosopher Georg Wilhelm Fredrik Hegel (1770–1831), among others, inspired intellectual investigations into the past, forged critiques of the present and set the goals for the future. Notably Hegel's dismissive comments were

---

[14] Matilal, *Epistemology, Logic, and Grammar in Indian Philosophical Analysis*, xii–xiii.

not part of a dialogue that Western scholars had with Indian thinkers. They were a response to German Romanticism, in other words, an integral segment of the debate between European scholars.

The German Romantics connected the classical past of India, China, Persia and Egypt with the making of modern Germany by focusing on common languages and shared traditions of the Indo-Germanic world. The fascination with India was perhaps expected, given the intellectual climate of the 19th-century Germany. Philology was one of the most important disciplines in German intellectual thought, and the study of ancient languages such as Persian and Sanskrit formed part of the study of languages. William Schlegel, a Sanskritist, was given a professorship at Bonn in 1818, and, in 1820, he established the first major journal on the Orient, the *Indische Bibliothek*. He held that European languages were descendants of Sanskrit, and the discovery of the Sanskrit literature was as important as the Renaissance discovery of Greek.[15] At the time Hegel was given a professorship in philosophy in Berlin, the Indologist Francis Bopp was given the chair in Sanskrit in the same university.

Hegel's professional life unfolded during a period of intense European interest in India in the 18th and 19th centuries. The English and French colonisation of India acted as a powerful incentive to study Eastern religions and philosophies. From the Romantics, Hegel inherited an attraction for the Orient, but he set out to demolish their assumptions. Accepting that chronologically, philosophy religion and art took root in the Orient that is in Persia, China, Egypt and India, he suggests:

> India, like China, is a phenomenon antique as well as modern; one which has remained stationary and fixed.... It has always been the land of imaginative aspiration and appears to us still as a fairy region, an enchanted world. In contrast with the Chinese state, which presents only the most prosaic understanding, India is the region of phantasy and sensibility.[16]

[15] Schlegal, 'On the Language and Wisdom of the Indians', 425–426.
[16] Hegel, 'The Philosophy of History', 219.

However, after explorers, missionaries, traders and commercial companies conquered India, and as the exotic became the known and presumably the mundane, it became clear that India had nothing to offer the world. European investigation into Indian knowledge systems, and European domination, heralded the end of the search for India's mythical wisdom and 'philosophy'. India cannot teach the West; its tradition is a matter of the past; it has never reached the level of philosophy and science, which is a genuinely and uniquely European achievement.[17]

Hegel did not know Sanskrit, and he had not studied any original Indian text. His considerable knowledge of India was derived from translations of Sanskrit texts, reports of the East India Company and the scholarship of his contemporaries. Over the years, his knowledge of India, writes Wilhelm Halbfass, became more nuanced and differentiated, and he incorporated this awareness into his later lectures and research on India. Hegel responded to the first of Henry Thomas Colebrooke's 1924 two essays on 'The Philosophy of the Hindus'. The essays dealt with the philosophy of *Samkhya* and *Nyāya-Vaiśeṣika* as a new basis for Western understanding of religion.

He saw these essays as examples of sober, thoughtful and thorough research, an indispensable precondition for Western philosophical interpretation and evaluation. Hegel also reviewed Humbolt's essay on the Bhagavad Gita in a long review piece that ran into a hundred pages. It was published in two instalments in 1827. The review went beyond the text to include reflections on the world view of the Gita, and the role of yoga and meditation, quoting profusely from the writings of William Jones, F. Wilford and J. Mill. This review is his testament to his understanding of India, concludes Halbfass.[18]

Hegel's opinion on Indian philosophy was shaped by two factors: his response to the very Indologists he drew upon and his profound ignorance about the great debates that accompanied the consolidation of the four sacred texts—the Vedas. Philosophies, such as *Cārvāka*, *Samkhya*, *Buddhism* and *Jainism*, repudiated the moral authority of the

---

[17] Cited in Halbfass, *India and Europe*, 2.
[18] Ibid., 86.

Vedas, the Bhakti Movement challenged Brahmanical authority and Buddhist philosophers, like Nagarjuna in the 2nd century CE, gave to the world a sophisticated and rational philosophy. But the impact of these philosophies on colonialism and interpretations of Hinduism was practically negligible.

Significantly, Hegel's reflections on India were profoundly influenced by his belief in the mission of philosophy in Europe. India had remained stagnant because its philosophy did not follow the path that Hegel believed universal history should follow to qualify as philosophy—that of the unfolding of the universal spirit and the realisation of freedom. For Hegel, the form that Indian philosophy took was 'substantial, without inward division, and it arises in natural communities, patriarchally governed'.[19] The notion of substantiality refers to the unity and ultimacy of one underlying substance. The religions of India find in God the ultimate substance, as a pure, abstract, being-in-itself, which contains finite and particular beings as non-essential modifications. Individuals are left without an identity or dignity of their own, because they are merged into the divine. Hegel insists:

> The spread of Indian culture is prehistorical, for history is limited to that which makes an essential epoch in the development of spirit. On the whole, the diffusion of Indian culture is only a dumb, deedless expansion; that is, it presents no political action.[20]

India was the birthplace of philosophy, but once philosophy left its shores and migrated to Greece, it stagnated. From Greece, philosophy acquired momentum as the unfolding of freedom. Although the consciousness of freedom first arose in Greece, it reaches its apogee in German nations under the influence of Christianity.

The history of philosophy in India, therefore, concludes Hegel, is but the pre-history of Europe. There is nothing left in India, or indeed in the Orient, because philosophy can never return to the past, it can only incorporate the past, it is but the history of philosophy. 'It

---

[19] Hegel, *The Philosophy of Right*, 112.
[20] Ibid., 221.

is (therefore) the necessary fate of Asiatic Empires to be subjected to Europeans', he wrote.[21] In sum, even though he interpreted India as a country with a rich past but an indifferent present, Hegel continued to be taken up by India as the birthplace and seat of philosophical learning almost 3,000 years before Christ. After that, he suggested, India stagnated, ripe for conquest.

How Did Indian Intellectuals React?

Although *the* philosopher of modernity Hegel continued to be fascinated with Indian society till the end of his life, he was contemptuously dismissive of the India of his day. Ironically, his thesis on decline legitimised the colonial project that India had to be saved from its own propensity towards collapse. It also motivated the endeavours of Indian intellectuals and nationalists to return to a once glorious past. This is not surprising when we recollect that the philosophies of G. W. F. Hegel, Emmanuel Kant and British idealism ruled the world of academics after the establishment of the university system in India in the early 19th century. Given the dissemination of Western scholarship that travelled throughout the colonised world through journalism, literature, political discourses and academics, the minds of generations of Indians were bound to be shaped by European knowledge systems and categories of understanding. This is explicit in the discourse of the nationalists that took from European thinkers the thesis of the greatness of ancient India and consequent deterioration.

Their thought went a long way in forging a spirit of nationalism and critical enquiry into Indian traditions. The culture of ancient India was the touchstone against which the Hinduism of their day had to be measured and evaluated. Public intellectuals were impelled to go back to the past to resuscitate the present and forge a future modelled on eternal truths embodied in the textual tradition emphasised by colonial agents as the soul of Hinduism. Aurobindo Ghosh wrote:

[21] Ibid., 221.

If an ancient leader of the time of the Upanishads, the Buddhist period or later classical age were to be set down in modern India, he would see his race clinging to forms and shells and rags of the past and missing nine-tenths of its nobler values … he would be amazed by the extent of its later degeneracy, its mental poverty, immobility, static repetition, the comparative feebleness of the creative institution, the long sterility of art, the cessation of science.[22]

Earlier, this mood of despondency had been expressed by Ram Mohan Roy, popularly hailed as the father of the Indian Renaissance. Roy (1772–1833) was among the first of these intellectuals to ask the question: Who are we? His response catapulted the thorny issue of how Indians could reconnect with history and discover a collective self into a nascent public sphere. Given the context of his times, he launched the project of understanding the past in order to speak to Western audiences and to counter attacks by Christian missionaries on what they considered an inferior form of religion. He began his exposition by accepting that the Hinduism of his day was sadly wanting. Writing in a deeply regretful tone to a friend John Digby in England on 18 January 1928, Roy complained that the Hindu community was immersed in 'gross idolatry' and peculiar beliefs:

> I regret to say that the present system of religion adhered to by the Hindus is not well calculated to promote their political interest. The distinction of castes, introducing innumerable divisions and sub-divisions among them has entirely deprived them of patriotic feeling, and the multitude of religious rites and ceremonies and laws of purification have totally disqualified them from undertaking any difficult enterprise…. It is, I think, necessary that some change should take place in their religion, at least for the sake of their political advantage and social comfort.[23]

He concluded with the observation that there was nothing to equal the sublime principles of Christ.

---

[22] Sri Aurobindo, *The Foundations of Indian Culture*, 29.
[23] Cited in Ghosh, *The English Works of Raja Rammohun Roy*, 929.

It is well known that Ram Mohan Roy was influenced by one strain of Christianity, Unitarianism, which posed a challenge to Christian orthodoxy, particularly the belief in the Trinity. The universal precepts of Unitarianism hold that the principles of Christ's teachings are separate from the culturally specific and institutional trappings of the religion. In a similar fashion, Roy had, at a fairly young age, abstracted the original teachings of Hinduism from contemporary social practices that he found degenerate and a departure from the tenets of Hinduism and held them up as a mirror to contemporary practices.

Christianity, however, was not the only system of thought to impact the development of his system of ideas. Roy had received a traditional education and was familiar not only with Hindu thought, but also with Persian and Arabic theology that contained secular Aristotelian influences. His ideas on theism and on the nature of the divine were significantly impacted by inductive reasons and the requirement of empirical proof by rationalist schools of thought in Islam. His first published work at a fairly young age was *Tuhfat-ul-Muwahhdin* or a *Gift to Theists* (1803–1804). The work was written in Persian, and the preface was authored in Arabic. In this work, Roy exposed and chastised dogmas that focused on revelation, in miracle-inducing acts such as worshipping at shrines and bathing in rivers, and on the widely held belief in prophets. And above all, he castigated the many rituals such as fasts and imposition of privations that defined the sort of lives people should live, notion of what is or is not propitious, and rank superstition.

In 1816, Roy translated the Vedanta into Bengali, Hindustani and English. The translation was accompanied by a comprehensive introduction and an equally comprehensive commentary. In the introduction, Roy launched a critique of extant Hindu practices. He wished to prove to his European friends that 'the superstitious practices which deform the Hindoo religion have nothing to do with the pure spirit of its dictates'. He also wanted to establish that the temples that had been erected to many gods and goddesses, and the rituals that were performed to propitiate them, had deviated from the norms of Hinduism. It is my design to prove, he wrote, that 'every rite has its derivation from the allegorical adoration of the true Deity; but at the present day all this is forgotten, and among many it is even heresy to mention it'.[24]

Roy was a pragmatic thinker, and he intended that his interpretation of Hinduism as theism could catalyse social transformation. If his early discomfort with Western criticism of idolatry and superstition inspired an investigation into Hinduism and recovery of the meaning of the Vedanta, the retrieval of the meaning was deployed to attack what, in his view, were irrelevant and useless rituals that inexorably led society into irrationality and delusions. He was the first of the great tradition of social reformers to engage with current practices through the prism of the wisdom of the ancients.

That is, his ideas of social reform were derived from the method of immanent critique and not from the establishment of a priori principles or abstract normative standards of what a religion should be. Roy did not morally condemn the religious practices of his day and leave it at that, nor did he confront fellow men and women with new doctrines and ask them to kneel before novel and discovered wisdom. The standards he applied to examine and critique practices of his time were internal to Hinduism. Throughout his study and admiration of the intellectual strains of Islam and Christianity, Roy remained committed to Hinduism. He gained a formidable reputation as a defender of the faith against attacks by Christian missionaries. One of these missionaries was his friend Alexander Duff. Duff, incidentally, had acquired considerable renown for converting an impressive number of Indians to Christianity.

Although he was certainly influenced by the liberal tradition, there was much more to Roy's intellectualism. He brought together worlds that technically belonged to different religious traditions, because they converged on theism which formed the essence of the Vedanta. More than familiar with the contemptuous dismissal of Indian religion and philosophy by Christian missionaries, many of whom were his friends, Roy was undoubtedly inspired by the essentially modern conviction

---

[24] Roy, Translation of *An Abridgement of the Vedant*, 4.

that persons should be able to evaluate the religion they subscribe to. He chose to do so by 'stepping back' from current practices and by reclaiming the original formulations of Hindu texts.

In the 19th and early 20th centuries, public intellectuals, riled by the criticism of Hinduism by missionaries and administrative officials, had taken on the task of social reform and invoked a Golden Age to critique present-day practices. The shadows of Hegel and Indologists, who had acclaimed a Golden Age of Hinduism, and consequent regression, hovered over the attempts of social reformers. Their criticism of religious practices was unsparing, even though their attempts to resurrect the intellectual disposition of the classics remained confined to the urban intelligentsia, at least till the arrival of M. K. Gandhi onto the scene. The influence of Indologists and Western philosophers over their understanding of India was manifest. Keshub Chandra Sen (1838–1884), a leader of the Brahmo Samaj, established by Ram Mohan Roy, captured the spirit of this endeavour when he stated, somewhat baldly, about India:

> What we see around us today is a fallen nation, a nation whose primitive greatness lies buried in ruins.... As we survey the mournful and dismal scene of desolation-spiritual, social and intellectual-which spreads around us, we in vain try to recognise therein the land of Kalidas-the land of poetry, of science, and of civilisation.[25]

It is not surprising that the return to the past inescapably involved the invocation of the Vedas and the Upanishads or the Vedanta, both as an evaluative measure of the present and an aspiration for the future. Despite the onset of a restless modernity, and the consolidation of relentless materialism in India, this ambition remains a dominant project for the religious right till today. By the end of the 19th century, the Vedanta was tailored to suit contemporary times as neo-Vedanta. We find the fullest articulation of this philosophy in Swami Vivekananda (1863–1902) when he addressed the World Parliament of Religions in Chicago in 1893. Orthodox Hindu organisations, such as the Arya Dharma Pracharini Sabha and Prarthana Samaj had stressed the

---

[25] Cited in Heimsath, *Indian Nationalism and Hindu Social Reform*, 15–16.

universal nature of Hinduism. But when Swami Vivekananda, well versed in Western philosophy, the sacred texts and Bengali literature, presented the Vedanta to the world; he gave to Hinduism the status of not only a world religion, but also that of a supra religion that could teach other belief systems how to live with each other in toleration and harmony.

He spoke of Hinduism as an ancient religion that taught acceptance and understanding of each other, 'I am proud to belong to a religion which has taught the world both tolerance and universal acceptance'.[26] The precept integral to Hinduism, he said, is pluralism and toleration, 'Oh Lord, the different paths which men take through different tendencies, various thoughts though they appear, crooked or straight, all lead to thee'.[27] He spoke of a universal religion that had no limits of time or space, and of a religion that united the whole credo of the human spirit, from the fetishism of the savage to the liberal creative affirmations of modern science.

Having provided the emerging national movement with a religious identity, which was no longer a source of embarrassment but one of pride, Vivekananda made it very clear that Hinduism needed to be cleansed of all contradictions and schisms that led to poverty and misery. His Vedanta did not tolerate the existing gap between its commitment to human liberation and material deprivation. Material well-being was an essential precondition of individual liberation or moksha.

In the early years of the 19th century, Ram Mohan Roy had retrieved the essential teachings of the Vedas to restore the glories of Hinduism that had been subjected to critique and dismissal. He subsequently theorised the sacred texts as a touchstone to evaluate extant practices. By the closing years of the 19th century, the intellectual wheel had turned full circle. Vivekananda pronounced the superiority of Hinduism as a universal religion. The wisdom of this universal religion transcended identities of specific religious groups but respected

---

[26] Vivekananda, 'Addresses at the Parliament of Religion', 3.
[27] Ibid., 4.

all of them. We believe, he said, not only in universal toleration but we accept all religions as true.

The trajectory of modern Indian political thought was succinctly described by Aurobindo Ghosh in his *Renaissance in India.* He wrote that the first effect of European entry into the country was the destruction of much that had no longer the power to live. A new activity was at first crudely and confusedly imitative of foreign culture. But whatever temporary rotting and destruction this crude impact of European life and culture has caused, it revived the dormant intellectual and critical impulse; it rehabilitated life and awakened the desire of new creation. Aurobindo Ghosh wrote:

> The national mind turned a new eye on its past culture, reawoke to its sense and import, but also at the same time saw it in relation to modern knowledge and ideas. Out of this awakening vision and impulse the Indian renaissance is arising, and that must determine its future tendency.[28]

The recovery of its old spiritual knowledge and experience in all its splendour, depth and fullness is the first work, he wrote. The second is the flowing of this spirituality into new forms of philosophy, art, literature, art, science and critical knowledge. The third task is original, dealing with modern problems in light of the Indian spirit and endeavours to formulate a greater synthesis of a spiritualised society. Its success on these three lines will be measured by the way it contributed to the future of humanity.[29]

A Flawed Doctrine

Surprisingly Indian intellectuals joined the Orientalist acclaim of a rich and sophisticated Vedic tradition without acknowledging its adverse impact upon society, that is, the consolidation of Brahmanical superiority. Nor did they take into account debates around the consolidation of the sacred texts. If the textual tradition provided an anchor for

[28] Ghosh, *The Renaissance in India in Nalini Bhushan and Jay Garfield*, 48.
[29] Ibid.

the recovery of the collective self, the self was deeply fractured along lines of contestation. The philosopher J. N. Mohanty tells us that the Vedas that developed around 2,000 years BCE cover an entire range of subjects, but above all they represent an exemplary spirit of enquiry into the 'one being' or '*ekam sat*' that underlies the diversity of empirical phenomenon, and into the origin of all things.[30] These themes were philosophically developed in the Upanishads, a group of texts that ranged from 1,000 BCE to the time of Gautama. These texts cover a range of themes from cosmology to psychology, but central to them is the defence of a main philosophical thesis, that is, the identification of the *Brahman* (the highest and the greatest that is the source of all things) with the *atman* or the self.

The Vedas had laid out the philosophical thesis that, in the beginning of things, there must have been a being and not non-being, for nothing can emerge out of nothing. This being was identified as the spirit within us. Therefore, the highest wisdom lay in realising the identity of the subject and the object (*tat tvam asi*). But if the real that we find behind the empirical nature is the universal spirit within, then what is the nature of the empirical world? This, suggests Mohanty, became the leading disputational question among commentators on the Upanishads and various schools of Vedantic philosophy.

The lessons in wisdom given by the Vedas were challenged both by supporters and opponents of the philosophy. Towards the end of the Upanisadic period was born Gautama, the founder of Buddhism (560 BCE). His teachings, after he attained the Enlightenment, were devoted to the central question of how to escape suffering. Although he renounced the notion of the soul, because he believed that all phenomena, material or non-material, are impermanent, he continued to believe in *karma*, in *rebirth* and in eventual deliverance or *moksha*. The emergence of Buddhism was politically significant because it represented generalised discontent with Brahmanical power and the monarchical state. The philosophy mounted a strong challenge to the superiority of the Brahmanical class, to ritualism and to the caste system that had banished its own people to the margins of society.

---

[30] Mohanty, *Classical Indian Philosophy*, 1–5.

The challenge to hierarchy was neutralised when Indian intellectuals began to appropriate Buddhism. Vivekananda, in his famous *Address at the Parliament of Religions* in Chicago, suggested that Buddhism had completed the highly metaphysical task of the Vedanta. In a short period of time, Buddha came to be seen as the eighth avatar of Hinduism. The critical edge of the philosophy had been blunted, somewhat alarmingly.

The main lines of division were drawn between philosophical schools that believed in the Vedas and those that did not or the *Sramanic* tradition. But within the tradition, according to Mohanty, we see considerable sceptical self-criticism. Both Mahavira, the founder of Jainism (599–527], and Gautama were influenced by intellectual dissenters within the Vedic tradition. These dissidents rejected sacrificial rituals as well as *Upanisadic* monism. For example, an influential philosophy that belonged originally to the Vedic tradition had a strong strain of atheism and naturalism. This was *Samkhya* philosophy associated with the legendary figure of Kapila. The philosophy eschews notions of the Brahman and subscribes to theories of the five elements. Other sceptics refused to accept the claim that the Vedas coded absolute knowledge, questioned the doctrine of omniscience, and believed that the conclusions of these texts were contradictory, as well as controversial.

Also excluded from the dominant and metaphysical conceptualisation of Hinduism was the heretical materialist school of *Lokayata* or *Carvaka* philosophy. This philosophy was originally one of the branches of Vedic learning, but over time it developed an anti-Vedic materialism. The origin of *Carvaka* philosophy is the thesis that the self is the body not the soul. This school of philosophy was left out of the dominant constructions of Hinduism, both by the colonialists and the nationalists. It just did not fit into the model of theism and of the ultimate objective of the merger of soul with the divine.

Pradeep Gokhale argues that though the *Carvaka* school of philosophy is comparatively neglected and disrespected, it represents the true philosophical spirit of the eternal quest for truth. All other schools accept certain authentic texts as their own, and they hesitate to question the goals of life, or the maxim of life after death, justified as these are in in trans-empirical terms. But if the true philosophical spirit lies in questioning and examining dogmas and religious beliefs, this spirit is embodied in *Carvaka* philosophy.[31]

The marginalisation of critical and rational philosophical schools both by the Indologists and nationalists gives us cause for considerable thought. If a rational, materialistic, empiricist and sceptical philosophical school such as *Carvaka* had been given prominence in the forging of a Hindu tradition, perhaps India would have escaped being slotted into the spiritual versus materialist dichotomy. This stereotyping of Indian society as exotic and other-worldly has not helped us forge an equitable future. India with all its material inequities, communalism and casteism, which erupt into conflict over material needs at the veritable drop of a hat, has been slotted into a spiritual pigeonhole. Till today Indian society has failed to accept the enormity of material inequities, fascinated as it is with the metaphysical spirit. In short, the privileging of a highly metaphysical tradition as the public philosophy of India leads us away from social oppressions and power. It cannot help us to pinpoint power equations, or remedy inequities.

Colonialism had politicised religion, or more precisely Hinduism, because projects gave form and shape to a set of loose, plural and decentred traditions, cast them in the modern mould of religion and created a 'unified' body of Hinduism. A homogenous Hinduism was to become the basis of a collective political identity. Public debates over religion inevitably led to the politicisation of religious identities, as people who lived in face-to-face communities and practised localised customs became aware of their identity as members of not only a religious but also a demographic group. Colonial policies gave an added flip to this politicisation. From the middle of the 19th century, in the public sphere, Hinduism and then Islam were foregrounded by intellectuals, leaders and political organisations for many reasons: to regenerate and reform Indian society, to serve as an anchor for the national project or rather projects, as a dominant language that enabled leaders to forge a constituency among the people, as a repertoire of

---

[31] Gokhale, *Lokaya/Carvaka*, 1–48.

symbols to restore confidence in the greatness of a civilisation and to mobilise opinion against the colonial power. Religion became more not less relevant to multiple political discourses.

The Making of a Contested Public Sphere

How does this brief delineation of colonial constructions of Hinduism and the nationalist response connect with the theme of this work—the project of civil coexistence? The discussion is intended to be a prelude to a discussion of the unification and the politicisation of religion. The Scottish philosopher of political economy and moral philosophy Adam Smith wrote that the zeal of religious teachers can be dangerous and troublesome when there is but one sect tolerated in society, or where the entire society is divided into two or three great sects, the teachers of each acting in concert and under a regular discipline and subordination. But that zeal must be altogether innocent when the society is divided into 200 or 300, or perhaps into as many thousands small sects, of which no one will be considerable enough to disturb public tranquillity. Teachers of each sect will act with modesty, surrounded as they are by as many adversaries as friends. This is not the case with large sects who are venerated by followers, disciples and humble admirers. Leaders of smaller sects are disposed to moderation and over time reason, unlike teachers and leaders of large sects.[32] The insight holds lessons for India: If the multiple sects that conceived of themselves as Hindu had been left alone, and not flattened out in the cause of a unified Hinduism, would we have been a more democratic and a more egalitarian society? Would people have the freedom to move between sects or even subscribe to the teaching of two or more religious gurus? Today, a 'unified' Hinduism in the form of Hindutva has pre-empted this freedom, expended enormous energy into the cause of constructing this temple or that, expended even more energy in identifying enemies, and become a highly intolerant and even an intemperate ideology. Instead of promoting a critical sensibility, sensitivity and pain to the

[32] Smith, *An Inquiry into the Nature*, 387.

suffering of others, dominant ideologies encourage us to think in terms of friends versus enemies.

Adam Smith had warned against precisely this development. He had recommended that wise legislators will prevent clergy from governing the minds of the people, because each ghostly practitioner seeking to render himself sacred in the eyes of his supporters will inspire them with abhorrence for other sects and try his best to excite their languid devotion. Organised religion, in Smiths words, modifies tenets to suit the disorderly affections of the human frame. This means that an organised religion has a tendency to accumulate power by appealing to the sentiments of followers. The best antidote to this form of power is to encourage numerous small sects that will remain in their own place. In India, the State and religion under the dispensation that came into power in 2014 have come together to uphold a vulgarised and thinned-out concept of Hinduism in the form of Hindutva. This has diminished not only its followers but Hinduism itself. The roots of this coming together can be traced to the colonial and the national periods.

Nationalism and Identity Formation

History proves that anti-colonial nationalism seldom erupts onto the stage of history fully fashioned like the Greek goddess Aphrodite.[33] The processes by which a territorially bounded community begins to view itself as a nation and generates the ideology of anti-colonial nationalism are multiple, complex, contradictory and complementary. The transformation of an otherwise fragmented, hierarchical and divided society into a nation that demands the right to determine its own future involves parallel and interlocking processes that predate nationalism. The link between these processes and nationalism might

---

[33] Strictly, Aphrodite's birth was also the outcome of a series of developments. According to Greek legend, Cronus, the leader of the Titans, on the behest of his mother Gaia, the Goddess of the earth, committed parricide by killing his father Uranus. Subsequently, Cronus threw his father's genitals into the sea. Out of the sea foam or *aphros* that followed this act emerged Aphrodite.

well be contingent. We cannot say with certainty that the process X led inexorably to the process Y.

Arguably, however, a public interrogation of, and engagement with, Hinduism both by agents of colonialism and Indian intellectuals in the first half of the 19th century generated and fostered the consciousness of the collective self. Collective self-consciousness was nurtured by intense and often acrimonious debates on what it means to be Hindu. Indian nationalism followed the dominant construction of an Indian identity around the axis of religion, the assertion of this identity as a means of rehabilitating the status of Hinduism and consequent battles between opposing world views. This intellectual exercise predated the making of the Indian nation. Both projects were, as a matter of course, plural and contested.

Religious identity might have acquired a covert tone, in some sections of the freedom movement, and an overt one in groups professing a commitment to Hindutva and to an Islamic nation. Above all, the contribution of colonial policies to the making of divisive political identities cannot be underestimated. Atavistic sentiments were played up by the colonial power by attributing the degeneration of India to Muslim invasions, by interpreting cases of conflict as communal and by the introduction of separate structures of representation.

Distrust between Hindus and Muslims was built up and sharpened by colonial policies, particularly the policy of separate electorates. Colonial modes of categorising, defining and interpreting identities and interests took this trend to its logical conclusion. Whereas moderate intellectuals and leaders succeeded in subsuming an aggressive Hinduism into a wider national project, the exclusion of the Muslim community from the national project was explicit in the writings of the founders of the ideology of Hindutva, such as Veer Savarkar and Madhav Sadashiv Golwalkar.

As suggested in the opening part of this chapter, in the early 19th century, Indians saw themselves as the members of a caste group or a *biradari*, as the residents of a locality/region or as the speakers of a language. By the turn of the 20th century, nationalism was anchored in the religious idiom. Although large numbers of Muslims preferred to stay behind in India after Partition rather than migrate to Pakistan, the fractures in the body politic and in the soul of India were never completely healed. In retrospect, the project of constructing a unified religious tradition was deeply imperfect, even defective. Our public intellectuals fell into a conceptual trap. They joined the Orientalist acclaim of a rich and sophisticated Vedic tradition without taking into account the internal criticism of the tradition. The identification of and the consequent privileging of selected texts that went into the making of Hinduism were shorn of plurality, and abstracted from debates and contestations.

This narrow construction of nationalism was based on an authoritative canon created of texts within the Vedic and Upanisidic traditions. Indian public intellectuals reiterated, filled in and transformed these great traditions into a public doctrine. This became the basis of a nationalist identity. A standardised version of a highly intellectual and Sanskritised Hinduism was produced and reproduced by a host of agents. The making of the canon has had a lasting impact, and till today the dominant definition of Hinduism as the Vedanta tradition continues to govern the fate of lesser traditions that were relentlessly relegated to the margins.

The integration of a rational, sceptical and empiricist tradition might have pre-empted the collapse of many traditions into a uniform ideology, which over time, was defined in opposition to Islam. A critical tradition could have helped us to challenge the authority of Brahmins, identified the lacunae in a transcendental philosophy, and become more sensitive to empirical realities of inequality, injustice, plurality and minority rights. But for our intellectuals and leaders, neo-Vedanta fitted the demands of both modernity, abstract and metaphysical, and tradition or fidelity to the Vedas. The tradition is theistic, intellectual, consistent and even scientific in its rejection of mindless ritual and idolatry, superstition and beliefs. Public intellectuals could finally bring together the worlds of the past and that of a colonised present through a philosophy that was abstract enough to challenge the claims of Christians to belong to a superior religion. But this tradition found it difficult to come to terms with non-Hindu identities of India.

Although traditions and figures that had been marginalised by this construction of Hinduism were later taken up by the subalterns and used to counter Brahmanical interpretations of the religion, a hierarchy had been created between high and popular Hinduism. This was produced and reproduced over time. The selectiveness with which Sanskrit texts were studied and interpreted, and scholarship on Vedic rituals and superstitions, served to privilege one strand of Hinduism—fix the nature of the religion and fulfil one of the objectives of the colonial project, to standardise religion and culture. The celebrated notion of an unchanging nature of Indian civilisation, which was in sharp contrast to Western individualism, rationalism, universalism and dedication to scientific methods, literally called out for colonial intervention. The transformation of culture, economy and the spirit of India could only be carried out by an external agent who was endowed with superior wisdom and modes of cognition. This was Hegel's precise remedy for the decline of a once great Indian civilisation.

The intellectual labours of Indologists, Sanskritists, colonial officials and missionaries shaped a public discourse in India in the early decades of the 19th century in at least two ways. First, the dominant tradition of Hinduism was identified with the tradition of the Vedanta. Second, the greatness of India rested in her past. If modern India had to be shaped in ways that could fetch acclaim and stave off criticism, contemporary India had to be returned to the past or be forged in the image of the cultural, religious and social traditions of ancient India.

Even as public intellectuals tried to discover a collective self that would legitimise their claims to independence, they were compelled to realise that this self was deeply fractured. Within the space of Hinduism, the collective self was fractured along the lines of caste hierarchies, which refused to be reformed. Caste, as Dr Ambedkar was to argue, had to be eradicated, but this was a task that the nationalist leadership was unable to take up. Dr Ambedkar had to perform a dramatic exit from Hinduism for the issue of caste to be taken seriously.

Within the political community, the collective self was fractured along the lines of religion. The overt Hindu symbols and imaginaries of political rhetoric, the collapse of religious ceremonies into political rallies and the hate-filled attacks of the aggressive right-wing Hindu faction sent shivers of apprehension along the spine of the Muslim community. The community consequently mobilised itself around Islamic identity and the two-nation theory. The path followed by extremist organisations of the Hindu right and the Muslim right could only lead in one direction, Partition, with all the attendant horrors that accompany the splitting up of territory in the pursuit of a state of one's own. The coming together of two forms of power, religion and nationalism was played out at the turn of the 20th century in the public sphere, which was increasingly dominated by religious politics.

The public sphere is a metaphorical space, constituted by multiple discourses occurring at different sites or the same site of contestation and affirmation. The sphere, relatively independent of the State, of the household and of the market, became the launching pad of a number of initiatives, new forms of associational life, new political vocabularies that lent a politically dangerous edge to debates and new projects. If, on the one hand, the sphere was dominated by responses of the intellectual elite to Western scholarship, it was equally dominated by oft-bitter debates between rival groups and schools on the nature of Hinduism, on the other hand. Reformist groups tried to establish new modes and places of worship, institute ancillary organisations such as youth and women associations, establish educational institutions and medical organisations and, in the case of Arya Samaj, cow-protection societies.

For practically every reformist, cult arose an orthodox cult to oppose it. For example, in 1887, the Bharat Dharma Maha Mandal was formed to defend idol worship and the position of Brahmins against Arya Samaj in Punjab. In Calcutta (now Kolkata), the Dharma Sabha led by Radhakanta Deb opposed the Brahmos. These are but a couple of examples of the arguments and counter-arguments offered by reformists and the orthodox, though both schools often agreed on the need for social reform. Interestingly, in India, modernity arrives through processes of intense reflection on, critique of, remaking of, and conversations between adherents of the same, and of different religions. Religion became a public affair. Religion as faith had been transformed into religion as politics.

Of course, religious debates were not the only mode of expression and articulation in this space. Indians debated on the profits that accrued to the use of the English language, economic exploitation, education, women and workers' rights, modes of representation, the nature of colonialism, nationalism, and the constitutional and political design of an independent India. A plurality of perspectives marked debates in the public sphere. In Western India, social practices were critiqued from a rational perspective and were unmarked, as Heimsath remarks, by personalised philosophes of spiritual salvation. In Maharashtra, Sardar Gopal Hari Deshmukh known as Lokhitwadi (1823–1892) launched a critique of extant social practices, particularly the Brahmanical monopoly over knowledge from the perspective of rationalist philosophy. The editor of the Anglo-Marathi newspaper, *Sudharak*, Gopal Ganesh Agarkar (1856–1895) urged that reason is the only proper guide to action. He stigmatised the reliance on knowledge found in Sanskrit text-books as narrow-minded. Even though educated Indians were aware of other philosophies, they concentrated on their own religious philosophy.[34] Markedly, however, religion did not stray too far away from circles that proclaimed themselves non-religious. Since social practices of hierarchy and discrimination were tied organically to religion, at some point public intellectuals had to come to grips with religion, either impatiently as Nehru did or innovatively as Gandhi did.

In sum, the hold of religion on the collective psyche became more than evident in the latter half of the 19th century in the public sphere. Even as an intellectual project of investigating Hinduism, as evident in the intellectual labours of Ram Mohan Roy, was transformed into a political project of nationalism, the public sphere became the site of anti-colonial ideologies through an assertion of Indian but also a religious identity. Leaders concentrated on public spectacles to tap public sentiment. Ironically, the project of launching a nationalist project on

---

[34] Cited in Heimsath, *Indian Nationalism and Hindu Social Reform*, 16–17.

the backs of religious identities by prominent leaders sharpened both anti-colonial sentiments and the sentiment of belonging to 'this' or 'that' religion.

In a fairly short span of time, the eruption of insane political violence under the banner of 'this' or 'that' religion, the suspension of civil ties between erstwhile neighbours, and the merciless brutality inflicted upon the bodies of children, men and women, should have taught subsequent generations a lesson. Religious identities, once evoked, cannot be controlled. The history of religious strife across the world establishes that the trajectories of identity politics are unexpected, and they can take unforeseen and shocking routes. One of these routes inevitably leads to the destruction of social harmony, howsoever fragile this harmony might have been. India should have learnt from a bitter history that led inexorably to the partition of minds and bodies, and that culminated in the Partition of India in 1947.

CHAPTER 5

The Evolution of Minority Rights and Secularism in India

We talk about a secular state in India. It is perhaps not very easy even to find a good word in Hindi for secular.[1]

Reading Orhan Pamuk, a Turkish novelist, screenwriter, academic and recipient of the 2006 Nobel Prize in Literature, is a fascinating and an absorbing experience. His grasp of history, his political sensibilities, the range of his imagination, the elegance of his prose, and the sheer power of his vocabulary are unparalleled. We in India have much to learn from at least one of his novels *Snow*. In this novel, Pamuk charts the debate between secularists and the religious revivalists. At one point, Muhtar, a friend of the protagonist Ka, says, 'After my years as a leftist atheist, these people [Muslim conservatives] come as such a great relief. You should meet them. I' m sure you'd warm to them too'. 'Do you really think so?' asks Ka. 'Well, for one thing, all these religious men are modest, gentle, understanding. Unlike Westernised Turks, they don't instinctively despise the common people; they're compassionate and wounded themselves. If they got to know you, they'd like

[1] Gopal, *Jawaharlal Nehru: An Anthology*, 330.

you. There would be no harsh words' replies Muhtar. Pamuk describes Ka's response in the following sentence:

> As Ka knew from the beginning, in this part of the world faith in God was not something achieved by thinking sublime thoughts and stretching one's creative powers to their outer limits; nor was it something one could do alone; above all it meant joining a mosque, becoming part of a community. Nevertheless, Ka was still disappointed that Muhtar could talk so much about his group without once mentioning God or his own private faith.[2]

This is precisely what ails the religious right in India—the transformation of religion into a political weapon without any reference to the basics of the religion it swears by. However, the more interesting question that is raised by Pamuk is different: Is political secularism inappropriate for religiously inclined societies? Are the secularists out of sync with the people they seek to deliver justice to? Is secularism fated to be relevant only for the West which has undergone a process of secularisation? This particular debate is discussed in the first section of this essay.

The second debate revolves around the issue of what the implications of secularism are. We could negotiate this question in two ways. We could adopt the US President Thomas Jefferson's position that a 'wall of separation' exists or should exist between the state and religion. Alternatively, we could carry out historical investigations and see how a concept that originates in particular sorts of practices in one part of the globe is reshaped in different social and political contexts. This essay seeks to explore the specific features that the concept has historically acquired in India, and what implications this historical experience holds for the generic concept.

The third debate is related to the second. If secularism means that all religions, and it is well known that the major religions of the world have found a home in India, are equal, what precisely does equality mean? What does it mean to treat religious groups equally? Does the State stay away from religious beliefs and practices equally? Or does it

---

[2] Pamuk, *Snow*, 60–61.

intervene in the internal affairs of religious groups, for whatever reason, equally? Does not the equal treatment of religious groups reproduce the empirical fact that one of these religious groups is numerically dominant and culturally hegemonic, and that minority groups are at risk because they are vulnerable to assimilation, on the one hand, and cultural domination of the majority, on the other? Does equality in other words imply that minority groups should be granted special protection to their culture and religion to protect them against advertent or inadvertent assimilation? What is then the relationship between secularism and minority rights?

The central argument of this essay is that secularism is not and cannot be a *stand-alone* concept. It is best thought of as derived from and justified by reference to a core concept of political theory. What that core concept is elaborated below. Here, let me just say that secularism is a complex and a somewhat muddled concept. But it is just as well that we recognise the untidiness of political concepts. If political theory as a critical activity is geared to addressing and reflecting on intractable political problems and dilemmas, then theorists simply cannot afford to live and work in rarified conceptual spaces or theoretical debates shorn of the complexities of actually existing social, economic and political worlds. In any case, in a world that is stamped by inflexible political predicaments, can the theorist resort only to formal propositions and hypothetical examples to illustrate the finer points of theory? Does he or she have any other option except philosophically reflecting on, and trying and sorting out the ambivalences, uncertainties and contingent nature of the political world and concepts that try to organise this world? This is more than true of secularism, which is a difficult concept; let us see why.

Is Secularism Appropriate for India?

Since the 1980s when the religious right began to manoeuvre its way into the centre stage of Indian politics, a troubled and troublesome question began to stalk the conceptual debate on secularism. Considering the pervasiveness of religious sensibilities in India, is secularism appropriate for the country? Correspondingly, has secularism proved capable of warding off the communalisation of Indian society and polity? Does it have the capacity to do so?[3] Regrettably, the communalisation of society has been paralleled by the communalisation of the polity. The role of individual administrators and police officials in the communal riots that have scarred the body politic since the late 1960s has been well documented. But in 1984, the *State* came to be seen as complicit in the genocidal attacks on the Sikh minority. In 1992, not only was the central government inactive when mobs demolished the Babri Masjid, but both the central and state governments failed to prevent massive riots, which following the demolition targeted members of both communities. In 2002, in Gujarat, about 1,000 Muslims were killed in a massive pogrom against the minority. The pogrom followed the death of a number of Hindus when a train compartment in which they were travelling was set on fire by a Muslim crowd at Godhra Junction railway station. Rather than waiting for the law to take its course, the Hindu right wing initiated a programme of brutal vigilante justice.

The inability of the state to prevent communal riots and the role of state officials in fomenting communalism have necessarily caused a great deal of consternation and apprehension. Has secularism been able to safeguard the life, the property and the dignity of citizens? Does secularism have the capacity to ensure inter-religious harmony? Given the communalisation of Indian society and of the polity, it is not surprising that scholars wonder whether secularism is appropriate for the country at all. Others rush to defend secularism as the only option for a society that has repeatedly been bitterly divided over religion. In effect, the academic community has been deeply and more often than not caustically divided on the issue.

In a piece provocatively titled 'An Anti-Secularist Manifesto', Asish Nandy argued that secularism provides us with an impoverished public sphere devoid of any substantive system of meaning. Therefore, the entry of religious identities into the public sphere diminishes religion, which is subordinated to political pursuits. Societies are left with few

---

[3] The collection of essays in Needham and Rajan, *The Crisis of Secularism in India*, deals with this and other such questions.

substantive resources which can enrich individual or collective lives, negotiate relationships between religious communities and control pure politics. Nandy finds an alternative to the twin ills of secular public spaces filled with crippled and truncated personalities and religious zealots using religion for their own narrow partisan ends, in the recovery of tolerance which exists in and through unarticulated but lived faiths.[4]

T. N. Madan is often lumped together with Nandy as anti-secularist. And his critics quote one of his aphorisms as evidence of the fact, 'I believe that in the prevailing circumstances secularism in South Asia as a generally shared credo of life is impossible, as a basis for state action impracticable, and as a blueprint for the foreseeable future impotent'.[5] Madan cites three reasons for this belief. First, the majority of people living in the region are active adherents of some religious faith. Second, Buddhism and Islam have been declared state religions. Third, secularism is incapable of countering religious fundamentalism. Yet there are major differences between Nandy's and Madan's position, notably that Madan does not give notice to secularism as Nandy does. At the end of the essay, Madan adds that he was not advocating a Hindu Rashtra. However, secularism will have to imply that those who profess no religion have a place in society equal to those of others, not higher or lower. What he had done was to caution against the 'easy confidence of secularists regarding [the] unproblematic adaption' of secularism'.[6] The only way that secularism may succeed is if we take both religion and secularism seriously, and not reject the former as superstition and reduce the latter to a mask for communalism or mere expediency.

These critiques of secularism have not gone unchallenged. Akeel Bilgrami accused Nandy of practising both nostalgia and skewed historiography.[7] Achin Vanaik suggested that both Nandy and Madan support a form of religious communitarianism which celebrates the

---

[4] Nandy, 'An Anti-Secularist Manifesto', 34–60.
[5] Madan, 'Secularism in Its Place', 298.
[6] Ibid., 318.
[7] Bilgrami, 'Secularism, Nationalism, and Modernity', 345–379.

traditional idea of the embedded self, rather than the modern idea of the free, equal, individuated self. The critics of secularism may be anti-communal, accepts Vanaik, but they land up sharing a discursive terrain with religious communalism.[8] The exaggerated criticisms of what were typed to be anti-secularist positions only make sense when we recollect the highly charged political atmosphere in the 1980s and 1990s. At this time, the religious right appeared on the political scene to mobilise civil society in the name of Hindutva, a mobilisation that resulted, on the one hand, in the destruction of the Babri Masjid and, on the other, in the ascent of the BJP to power in the central government in 1996. The polarised debate served to obscure what was significant in Nandy's and Madan's arguments. Both theorists sought to grapple with the uncomfortable fact that the grip of religious identities on popular imaginations has lasted longer than might have been once hoped, and that this has led to incivility, violence, riots and murderous assaults. Can secularism help us to ward off the communalisation of society and the polity?

Other arguments that hinge on the mismatch between secularism and non-secularisation of the Indian polity recognise the salience of religious identities, but they go in different directions. Vanaik proposes that traditional beliefs and practices are responsible for undermining the secular state, because they have blocked the project of rationalisation and democratisation of society. Secularism in India must mean three things: the right to freedom of worship, the primacy of citizenship and the non-affiliation of the State to any religion and impartiality.[9] Bilgrami suggested that secularism has run into trouble because it stands in a conceptual and political space which lies outside the sphere of substantive political commitments. It was adopted from an Archimedean point. And it is precisely this feature that makes it unsustainable. Had secularism been grounded in debate and the understanding of different communities, it would have proved more compelling, for all groups would have had reason to subscribe to the notion of secularism.[10]

[8] Achin, *Communalism Contested*, Chapter 4.
[9] Ibid., 171.
[10] Bilgrami, 'Secularism, Nationalism, and Modernity'.

In the highly polemical exchanges that followed, it was overlooked that Nandy and Madan had raised two sets of distinctions to the forefront of debate: between secularism and secularisation, and between the state and civil society. If India's civil society is deeply religious, then this poses a problem for secularism as a state project. Accordingly, both theorists sought the answer to communalism in the practices of civil society, particularly that of tolerance. Although Nandy dismissed secularism altogether, Madan suggested that State practices of secularism have to be based on the recognition of religious practices. This has to be buttressed by discovering and strengthening internal resources of religious pluralism and tolerance. But in the end, both theorists ground their understanding of tolerance in largely undefined and unarticulated lived practices. That these practices may have changed or degenerated in the context of competitive electoral politics, and an equally competitive market economy, is something that they would rather not take into account.

In the years that followed these exchanges, secularism came to be questioned simply because it has been identified as quintessentially a part of the project of modernity. In the process, it has often been forgotten that political secularism gains even more importance and relevance in multi-religious societies because it pre-empts the mixture of two forms of power: political power and religious power. It has also been forgotten that political practices and policy can also shape popular sensibilities. India is no longer the exotic 'Other' of the modern materialist West, it is now a country riven by competition for material and symbolic domination. The case for political secularism becomes even more compelling, and the case against political secularism on grounds of some essentialised spiritual Indian identity becomes even less compelling.

What Is Secularism About?

Despite the onset of a rich and textured debate on secularism in the 1980s, scholars do not really seem to share the understanding of what secularism means in and for India. The uncertainty that dogs secularism, however, breeds unfortunate consequences. As Madan points out, though the ambiguity of secularism was at one point considered its strength, now its vagueness is a poor foundation for clear-headed public policies.[11]

For instance, it is clear that Nandy hinges his critique of secularism on the separation of religion and politics. Even though he accepts that secularism holds another meaning for India, the idea of equality of all religions,[12] for some inexplicable reason, he puts aside the second conception of secularism as an 'avoidable Indianism' and uses secularism in its 'proper English sense', presumably as contingent upon secularisation. Yet secularism and secularisation are to some extent independent of each other. Kemal Atatürk did, after all, establish a secular state in religious Turkey. And the leaders of the freedom struggle in India sought a way out of religious conflict in and through the adoption of the principle of secularism. In other words, the extent of religious belief or unbelief does not necessarily translate into a distance between the state and religion or even control over religion by the State. In India, as we shall see, the principle of secularism reiterates the principle of equality between religions and State neutrality towards all religious groups. Secularism, thus, protects pluralism and diversity through commitment that no one shall be advantaged because she is a member of a numerically significant community and no one will be disadvantaged because her community lacks numerical strength. That is why the concept is seen as a companion to democracy, and it extends the principle of substantive equality to religious communities.

Development of Secularism and Minority Rights in India

In India, the concept of secularism was not defined till after Independence, but the spirit of secularism emerged as a constitutive principle of democracy in the 1920s. The making of a nationalist identity in which religion played a major role and the history of communal

[11] Madan, 'The Case of India', 65.
[12] Nandy, 'An Anti-Secularist Manifesto', 34–35.

riots in the country formed the backdrop of not only secularism, but also the rights of minorities to their religious community and practices. The two concepts, it was expected, would act as a brake on arbitrary and wilful majorities, whether ethnic or elected. Although the history of secularism in India is a thorny one, in retrospect, the decision to adopt the concept was politically wise. Secularism allows people belonging to different persuasions to live together in a measure of civility, particularly when religious identities have been politicised and harnessed to nation-making projects. Even though secularism has been breached time and again by murderous mobs wreaking havoc on other communities during riots, the norm continues to set a gold standard on how the State should treat religious groups, and how religious groups should treat each other.

The period of 27 years between 1920 and Independence was significant for several reasons. Increasing numbers of Indians were granted representation in legislative and executive institutions. Of equal importance was the expansion of the freedom movement into geographical areas that, till then, had been left untouched by popular mobilisation. M. K. Gandhi who had emerged as an outstanding leader of the Indian National Congress had the unusual ability to touch hearts and harness political imaginations in the cause of freedom. Under his leadership, the scale of the freedom struggle expanded exponentially. But in the first half of the 20th century, India also witnessed the unleashing of rabid communal violence and a hardening of political/national positions. In the 1920s, the leadership of the Indian National Congress took steps to halt the sharp deterioration in inter-community relations. Officially, the Congress had adopted policies of toleration and of religious coexistence, even if individual members of the Congress were simultaneously members of religious organisations. This dual identity was possible because the Indian National Congress was constituted as a federation of 'big men', landowners, merchants, industrialists, and caste and religious leaders. These leaders shepherded into the organisation their followers: tenants, members of communities, workers and peasants. The leadership of the party relied upon these 'big men' to ensure the implementation of political strategies of resistance and to take care of the suspension of strategies if the need arose. Given the layers of membership and hierarchy in the party, at the grass roots, members could be ardently Muslim, or fiercely Hindu, without overtly impacting policies drafted by party leaders. The leadership continued to swear by secular or non-religious principles of statecraft, and at the same time leaders and their followers espoused the cause of religion-based nationalism. The national movement was not neatly divided into pro- and anti-religious factions; religious affiliations cut through different organisations, even if some of them proclaimed their secular credentials. Ideologically, however, the Congress and its main leadership were committed to social harmony. The history of secularism is proof of this commitment.

The Nehru Constitutional Draft

Even as the relationship between Hindus and the Muslims worsened in the aftermath of the institutionalisation of separate electorates introduced by the Constitutional Act of 1909, a group of Indian liberals in the second decade of the 20th century took on the task of drafting the basic principles of a constitution for India. The exercise in constitution making followed a flurry of widespread discontent over the visit of the Statutory Commission, headed by Sir John Simon, to India in 1927. The British Parliament requested the Commission to consider and report on the prospect of further constitutional advance in India. Although a number of accomplished Indian lawyers and constitutional experts had emerged onto the horizon of nationalist politics, Indians were not represented in the committee. The deliberate exclusion of Indians from a body which was given the mandate to conceptualise the political future of the country deeply riled the leadership of the freedom struggle. In a major show of solidarity, all sections of Indian society joined hands to oppose the Commission. The Simon Commission travelled across the country to elicit opinion and participate in an exchange of views. Everywhere, its arrival was met by hostility, anger and black flag demonstrations.

Amidst a surge of intense anger at the latest episode of colonial arrogance, Lord Birkenhead, the then Secretary of State for India, threw a challenge at the leaders of the freedom struggle. He dared them to produce a constitution that would fetch approval across the board. The Secretary of State believed, or so it appears, that no constitution would ever be acceptable to both Hindus and Muslims. He was fated to disappointment.

The leaders of the Congress Party rose to the challenge and in the 1927 Madras session decided to draft a constitution in association with other political groups. An All-Parties Conference under the Chairmanship of Dr M. A. Ansari was set up to supervise the task. On 19 May 1928, the Conference appointed a committee of nine members with Pandit Motilal Nehru as the chairman.[13] The mandate of the committee was to consider and determine the basic principles of a future constitution with (a) special reference to the communal problem and (b) the question of Dominion Status/Responsible Government. The committee submitted its report in August 1928 to the All-Parties Conference.

The Madras Congress session had stipulated that a Declaration of Fundamental Rights should form the basis of any proposed constitution. The committee accordingly took care to conceptualise a list of inalienable fundamental rights. None of these rights could be withdrawn at any point of time. Strikingly, the committee conceptualised an integrated schedule of civil, political, social, individual and group rights. The list, in other words, bridged the traditional divide in rights talk. When the report was submitted to the All-Parties Conference in August 1928, two recommendations aroused a great deal of interest. These referred to the demand for Dominion Status and the grant of group rights to minorities or minority rights.

---

[13] The other members were Sir Tej Bahadur Sapru, Sir Ali Imam, Shri Pradhan, Shri Shuaib Quereshi, Shri Subhas Chandra Bose, Shri Madhao Shrihari Aney, Shri M. R. Jayakar, Shri N. M. Joshi and Sardar Mangal Singh. The Committee acknowledged that it had drawn freely upon the constitutions of the Dominions as well as on earlier drafts such as Dr Besant's Commonwealth of India Bill, the drafts prepared by Messrs. Vijiraghavachariar, Srinivasa Iyengar, Ramaswamy Iyengar, the committee of the Independent Labour Party and the Government of India Act, to which it has made alterations; Kumar and Sharma, *Selected Works of Motilal Nehru*, 74 (hereafter, the Nehru Report).

Whereas the first recommendation aroused criticism because the Congress had begun to think of independence instead of Dominion Status, the second was hailed as a possible resolution of the communal question. 'We', stated the introduction to the 'Report', do not wish to exaggerate the minority issue but we have to face it. In order to resolve the issue, members of the committee provided for the protection of the rights of the minorities in the Declaration of Rights. They also provided for group representation in the legislatures. Notably, minority rights were granted in addition to universal rights; they supplemented universal rights and were not a substitute for them. Other countries, the 'Report' continued, have the same problem of minorities and majorities, but this has never been seen as a valid reason for withholding self-government from them.[14]

Paramount among the rights recommended by the committee was universal adult suffrage. This, recorded the report, was in direct contrast to the recommendations of the Ceylon Reform Commission. The Commission had provided for universal manhood suffrage and restricted franchise for women over 30 years of age. This idea was firmly rejected. According to the Motilal Nehru Report:

> Any artificial restriction on the right to vote in a democratic constitution is an unwarranted restriction on democracy itself. It is quite a different thing to say that a system of universal adult suffrage is difficult to work. But this difficulty howsoever great has to be faced if what is contemplated is full responsible government in its true sense and with all its implications.[15]

The makers of the constitutional draft had grasped the significance of the right to vote. They agreed that the right is a precondition for the exercise of other rights. Unless citizens have the right to participate in the electoral and the political processes, and the right to elect and monitor their representatives, other rights are at risk. The enumeration of civil rights in the Nehru Draft was inaugurated with the classic right to liberty and privacy. Clause II of Fundament Rights stated that no person shall be deprived of his liberty, nor shall his dwelling or property

[14] Introduction to the Nehru Report, 12–13.
[15] The Nehru Report, 69.

be entered, sequestered or confiscated, save in accordance with law.[16] The constitutional draft further guaranteed freedom of conscience, and the free profession and practice of religion subject to public order or morality. Also granted was the right to free expression of opinion, the right to assemble peaceably and without arms, and the right to form associations or unions for purposes that were not opposed to public order and morality. All citizens were assured equality before the law and granted equal rights.

The primacy of secularism as the organising principle of the polity was given due recognition in spirit, even if the concept was not given a name. Clause XI of the Fundamental Rights section of Chapter VII stated that there shall be no state religion for the Commonwealth of India, nor shall the state either directly or indirectly endow any religion or give any preference or impose any disability on account of religious beliefs and religious status. No person shall be obliged to attend religious instructions in schools receiving state aid or public money. According to Clause XIII, no person shall by reason of his religion caste or creed be prejudiced in any way with regard to public employment, office of power or honour and the exercise of any trade or calling. Subsequent clauses guaranteed non-discrimination in the use of public roads, public wells and places of public resort. All citizens were granted equal rights.[17]

The Muslim League had agreed to join the deliberations on the condition that the committee should accept separate electorates. Given the reluctance of the Congress to acknowledge, let alone institution-alise separate electorates, the leaders chose to offer to the Muslim community the protection of their religion and culture in the form of minority rights. In addition to the Declaration of Rights assuring religious and personal liberty to all citizens of India, the constitutional draft made provisions for the reservation of seats for Muslims, if so desired by them, in strict proportion to their population, in the central and provincial legislatures for 10 years. The exception to this rule was Bengal and Punjab where Muslims were in a slight majority. Members of the community also had the right to contest general seats. The

[16] Ibid., 75.
[17] Ibid., 74–75.

Report established that reservation of seats for non-Muslim minorities would be institutionalised in the North-Western Provinces. Electoral reservation, accepted the authors of the Report, is a necessary evil, at least for some time.[18] This was the first step towards minority rights and substantive equality that lie at the heart of Indian secularism.

The recognition that minorities needed special protection was the outcome of the troubled history of India in the first decades of the 20th century. The minority issue, the question of what the future of the Muslim minority was in a Hindu-dominated India, was propelled to the forefront of the political scene, a dark shadow on the future of the country as a plural society. The reason for institutionalising minority rights was essayed by Pandit Jawaharlal Nehru in 1930. He authored an elegant and perceptive note on the issue in *Young India*. The history of India and Europe, he wrote, has demonstrated that there can be no stable equilibrium in any country if attempts are made to crush minorities, or force them to conform to the ways of the majority. There is no surer way of rousing the resentment of the minority, and keeping it apart from the mainstream, than feeling that it has not got the freedom to stick to its own ways. We in India, he continued, are clear that our policy is based on granting this freedom to minorities. Under no circumstance will any coercion or repression be tolerated, nor will any unfair treatment of the minority be tolerated. 'Indeed we should go further and state that it will be the business of the state to give favoured treatment to minority and backward communities'.[19] Nehru reiterated the commitment of the 1928 Nehru Draft of minority rights that the religious, cultural, linguistic and educational rights of the minorities would be safeguarded in an independent India. This was the promise of the future prime minister (PM) of independent India to an anxiety-ridden Muslim community.

The Aftermath of a Riot

This commitment to minority rights, as well as secularism, was reiterated in 1931 after the savage Hindu–Muslim riots in Kanpur. The Kanpur riot left 400 dead, parts of the city were destroyed, mosques

[18] Ibid., 43.
[19] Nehru, 'Notes on Minorities', 259–260.

and temples were damaged, and houses burnt. A miasma of devastation and gloom hung over the city. In the aftermath of the Kanpur riots, the Indian National Congress established an enquiry commission to explore the reasons for the violence. A small committee of the prominent Congressmen, Purshottam Das Tandon, Khwaja Abdul Majid, T. A. K. Sherwani, Zaraful Mulk, Pandit Sunderlal and Bhagwan Das, authored a report that has been described as an elaborate, contemporary nationalist statement on the history of Hindu–Muslim relations in India.[20] Communal riots are an outcome, the report argued, of certain historical and social processes that have been sparked off by colonial rule. The argument overturned the assumption, widely disseminated by the colonial government, that Hindu–Muslim enmity is endemic to India. Therefore, the maintenance of peace required the presence of British rule.

Historians tell us that the pejorative term 'communal' was practically invented by the colonial government. The Indian National Congress uncritically accepted the term 'communal', but held that it was the British policy of divide and rule that was responsible for violence, loss of lives and destruction that was a direct outcome of communal riots. The official Congress position was that India was home to both Hindus and Muslims, and that it was possible to put an end to the conflict. For this, minorities had to be sure that their rights to religion and culture would be given full protection in an independent India.

In the shadow of the Kanpur riot, the Congress drafted the Karachi Resolution on Fundamental Rights. The declaration emphasised the right to religion and the freedom to profess, and practise any religion. The new additions to the list of minority rights were the right to cultural autonomy and equal access to educational facilities. On 31 March 1931, Gandhi moving the resolution on fundamental rights in the open session of the Congress at Karachi spoke on the issue. Although Islamic and Aryan cultures are not mutually exclusive, he said, we must recognise that Mussalmans look upon Islamic culture as distinctive from Aryan. Let us, therefore, cultivate tolerance.[21]

[20] Pandey, *The Construction of Communalism in North India*, 250.
[21] Gandhi, 'Speech on Fundamental Rights', 372.

Religious neutrality is another important provision, he continued. Swaraj will favour Hinduism no more than Islam, nor Islam more than Hinduism. Let us from now on, he concluded, adopt the principle of State neutrality in our daily affairs.[22] For Gandhi, the route of toleration led straight to religious neutrality, popularly understood as the first principle of secularism.

The report of the Sapru Committee set up by the non-party conference in November 1944, recommended full religious tolerance, non-interference in religious beliefs, practices and institutions, and protection of the language and culture of the communities. The report proposed that in every state, and at the Centre, a commission consisting of a representative of each minority community would be set up to keep watch on the affairs of the minorities.

Three features distinguish the official position of the Congress on communal violence. One, the leaders accepted that the Hindu majority was as guilty of communal sentiments and violence as the Muslim minority. Two, the state had to be neutral towards religions. Three, group rights for minorities were not only an essential precondition for individual rights, but also important in themselves. In other words, religion was seen as a significant good to which all people had a right. In a society where the Hindu community had the advantage of numbers, minorities had to be protected against the onslaught of majoritarianism.

The trail of repeated communal riots in the 27 years before Independence had traumatised the body politic. Religion as politics or politicised religion could not be brushed away as a minor or even a major inconvenience. It was futile to hope that religion would be privatised at some time in the future, and the public sphere would be free of constant threat of communal violence. It was precisely this violence that prompted India's tallest leader Jawaharlal Nehru to write in his diary while in prison in 1935. 'What a disgustingly savage people we are', he wrote, '... politics, progress, socialism, communism, science-where are they before this black religious savagery?' His biographer

22 Ibid., 373.

S. Gopal concluded that Nehru was extremely impatient with religion. It might be an anchor for some, but he did not seek harbourage in this way. I prefer the open sea, wrote Nehru, with all its storms and tempests.[23] Nehru was to change his mind after the communal fury that accompanied the Partition of India. S. Gopal cites a letter written to Jinnah by Nehru, in which he expressed extreme discomfort with the great role played by religion in the lives of people. I, he wrote, have lost confidence and the last few years have had a powerful effect on me. My own mind moves in a different plane and most of my interests lie in other directions. However, I have, he continued, given much thought to the problem, and understand much of its implications. But I feel like an 'outsider', and 'alien in spirit'.[24]

One would have expected Nehru, a secularist in the Western mode, to banish religion from the public sphere of politics as Kemal Atatürk had done in Turkey, and force the notion of religion as private faith upon his people. But that would have been bad history as well as bad politics. Religion in India was not simply faith. An entire brand of politics that ranged from the awareness of religious identity and consequent politicisation to competitive nationalism and to Partition had been constructed around religion. Since both the pervasiveness and the political potency of religion had caught hold of the public mind, Nehru could hardly ignore the command of religious politics in the public sphere. Nor could he abdicate his responsibility—that of calming down religious passions. What he could do was to oversee that the future of India was civilised, civil, secure, democratic and secular.

In the Constituent Assembly

Although Congress leaders used the term secularism in the pre-Independence period often enough, oddly enough, the concept was never spelt out or elaborated as a principle of state policy. Nor did it form part of the Preamble to the Constitution till 1976, vide the 42nd Amendment. But the seeds of secularism were present throughout

[23] Cited in Gopal, 'Nehru and Minorities', 2466.
[24] Ibid., 2466.

the debates in the Constituent Assembly, for instance, most members agreed that the Preamble to the Constitution should not contain any reference to God. On 17 October 1949 during discussions on the wording of the Preamble, H. V. Kamath moved an amendment that the Preamble should begin with the phrase 'In the name of God'. Similar amendments were moved by Shibban Lal Saxena and Pandit Madan Mohan Malaviya. Other members objected, and a majority of the members expressed their conviction that religion was a matter of individual choice and not the signpost of a collective.[25] Pandit Hirday Nath Kunzru regretfully stated that matters concerning our innermost and sacred feelings have been brought into the arena of discussion. It would have been far more consistent with our beliefs that we should not impose our feelings on others, and that the collective view should not have been forced on others. 'We invoke the name of God, but I make bold to say that while we do so, we are showing a narrow sectarian spirit, which is contrary to the spirit of the Constitution'.[26] The amendment moved by Mr Kamath was defeated.

It is quite puzzling that though copious references were made to secularism, no one seemed to be quite sure what the concept stood for. On 15 November 1948, K. T. Shah (Bihar, General) moved an amendment to Article 1. The amendment held that Clause 1 of Article 1 will read as follows: 'India shall be a Secular, Federal, Socialist Union of States'. We, he stated, have been told time and again, from every platform, that ours is a secular State. If that is true, if that holds good, I do not see why the term could not be added or inserted in the Constitution itself, once again, to guard against any possibility of misunderstanding or misapprehension.

Mr Shah argued that every constitution reflects the spirit and the tensions of its age. The pre-Independence period was scarred by communal riots, and Independence was accompanied by its unhappy twin—the Partition of India. To avoid a repetition of these experiences, the character and nature of the State, which is being constituted

---

[25] *Constituent Assembly Debates, 1989,* Official Report, vol. X, 17, New Delhi, Lok Sabha Secretariat, October 1949, 439, 444, 446.

[26] Ibid., 441.

by the Assembly, should assure all citizens that relations between citizens, the relation of the citizen to the State, and the relationship of the states inter se may not be influenced by any consideration, which might result in injustice or inequality.[27]

Dr Ambedkar (Bombay, General) in a longish reply to this observation focused on the implications of the term socialist, but completely ignored the suggestion that secularism should be institutionalised as the governing principle of democracy. The amendment was rejected on the plea that the Constitution is merely a mechanism for the purpose of regulating the work of the various organs of the State. The policy of the State and the organisation of society should be decided by the people themselves according to time and circumstance.[28] In the process, secularism remained undetermined, even though the concept was mentioned in three different contexts.

The first context was the discussion around the need to curtail the regime of religion in the interests of nation-building—of democracy and of rights. K. M. Munshi emphasised that religion must be restricted to spheres which legitimately appertain to religion. The rest of life must be regulated, unified and modified in order to build a strong and consolidated nation.[29] Dr Ambedkar asked for strict control over religion.[30] Religious conceptions in this country, he said, are so vast that they cover every aspect of life from birth to death. We should strive to limit the definition of religion so that it does not extend beyond beliefs and rituals of ceremonies. In sum, the role of religion in public affairs was sought to be depoliticised, and religion privatised, so that the public sphere and state policy could be governed by secular or non-religious politics.

[27] CAD, vol. VII, 15 November 1948, 399–400.

[28] Ibid. 'It was somewhat new to me', responded K. T. Shah on the same day, 'to hear that a Constitution is a mechanism for regulating the various organs of Government and their functions; and that any desire to include in it any aspiration of the people might be regarded as somewhat out of place' (p. 418).

[29] CAD, vol. VII, 23 November 1948, 548.

[30] It is generally agreed that the argument made by Ambedkar for control over religion is the source of the essential practices doctrine that judges have used to evaluate religious practices (CAD, vol. VII, 2 December, 781).

The second context for the discussion on secularism was the provision of minority rights first granted by the 1928 Nehru Constitutional Draft. We need to recollect that Constitutions are not only legal but also normative documents. They embody constitutional morality, and institutionalise norms that should govern, implement and arbitrate law. Yet these principles and values cannot be wholly abstract; they are often a response to empirical situations and dilemmas. The present of the deliberations of the Assembly was shaped inexorably by communal riots that accompanied the Partition of India. The discussions were carried on in the shadow of the breakdown of life in large parts of Northern, Western and Eastern India, and fear of further balkanisation. The debate was expectedly an uneasy one, given that deliberations in the Constituent Assembly traversed the past, scarred by bloodletting and destruction, and the future that would hopefully put an end to any vestige of communalism.

Predictably, the grant of minority rights by the 1928 Nehru Constitution became contentious. The most important task, stated K. M. Munshi, was to consolidate the nation. The British had destroyed the nation by statutorily fragmenting political India into religious communities, under the guise of protecting the minorities.[31] Secularism, which was largely identified with minority rights, was feared as potentially divisive. It threatened to further fragment an already divided society. Members opined that the state should observe secularism by distancing itself from all religious affairs. This conception came close to the Western concept of secularism.

The third context for the discussion on secularism was the debate on personal laws. Some Muslim members emphasised that secularism did not imply the abdication of personal laws and that the secular State should not do anything to interfere with the way of life and religion of the minorities. Mr Mohammad Ismail (Muslim League, Madras) pointed out that no group, section, people or community should be obliged to give up their personal laws. The right to follow personal laws, he pointed out, is part of the way of life of those people who follow such laws, part of their religion and part of their culture.

---

[31] Munshi, *Indian Constitutional Documents*, 197.

Precedents for such practices were already in existence. In Yugoslavia, treaty obligations enjoined the government to respect minority rights. 'The Serb, Crot [sic], and Slovene State agree to grant to the Musulmans in the matter of family law and personal status provisions suitable for regulating these matters in accordance with the Musulman usage'.[32]

Pocker Sahib Bahadur, the Muslim League member from Madras, pointed out that people seem to have very strange ideas about a secular State and that under such a State, there must be a common law observed by its citizens in all matters, including matters of their daily life, their language, their culture and their personal laws. That, he remarked, is not the correct way to look at the secular State. In a secular State, citizens belonging to different communities must have the freedom to practise their own religion and observe their daily life, that is, their personal laws should be left as they were. The British, he pointed out, were able to carry on the administration of the country for 150 years because they gave religious communities the guarantee that they would follow their personal laws. 'This is one of the secrets of success and the basis of the administration of justice on which the foreign rule was based'.[33] The argument, like the other two notions of secularism, stressed that the state should keep away from religion. But it ran against the idea that a secular state must impose a non-religious or secular law on all its citizens in all matters of daily life, language, culture and personal laws.

We get an indication of the many tasks that were going to be laid upon the slender shoulders of secularism. A secular State must control religious excesses that had wrought havoc on the lower castes, it should distance itself from religion, it should protect minority rights, but it should not interfere with religious laws or personal laws. That is, secularism was fated to shoulder many tasks that a democratic State should logically take on, removal of caste discrimination, protection of vulnerable sections and negotiation of personal law to ensure gender

[32] CAD, vol. VII, 23 November 1948, 540–541.
[33] Ibid., 544.

justice. Even before it had been spelled out, expectations of the concept were high. It had already begun to suffer from an overload.

It was on 24 January 1948 that PM Jawaharlal Nehru clarified the notion of secularism in a convocation address to the Aligarh Muslim University. In the middle of a fluid state caused by the Partition, he said, all of us have to be clear about our basic allegiance to certain ideas. Do we, he asked, believe in a national state, which includes people of all religions and shades of opinion and is essentially a secular as a state, or do we believe in the religious theocratic conception of a State that considers other people as beyond the pale? The idea of a theocratic State was given up some time ago by the world and it has no place in the mind of a modern person. And yet the question has to be put in India, for some of us have tried to jump to a bygone age. Whatever confusion, he said, the present may contain, in the future, India will be a land, as in the past, of many faiths equally honoured and respected, within a tolerant, creative nationalism not a narrow nationalism living in its own shell.[34]

In 1961, in a preface to a work on secularism, *Dharam Nirpeksh Raj* by Raghunath Singh, PM Nehru further elaborated the concept of secularism. We, he said, call our State a secular State. There is no good Hindi word for secular. Some people think it means opposed to religion. But this, he wrote, is not the correct notion of secularism. It means a State that honours all faiths equally and gives them equal opportunities, that is, as a State it does not allow itself to be attached to one faith or religion, which then becomes the State religion. This is a modern conception. In India, we have a long history of toleration, but this not the all that secularism is about.[35]

Strictly speaking, we do not need to proclaim secularism in order to grant religious freedom. This freedom can emerge from, and form part of Article 19, guaranteeing the fundamental right to liberty that is assured to every citizen. But a secular State cannot stop at granting the right to religious freedom. The principle of secularism goes further and establishes *equality* between all religious groups. Certainly, the

[34] Nehru, 'A Common Cultural Inheritance', 26.
[35] Nehru, 'A Secular State', 330.

generic right to equality, granted by Article 14 of the Fundamental Rights Chapter, can protect equality among religious communities. If we were to stop at this, secularism would be rendered unnecessary, and it could well be collapsed into democracy. Secularism extends beyond equality and freedom in two ways. First, as a companion concept of democracy, secularism extends individual rights to equality to religious communities and guarantees equality among them. Second, the State is not aligned to any religion. These *commitments establish the credentials of a secular State.* Or secularism, we can say, promises that the State would neither align itself with any one religion, especially the majority religion, not pursue any religious tasks of its own and ensure that religious minorities are treated equally by the State.

The second and the third components of secularism, that is equality of all religions and the distancing of the State from all religious groups, were specifically meant to assure the minorities that they had a legitimate place as citizens in the country and that they would not be discriminated against. Correspondingly, secularism established that the majority group would not be privileged in any manner. The creed simply discouraged any pretension that a demographically numerous religious group had any right to stamp the body politic with its ethos. It is this political task that was allotted to secularism in a plural society, and it is the significance of this political task that is overlooked by critics of secularism in India.

In sum, the concept of secularism that emerged in India possesses four substantial components as follows:

1. The State will not attach itself to any one religion, which will thereby establish itself as the State religion.
2. All citizens are granted the freedom of religious belief.
3. The State will ensure equality among religious groups by ensuring that one group is not favoured at the expense of another. Correspondingly, the minorities will not be discriminated against in any way.
4. Members of minority groups that are at risk have the right to their religion and practices, and the community has the right to maintain and perpetuate its collective self.

CHAPTER 6

Equality and the Rights of Minorities

I believe implicitly that all men are born equal. All whether born in India or in England or in America, or in any circumstance whatsoever have the same soul as any other. I consider that it is unmanly for any person to claim superiority over fellow-beings.[1]

I have suggested in this essay that secularism cannot be seen as a stand-alone concept and that it has to be located in democracy or rather as an extension of the principle of equality. In Europe, the hinge for the concept of secularism was secularisation or the privatisation of religion. If religion had been privatised, and the public sphere had been emptied out of religious imageries, vocabularies, idioms and rhetoric, it was relatively easy for the State to adopt the principle of neutrality towards all religious groups. Although secularisation—as a social principle—and secularism—political principle—have been treated as synonymous in the European debate, in India, the concept of secularism formed part of the effort to neutralise the communalisation of society. One of the basic preconditions was that the State should not adopt a religion as the official religion. It was hoped by many, most of all by Jawaharlal Nehru, that Indians would set aside their ancient

---

[1] Gandhi, *Young India*, 385.

religious prejudices and biases, and metaphorically enter the public sphere as unencumbered beings. In this sphere, modes of reasoning on issues that pertained to the common good would rely on scientific and rational modes of argument and persuasion. Secularism, in other words, would encourage the development of a secular spirit as an alternative to religion in society.

There is more, the leadership in India had accurately gauged the troubled political climate of the day when they set out to draft the Motilal Nehru Constitution in 1928. Consequently, they provided for both minority rights and the spirit of secularism in the constitutional draft. But nowhere, as suggested above, was secularism defined and clarified in an unambiguous manner till 1951 when Pandit Nehru conceptualised it as an integral part of the democratic State, which protected the right to religion, including the right to be non-religious and that did not distinguish between groups on the ground of religion. The Supreme Court, as we shall see, has followed precisely this form of reasoning and interpreted secularism as equality of all religions.

However, at precisely this point of time, we are confronted by a crucial question: What does equality mean? Equality as a moral principle creates the foundations of a democratic society. This is best exemplified in the precept of one person one vote. Each person has only one vote, and each vote will count for only one. The background presumption of the one-person-one-vote principle is impersonality and impartiality. Given its centrality to democracy, it is not surprising that the right to equality leads the list of Fundamental Rights granted by the Indian Constitution in Chapter 3 of the Constitution, that is, Article 14. Rights do not exhaust the space of political morality. Sentiments that are independent of a rights-laden tongue, such as care, benevolence, charity, sympathy, pity and love, are good in themselves. Any society which is not marked by the presence of these sentiments would be poor indeed. But unless we recognise that our duty to extend solidarity to our fellow citizens flows from their right to freedom or equality, the recipient of obligation is rendered dependent on our 'care' or 'generosity'. We might feel that whereas P deserves our sympathy and, therefore, we have a moral obligation to her, Q does not evoke quite the same sensibility and, therefore, we owe her nothing. That is Q's status, or rather her lack of status, is neither here nor there as far as we are concerned. Bearers of rights, on the other hand, possess irreducible standing as persons who matter, or at least who should matter, equally. That is obligations are not attached to either P or Q as persons with specific traits, but because both belong to a category that we term human. Therefore, they are bearers of rights, and this is independent of subjective evaluations of who deserves rights. Our obligations, therefore, flow from rights.

At this stage of our history, we do not have to defend the proposition that all human beings are equal. It is enough if we recognise that individuals are equal because all individuals share something in common. For example, each individual has the capacity to make his or her own history along with others. Of course, the history they make may not be the history they wanted to make in the first instance, but that is not important. What is important is the capacity of each individual to make his or her own history and do that by speaking back to histories made by others.

The recognition that all individuals possess the capacity to make their own histories, even if this is, as Marx famously said, not in circumstances of their own choice, gives us enough reasons to see them as equal. The principle of equal standing in society generates two robust principles of political morality. For one, equality is a relation that obtains between persons in respect of some fundamental characteristic that they share in common. Equality is, morally speaking, a default principle. Therefore, and this is the second postulate, persons should not be discriminated against on grounds such as race, caste, gender, ethnicity, disability or class. These features of the human condition are morally irrelevant because individuals do not choose which community they wish to be born into. This is particularly relevant for India, for more often than not, individuals are harmed because of their community of birth.

The concept of equality in other words refers to the value we place on human beings. This is not an empirical fact the way the proposition that all individuals have two eyes is an empirical fact; it is rather a statement of the respect that human beings are entitled to. This is so self-evident at this point of our history that anyone who believes that humans are not of equal standing in society should be asked to establish this point. Therefore, if someone were to ask 'equality *for* what', we can answer with confidence that equality ensures equal standing and respect, and respect is an essential prerequisite for the making of human beings who can participate in the multiple transactions of society from a position of confidence and self-respect.

This proposition of equal standing in society carries two more implications. One, the right to equality as a right does not imply that people are the same. An egalitarian does not seek to prevent people from pursuing and enjoying what they consider a life worth living. People have different talents, skills and tastes, different interests, and different persuasions. One among three friends might be a skilled cricketer, the other a good musician and the third might not do anything spectacular except live his or her life in the best way he or she can. Living life well is an exceptional talent and one we should learn to respect this the way we respect gifted sportspeople or musicians. But this also does not mean that a cricketer should complain of discrimination if he or she does not get a place in an orchestra, and his or her musician friend does.

Equality is significant because it establishes that people should be treated equally in morally relevant respects: the right to freely express her or his opinions, the right to worship which God he or she opt for, the right to work in a job he or she is suited for, the right to live wherever he or she chooses to live, the right to move freely around the country and abroad, and the right to be respected not despite but irrespective of his or her gender, caste and religion. Therefore, the police cannot arrest P for no reason because he or she is a citizen of India and they cannot arrest Q for the same reason even if Q belongs to a different ethnic community or a different religious group. We have reason to act in the same way towards different people in different situations if these situations are alike. This is the principle of equality as fairness. The second implication of equality is that all people should have access to social, economic and political institutions, enjoy the rights and benefits of citizenship, participate in the social, economic and political transactions of their society, and be equally protected by the rule of law. This is the principle of equality of opportunity. We have made two propositions here (a) that human beings possess equal standing in society and must be treated equally, and (b) that all should be given the right to equality of opportunity. Secularism extends the democratic principle of equality to the relationship of the State with religious communities and the relationship of religious communities with each other. Secularism is a companion concept of democracy insofar as it is an extension of the equality principle.

The Rights of Minorities

The problem arises in the notion of secularism as equality when we recognise what have been called 'background inequalities' in society. People are unequal for many reasons, they are poor, they belong to a gender or a caste that has been stigmatised and they are members of a religion that has been constructed as the enemy. Will people who have been marginalised by social processes of hierarchy, domination and subordination possess the right to equality of opportunity? We have seen in the case of Ahmedabad that Muslim workers in the textile industry had to organise their own subunion because the TLA did not give them adequate representation. We have seen that the Muslim community in the city had to live in ghettos because life in residential areas that were contiguous to other residential areas was fearful and short. Because they were not treated equally, they did not possess the right to equality of opportunity. And because they were outside the pale of equality of opportunity, they were not treated as equal. And because they are not treated as equal, they live in insecure conditions.

People are, in this case, treated unequally because they belong to a religious community that has been demonised through vicious rhetoric and hateful actions. The demonisation of an entire community impacts the life of its members adversely. Individual members may not be able to get the jobs they want, rent or buy a house in the neighbourhood they want to live in, send their children to schools they think are desirable, and form warm and social relationships with others who they wish they could be friends with. Inequality of life conditions has shaped their lives, they are considered lesser than the members of the majority community for purely arbitrary reasons. They are not seen as individuals; they are reduced to the community of which they are members. They might possess the right to cast a vote, but the exercise of this right may not be enough to enable to live better lives. There is more, the religious codes of minorities are attacked, their commitments are mocked, and their identity as a member of a community is enough to debar them from jobs, from the membership of a prestigious club and from sentiments of mutual respect.

What law, what precept, what norm, which ruling have these individuals broken? In rights talk, our rights can only be suspended if we have violated some provision of law. A person whose basic rights of citizenship have been infringed is probably a law-abiding citizen, he or she has hurt no one, and he or she may be perfectly innocent of any crime known to humanity. But in times of covert communalism and overt communal violence, every right that legal and political philosophers have argued for so strenuously is neutralised. A person who belongs to a community that has been vilified and stigmatised is by definition stripped of his or her rights, except perhaps the right to vote, the power of which is sadly truncated because there is no one to listen to his or her voice.

We have to go beyond individual rights in such cases and recognise that the effectiveness of fundamental rights is contingent upon the existence of group rights. A member of a majority community is advantaged because his or her community is numerically larger than the others, and a member of a minority community, particularly a community which has been targeted by the purveyors of hate, is disadvantaged only because his or her community is numerically smaller and because it has been isolated and subjected to hate speech. Unless we commit to equality between communities, a democratic society is fated to majoritarianism. There is nothing democratic about the majority principle; it is workable, but it is not a formula that should be designed to trump the rights of minorities all the time. Democracy is about the rights of each citizen independent of his or her community. However, in India, individual rights are compromised because of his or her membership in a religion or a race.

When a society is stamped by tensions between the majority and the minority communities, the rights of individuals belonging to the latter community are bound to be overridden by the majority. We have to think in terms of the rights of that community to respect and regard— perhaps to existence itself in order to institutionalise preconditions for individual rights. Agents who trigger off communal riots build upon latent and often unrecognised prejudices and motivate people who had lived with one another in civility even if not in harmony to engage in indescribable violence. It is more than likely that perfectly innocent citizens get caught in the cross-fire. Communal conflicts have not been controlled by only democracy; we also need secularism and minority rights to ensure equality of groups and protection for vulnerable groups.

This allows us to accept that if a culture is under attack by majoritarian groups, which seek to annihilate it or marginalise it, it should be shielded through protective measures. It is not enough to grant the individual the right to community and leave it at that. It is equally important to institute supportive political and social environments so that the individual has access to a flourishing community. To grant the individual the right to his or her religious community and practices is of little account if the community is threatened by majoritarian elements. Likewise, if we allow communities to die out through indifference or neglect, if we allow them to decay or be overwhelmed by majoritarianism, we deprive their members of access to vital resources that deepen their cognitive and evaluative faculties. Communities dwindle because they have been subjected to sheer indifference, intentional neglect and deliberate targeting. Languages decay because their histories have been denigrated and dismissed. Communities lose self-respect because they have been stereotyped in perverse ways. The causes as well as the remedies for the decay of religious and or cultural communities have to be sought in the wider society. The responsibility for maintaining and reproducing the community in the form of places of worship, styles of worship, observance of holy days and, above all, respect for the members is not that of the group. Society and the State are responsible for it. A democratic State cannot allow majority groups to target the members and affect the fate of the community.

To extend this protection through policies of non-discrimination and equality, the State has to be secular as well, and it has to be committed to minority rights.

The Global History of Minority Rights

This is not a new idea at all. The history of minority rights goes back to policies adopted by some European states at the turn of the 19th century, and especially to the period after the end of the First World War and the establishment of the League of Nations. After the First World War, the rights of minorities to their religion and their culture were discussed as part of international jurisprudence. The collapse of the once great polyglot empires in Central and Eastern Europe and the emergence of multi-ethic societies threw the issue of how minorities should be protected against the brute power of the majorities onto the table. Ironically, whereas the states in these large multi-national empires had left various ethnic groups alone and shown no desire to merge them into the majority population, successor states exhibited no such rectitude. For instance, Poland contained not only the Polish people, but also German, Jewish and Lithuanian groups. Yet some majority groups, gripped by dreams of an ethnically pure Polish people, carried out a series of pogroms against the Jewish community and engaged in near war with the Ukrainians in 1918.[2] The leadership of the international community recognised at the Paris Peace Conference that unless the rights of minorities were especially protected and guaranteed under a system of international law, East Europe would be engulfed in civil war between different ethnic groups. Minority rights were included in the five peace treaties between the Allies and associated powers, on the one hand, and Poland, Czechoslovakia, Romania, Greece and Yugoslavia, on the other. Special provisions for minorities were incorporated in the peace treaties with Austria, Bulgaria, Hungary and Turkey. Albania, Finland and Iraq declared that they would protect their minorities. The entry of Eastern European countries into the League of Nations was made conditional on the grant of minority rights. The League was entrusted

---

[2] Chandhoke, *Beyond Secularism*, 276.

with the responsibility of ensuring that international commitment to the rights of minorities would be honoured.

The treaties provided a model for minority rights. Signatory states assured equality of treatment to all inhabitants without distinction of birth, nationality, language, race and religion. Minority groups were given the right to establish manage and control at their own expense charitable, religious, educational and social institutions, and the right to use their language and believe in their religion freely. Complaints could be brought before the International Court of Justice and the League could initiate action against offenders in certain specified cases.

The International Court of Justice played an important role in securing minority rights through two notable judgements. In 1930, the Permanent Court of International Justice in an advisory opinion on the Graeco-Bulgarian community case defined community in terms of religious, racial and linguistic traditions, and if the group wished to preserve and perpetuate through rituals, education and socialisation of the young. The existence of a community, stated the Court, is not dependent on recognition by law. If a community exists in the shape of a group of members united by cultural factors that are distinctive to them, and if the community is intent on maintaining these cultural markers, this is enough to see that group as a community.

The principles for minority protection were laid down by the Permanent Court of International Justice on 6 April 1936 in the case of minority schools in Albania. The objective of minority rights, stated the Court, is to secure for minority groups the possibility of living peacefully alongside the rest of the population, and cooperating amicably with them, while at the same time preserving the characteristics which distinguish them from the majority and satisfying their special needs. Equality in law, held the Court, precludes the discrimination of any kind, whereas equality, in fact, might involve the necessity of different treatment in order to attain a result which establishes an equilibrium between different situations. It is easy to imagine cases in which equality of treatment by the majority and the minority whose situations and requirements are different would result in inequality.[3]

---

[3] Ansari, *Readings on Minorities*, xvi.

It was in this context of global acceptance of minority rights that the Nehru Constitutional Draft outlined the rights of minorities, specifically in 1928, along with fundamental rights for all.[4]

The commitment to minority rights across the world lasted till the third decade of the 20th century. After the Second World War, the consensus seemed to have weakened. For one, most of these rights had been granted not to all minorities across the world but selectively. Whereas they were imposed upon countries of Eastern Europe which saw these rights as discriminatory, other countries perceived these rights as violations of sovereignty and encouragement of separatism. Oddly enough, a commitment to minority rights was not extracted from Germany and Italy, countries peopled by substantial numbers of minorities. Two, these rights did not prove conducive to international peace. The Nazis used minority rights as a pretext to intervene in other countries in the name of protecting German populations that resided there. The Nazis encouraged German minorities to escalate their demands on the governments of Czechoslovakia and Poland. The consolidation of anti-Semitism in Germany and the repression launched on the Jewish population there, hammered a further nail in the coffin of minority rights.

In the end, wrote a political commentator in *Foreign Affairs*, things came to an extraordinary pass. Totalitarian and dictatorial States like Germany, Italy and Hungary persecuted minorities in their own territories and at the same time posed as the protector of their own people who formed minorities in other countries.[5] After the Second World War, the great powers agreed that it was best to promote universal human rights and that this was enough to protect minorities. The Universal Declaration of Human Rights was adopted without a provision on minority rights, even though the subcommission had recommended these rights.

Later, however, the Covenant on Economic, Social and Cultural Rights and the International Covenant on Civil and Political Rights specified minority rights in 1966. In the latter Covenant, Clause 27 stated that in those states in which ethnic, linguistic and religious

---

[4] Chandhoke, *Beyond Secularism*, 274–280.
[5] Benes, 'The Organisation of Postwar Europe', 226–242.

minorities exist, people belonging to these communities shall not be denied the right in community with other members of their group to enjoy their own culture, to profess and practice their own religion and to use their own language. These rights are granted along universal rights to non-discrimination. After the Second World War, the issue was sidelined for a number of reasons. It reappeared on the agenda in the last decade of the 20th century in response to ethno-nationalist wars, ethnic cleansing and genocide that had spread their tentacles across the world after the end of the Cold War in 1989.

The Indian Case

In the first half of the 20th century in India, equality was considered to be inadequate for the protection of religious minorities. The leadership of the national movement recognised the precise problem. Partition had sparked off massive ethnic cleansing on both sides of the border, and the Indian government felt the need to protect Muslims who had opted to stay in India and chosen Indian citizenship over Pakistan. They were highly vulnerable in India. Consequently, the Government of India granted special concessions to religious minorities along with the right to their culture. They could retain their own personal laws relating to marriage, dowry, dissolution of marriage, parentage and legitimacy, guardianship, adoption, gifts, wills, inheritance and succession. The reasons why the minorities were allowed to do so are intricate and outside the purview of this essay, but the grant had to do with the political need to make the minorities secure in a Hindu-majority India. These were conceptualised as transitory, but over time it has become difficult to enact a Uniform Civil Code, or rather ensure gender justice for all women.

The problem is that immediately after Independence, the government set out to reform the personal laws of the Hindu community through the Hindu Code Bill. In other words, government intervention in the affairs of religious groups proved to be *selective*. Expectedly, the Hindu right attacked the government for practising pseudo-secularism. At that time, Hindu right did not dismiss secularism. The religious right argued that if secularism means equality of all religions, then minority rights and retention of personal laws violate the basic precepts of secularism as equality. It may appear ironic that the religious right, devoted as it is to the establishment of a majoritarian State, had till recently no problem with secularism as the doctrine of strict equality between religious groups, till we recollect that the doctrine of formal equality is profoundly indifferent to background inequalities. The natural consequence is that the equal treatment of un-equals reproduces inequality.

Matters came to a head in the mid-1980s with the Shah Bano case. Shah Bano, an elderly woman who had been divorced by her husband, appealed to the High Court of Madhya Pradesh that her former husband should pay her maintenance under section 125 of the Criminal Procedure Code (CPC). The High Court ruled in favour of Shah Bano. However, her husband Ahmed Khan, moved to the Supreme Court on the ground that he was *not* obliged to pay his former wife maintenance beyond the traditional three-month period of *iddat*[6] under Section 127 (3) of the CPC. This section rules that if under the personal law of certain communities, certain sums were payable to women in the form of *meher* or dower agreed upon at the time of marriage, then this along with maintenance for the period of *iddat* released the husband from further obligation. The Supreme Court in effect had to pronounce on the relation between Sections 125 and 127 (3) of the CPC, on the one hand, and the relationship between the CPC and personal laws, on the other. On 23 April 1985, a Supreme Court Bench under Chief Justice Y. V. Chandrachud confirmed the judgement of the M. P. High Court and stated that Article 125 of the CPC overrides all personal laws and that it is uniformly applicable to all women. The Court, thus, subordinated not only Section 127, 3(b), of the CPC to Section 125 but also personal laws to the civil code.

Expectedly, the leaders of the Muslim community and, in particular, the Ulama opposed the judgement on the ground that it constituted a disregard for the personal laws of the Muslim community based on the *Shariat*. The controversy snowballed into a major political problem, and PM Rajeev Gandhi's Congress government, then in power at the centre, bowed before the uproar. In February 1986,

---

[6] It means three months following divorce to see whether the woman is pregnant.

the government introduced a Bill in the Parliament which sought to exempt Muslim women from the protection provided by Article 125 of the CPC. The Muslim Women (Protection of Rights on Divorce) Bill in essence abrogated the limited right to maintenance under Section 125, because it stipulated that the husband at the time of divorce should pay the amount of the *meher* or dower, the properties given to his former wife by her relatives, friends, and husband and his relatives, make a one-time fair and reasonable provision for her as provided for in the Koran and provide two years maintenance for her children as well as three months payment. The woman could ask a magistrate to direct her husband to give her these properties. In case the woman could not maintain herself, the magistrate could order her relatives to maintain her if they were to inherit her property. Alternately the state wakf board would support her. If the woman and her husband so decided they could apply to be governed by Sections 125–128 of CPC.

The passage of the Bill aroused massive demonstrations as liberal, left and feminist sections who considered the Bill as regressive and as violative of gender justice mobilised against it. Oddly enough, the protestors shared a common ground with the religious right which attacked the Bill on the same grounds. In fact, the right argued even more vociferously than the feminists did about the need to subordinate personal laws of the minority to a Uniform Civil Code in order to secure for all women their basic rights. Although it became increasingly clear that right-wing forces were interested in gender justice less and in subordinating the minority identities to majority notions of one nation, one law, more, the argument proved persuasive to many right-thinking Indians. Those who defended the rights of the minorities to their own cultures and community identity were frankly on a weak wicket. How could the government or the defenders of secularism justify the retention of personal laws of the minorities when these violated the basic precepts of gender justice?[7]

[7] On 22 August 2017, the Supreme Court pronounced that instant triple talaq is unconstitutional. The Government of India piloted a Bill termed The Muslim Women (Protection of Rights on Marriage) Bill 2017, which banned instant triple talaq in the Lok Sabha. It was passed on 28 December 2017. It has still to be passed in the Rajya Sabha.

The process advocated for secularism was laden with two more theoretical tasks: first, to justify selective state intervention in religion and square this with secularism; second, to include minority rights into the secular project. This was absolutely essential to counter the onslaught of the religious right which grounded its arguments in the basic precepts of classical liberalism—non-discrimination, fundamental rights and individualism. Four different kinds of arguments were offered to negotiate the challenge both to minority identities and to the rights of the members within the minority.

Writing against the background of the demolition of the Babri Masjid and subsequent communal riots, in 1994, Partha Chatterjee raised the following crucial question: Is secularism adequate to counter the political challenge of majoritarianism?[8] If we accept that secularism means a strict separation of religion and politics, this particular meaning can prove fairly compatible with the persecution of and discrimination against minorities. But if secularism means equidistance from all religious groups, he suggested, then the political biography of the Indian State belies the norm. The State *has* after all intervened selectively in different religious communities. The dilemma is the following: If the State adopts secularism as separation, then minorities cannot be protected; however, if it interprets secularism as equidistance, its own practices violate the norm.

A better way to protect minorities, suggested Chatterjee, is through the establishment of the norm of toleration. But rather than looking to the practices of everyday life to discover toleration, he grounded the concept in the liberal precepts of autonomy and respect for persons and extended the principle to cover group rights. Provided a group gives reasons for what it does to its own members, it can refuse to give reasons for doing what it is doing in the public domain. Chatterjee in effect moves away from the normative principles of secularism to another normative principle—that of democratic accountability within groups—in order to build in minority rights into the principle of toleration.

---

[8] Chatterjee, 'Secularism and Tolerance', 380–417.

Rajeev Bhargava came to an understanding of why secularism necessarily involves different treatment for different groups from another theoretical direction. He began his argument by distinguishing between three kinds of secularism. The first kind, hyper-substantive secularism, seeks to bring about a separation between religion and the State, in the name of a package of ultimate substantive values, for example, autonomy, development or reason. The second kind, ultra-procedural secularism, separates religion from the State in the name of purely impersonal, value-free, rational procedures and rules, such as bureaucratic and technocratic rationality. The third kind, one that Bhargava clearly prefers over the other two, is contextual secularism. Contextual secularism implies the princ'pled or non-sectarian distance or non-absolutist separation between the State and religion. That is this avatar of secularism combines substantive values and procedures, without any commitment to the priority of either. Bhargava argues that contextual secularism, which is enshrined in the constitution, enjoins the State to exclude religion for some purposes as, for instance, in the decision to exclude separate religious electorates and to include it for others as, for example, in accepting personal laws. But contextual secularism is always guided by non-sectarian principles which are consistent with a set of values constitutive of a life of equal dignity for all.[9]

Amartya Sen defended secularism as part of a more comprehensive idea, that of India as an integrally plural country made up of different religious beliefs, language groups and divergent social practices. Secularism is, he suggested, part of a bigger project of recognising this heterogeneity. Engaging with six strands of critiques against secularism, Sen argued that any re-examination of the difficult question that relates to the principle of symmetrical treatment of different religious communities must arise within a commitment to secularism. 'Secularism is basically a demand for symmetric political treatment of different religious communities.... Balanced political treatment can be achieved ... in rather disparate ways'.[10] Although Sen accepted that this interpretation raised many questions which need to be explored,

[9] Bhargava, 'What Is Secularism for? 486–542.
[10] Sen, 'Secularism and Its Discontents', 484.

this by itself, he insisted, does not contradict the overarching argument for secularism.

I have suggested that secularism cannot be abstracted from the wider conceptual context of which it forms one part. It can only be understood as an intrinsic component of historical, constitutional and political practices of democracy and rights. Why should we subscribe to the notion that each individual/group is free to practise his/her/its own religion, and that this right is equally held by all, *unless* we subscribe to the generic right to freedom and equality? And why should a society subscribe to the right to freedom and equality unless it subscribes to the value of democracy? Secularism, in other words, is not an autonomous concept. Therefore, in order to unravel the meaning of secularism, we should first try to unravel the implications of the attendant concepts that give it (secularism) meaning—equality, freedom and democracy.[11]

Minority Rights as a Corollary to Individual Rights

Let me expand the argument for minority rights briefly given above. The right of individuals to enjoy their own culture and speak their own language can hardly be guaranteed if his or her community is threatened by majoritarianism. All rights are a right to some good, but what is the point of the right if the good is not secured. Vulnerable minorities cannot secure their own existence and reproduction if wider social and political processes threaten it openly or covertly, through coercion or through benevolent neglect. In that case, the democratic and secular State has to intervene to secure the good the right is a right to.

The universal right to equality and non-discrimination is extremely significant, but this right simply does not guarantee what we have an equal right to. The culture of the majority community in India is reproduced through various and diverse modes. Bollywood, classical music, symbolism in the public sphere, prayers in schools, enthusiastic celebration of festivals and the vocabularies of everyday life serve to perpetuate this culture. Minority cultures, especially cultures of

---

[11] Chandhoke, *Beyond Secularism*, 115–142.

communities that are subjected to viciousness, tend to be marginalised in public perceptions. Therefore, there is need for additional safeguards in addition to the classical approach to the protection of individuals. Recognition of this lacuna has brought back minority rights, especially the rights of communities, to exist and reproduce their practices onto various global agendas. This is significant because through access to common narratives of memories that tell people who they are and where they have come from, through access to a common stock of knowledge about the physical environment, and through ceremonies and rituals of belonging, members are linked together through dense networks of bonds.

On the other hand, such communities have hardly existed in history, even if they are spatially distant from the rest of the world. The sheer traffic of voluntary and involuntary migrations, tourism, entry of people searching for sanctuary, exiles, the informational revolution and the entire gamut of technology renders this notion of community a mirage. The dual movement that takes place today, that of tourists and capital from the West to the post-colonial world, and that of displaced people and refugees to the West, has dissolved the idea of an authentic place-bound community. Global flows of information and media images annihilate space and create a sense of spacelessness. The global restructuring of spaces under the impact of the current phase of capitalism has overwhelmed the notion of community as a tightly bound and space-based group of members who are dependent on each other for different reasons.

At the same time, communities continue to exist and inhabit the human imagination, the codes of communities continue to govern personal and social relationships, and the rich images of the community continue to haunt the memories of people who may have moved away from their own, but who still experience a sense of belonging to each other. Members of the community may never know each other and yet feel they share in common certain histories and traditions, and that they have a common destiny that is different from others. This consciousness of belonging tells us that we belong to a larger group.

The concept of community can be thought of in another way. Most of us belong to different and overlapping communities, the national, the professional, the social, religious and caste communities. We can count as many communities of which we are members as much as we count different sorts of interactions we are part of. Let us dwell on the community of first instance, religious communities into which we are born. This community is smaller than society and wider than other communities.

Such communities are typically characterised by two features. One, the identity of the community cannot be reduced to the identity of its members or thought of as an aggregate of individuals. They possess an identity which defines the identity of their members. Two, the well-being and respect of the members are closely tied to the well-being and respect of the community, and even dependent on it. The same features mark an ethnic or a caste community, but here I concentrate only on religious communities. What conditions should a group satisfy before it can be called a religious community? Sacred places, pilgrimages, rituals and rites of birth and death are one distinguishing feature. But objective features are not enough; people must feel that they belong to a community. These feelings may well be subterranean and unarticulated, or they may be unrealised. That is not important. What is important is people without access to their community feel bewildered, incomplete and homeless. They have little understanding of who they are or where they have come from, or what is it that they should do in identifiable and not so identifiable situations if they are denied access to their community. Communities give us the rudiments of a language which helps us understand who we are, how we interpret the world and our own place in it, and what we should be doing at crucial moments of our life. Our religion gives us meaning systems that help us to negotiate our life and experiences, to understand and to evaluate them. We are influenced by our community because it provides us with the basic cognitive and evaluative resources that enable us to perceive the phenomenon as valuable, or invaluable or without value. These become a resource in enhancing and deepening our personal faculties of reflection and judgement, as we comprehend the world, people who are like us and people who are not like us.

Of course, these meaning systems will not and cannot provide us with neat algebra like equations. There will be large grey areas in these meaning systems, which we can negotiate, make our own judgements and question the language of our community. We can do this because no community is bound off from others in a society. We learn from others, we modify our own understandings and we may even move to another meaning system. Our primary languages stay with us, and stay embedded in our consciousness, as a resource to be drawn on whenever we feel inadequate or lost. This does not mean that we cannot challenge and question handed down meanings. The relationship between a community and its members is complex; members are constituted by the languages of their community, but at the same time they can be motivated to question and to rework these languages.

The implication is that individuals are not completely and utterly subordinated to their community. The community provides them with basic meaning systems or a language, which interacts with other languages to provide a context for evaluation and judgement. An individual is not subordinate to a community, because the language he or she has learnt allows him or her to examine and contest the norms of the community. Yet cultural and religious communities are important for us because we acquire our basic languages that allow us to make sense of the world from these communities. When we deny the existence and the practices of the community to our own citizens, when we ask that minorities assimilate into the majority culture, we will have nothing but homeless individuals, individuals who have been torn away from the languages they were taught to speak and understand the world by our own hands. There is need to protect communities that are at risk. This is the least we owe our fellow citizens.

Let us now tie up the threads of the argument. Individuals should possess the right to their community, because this is a distinct good. But this holds little meaning unless the community is allowed to flourish and reproduce itself as an entity. Minority communities are particularly susceptible to multiple erasures. Therefore, it is important that these communities are protected. The caveat is that practices of a community should fall within the ambit of what is democratically permissible and within the domain of the rule of law. There is little need to argue for the existence of cult-like groups that exploit their own members. What is more significant is that if the religious community of which the individual is a member is made the object of perverse and demeaning stereotypes that make it vulnerable to disrespect, the individual becomes equally vulnerable. Individual lives, dignity and self-respect require as an essential precondition that his/her constitutive group be respected. This will require the establishment of measures that prohibit incitement to violence or harm. Finally, the efficacy of individual rights is dependent upon the grant of group rights. There is hardly any point in granting individuals the right to associations, unless the law permits associations as a distinct legal entity with certain rights and obligations. The right of a religious group to maintain and reproduce itself is a precondition for individual rights.

We, of course, do not need minority rights to regulate each and every area of human interaction. People and groups need not be treated differently in every respect. There are large and substantial areas in which individuals live and work together. They should benefit from the same kind of rights, the right to life, the right to dwelling, the right to participation, the right to an adequate living wage, the right to freedom, equality and justice. But if minority groups wish to preserve their identity, in circumstances where it is threatened, they should be enabled to do so.

It is possible to differentiate between two kinds of minority rights. The first right is negative, the right not to be harmed or disrespected through hate speech and violent actions for reasons that are not within human control. People have to be protected against acts that threaten their livelihoods, and their living spaces, their customs and rituals, their modes of prayer, and their interaction with like-minded individuals. The second sort of minority rights relates the right of the constitutive community to maintain and reproduce itself. The State is obliged to sustain languages that are in danger of dying out for want of attention, extension of funds to writers in these languages and encourage the community to celebrate its festivals along with others, including members of other communities. Minorities have the right to equality along with other communities, they have the right to their own distinctive cultural practices and they have a right to membership of a community that is allowed to flourish.

This brings us to the last issue that is great import to countries like India. What if the right of an individual member of a constitutive group, say the right to freedom of choice what profession to pursue or who to marry, conflicts with the norm set by the community? What if individual rights conflict with group rights? The clash between the two sets of rights is endemic to communities that seek to control the lives of its members. However, the vantage point of minority rights is that groups are good for the individual member. The right of a community to exist and thrive is an essential precondition for individual rights. The rights of the community cannot truncate the rights of the individual to a good life. Whether it is a life spent in accordance with the dictates of the community and its leaders, or a life led in relative autonomy from the community and its orders, the choice is that of the individual. We cannot replace individual rights with the precondition of these rights. The idea of group or minority rights is to cover some of the exposed flanks of rights theories, notably the violation of individual rights because his or her community has been targeted in perverse ways. That is, individual rights are incomplete in some cases without group rights, but group rights cannot substitute for individual rights.

CHAPTER 7

The Principle of Tolerance

It was India's way in the past to welcome and absorb other cultures. That is much more necessary today, for we march to the new one world of tomorrow where national culture will be intermingled with the international culture of the human race. We shall therefore seek wisdom and knowledge and friendship and comradeship wherever we can find them.[1]

The defence of minority or group rights is not entirely free of problems. One of the problems that has already been posed is a potential clash between individual and group rights. But as has been argued above, group rights are an essential precondition for individual rights, and in the case of conflict, it is the rights of the individual which will trump the rights of the group to order its members according to its own canons. Democracy establishes limits on the rights of groups to set boundaries to individual freedom. The other problem that confronts most defences of group rights, howsoever limited these defences may be, is how groups can live with each other in a society. Group rights can easily slide into ghettoism, and prevent the construction of a democratic political community, where groups can speak to each other.

[1] Nehru, *The Discovery of India*, 566.

One way of establishing such a multi-religious political community is to institutionalise secularism as a companion concept of democracy. The State should not be aligned to any religion, especially the majority religion. This is an essential precondition of secularism. But it is not enough. Laws and regulations do not always work to change social attitudes. Within society, we need to adopt the principle of tolerance. This, of course, begs the question of why tolerate? This section of the essay seeks to negotiate precisely this issue.

Secularism as Tolerance

Given that secularism had not been defined in the Constitution and did not form part of the Preamble till the 1970s, given that the meaning PM Nehru allotted to the concept was not codified in law and, above all, that the concept is neither self-evident nor self-explanatory, the task of defining and elaborating the concept of secularism has fallen upon the shoulders of the Supreme Court. On 25 October 2016, amidst an acrimonious legal debate on curbing the role of religion in electioneering, a seven judge bench headed by Chief Justice Thakur remarked that in a secular country any appeal to voter on the basis of caste cannot be in tune with our secular principles, and more dangerous than an appeal on the basis of caste or language.[2]

The Supreme Court reiterated what an earlier court had ruled in the case of S. R. Bommai versus the Union of India in 1994. Within general considerations of the federal principles, and the right of the central government to dismiss state governments' vide Article 356 of the Constitution, the complex of judgements established both the meaning and the significance of secularism in India. The political context of the elaboration of the secular principle was that of venomous communal violence. On 6 December 1992, cadres of the Hindu right destroyed a 16th-century mosque in Ayodhya, the Babri Masjid. The BJP had escalated a hysterical campaign in the late 1980s, by mindlessly reiterating the oppressions of Mughal rule

[2] *The Telegraph*, 26 October 2016.

in the distant past. Leaders and ideologues of Hindutva held that the mosque had been erected on the exact site of a temple that had been dedicated to the God Ram. They went further and argued that the mosque had been erected on the precise place where the God was born. This act or replacing a temple with a mosque, it was held, desecrated the religion of the Hindus, and the site had to be recaptured, if necessary, by force.

Although there is no historical evidence that the God had been born on that precise site, hysterical repetitions tend to breed an illusion of the truth and reproduce frenzy. Resultantly, the liberation of Ayodhya formed the dominant metaphor in a cluster of ideological formulations that challenged the themes covered by secularism, freedom of religion, equality between religious communities or equal citizenship and minority rights. Frenzy and heightened tension between the Hindu and Muslim communities stamped the intensification of the campaign. The upsurge bode ill for the future of a plural India.

The demolition of the mosque was followed by massive riots in parts of India. Hundreds of people lost their lives, property was destroyed, workplaces and residential areas were devastated, and once again India witnessed bloodletting and mayhem in the name of religion. Kalyan Singh the then Chief Minister of Uttar Pradesh resigned on the same day. He was later indicted by the Liberhan Commission that was established by the Central Government on 16 December 1992 to report on the destruction of the Babri Masjid. The Commission submitted its report to Manmohan Singh's government on 30 June 2009.[3] In 1992, three state governments of Rajasthan, Madhya Pradesh and Himachal Pradesh were dismissed, even though Himachal Pradesh had not witnessed communal riots. The Congress government that controlled Bombay, a city which experienced terrible

---

[3] He was identified as one of the key men responsible for the demolition of the Babri Masjid on 6 December 1992. Available at: www.the hindu.com/news/national/Kalyan.Singh-Unrepentant/art 16894027, 24 November 2009, accessed on 14 November 2018.

violence, was not dismissed. This notable omission occasioned charges of political bias. Clearly, the three state governments had been dismissed because the BJP, which was in power in these states, had supported the Ayodhya campaign. The party was held responsible for damage and loss of lives.

Although President's rule had been imposed on numerous states since the advent of the Constitution, the reason for dismissals was usually loss of majority of the ruling party, through defection of its members to other parties. For the first time in constitutional history, the dismissal of three state governments on 15 December 1992 was on the grounds of constitutional morality, specifically the principle of secularism. When appealed to, the Court upheld the political decision of the central government, and in the process held forth on the concept of secularism in some detail.

Secularism, ruled the Court, is part of the basic structure of the Constitution, a concept that had been declared by the Court in the 1973 case of Kesavananda Bharati versus the State of Kerala. The three erstwhile state governments, it was held, had subverted and sabotaged the concept of secularism enshrined in the Constitution. Since they had committed acts that run against the provisions of the Constitution, they can be lawfully dismissed by the President of India on the advice of the central government.

One of the tasks confronting the Court was defining secularism. What, asked the counsel of one of the dismissed states, Ram Jethmalani, is secularism? It is a vague, ill-defined concept, a vacuous word, a phantom concept that will not bear the weight of the actions undertaken in its name. It cannot furnish a basis for taking action under Article 356, the provision of the Constitution that empowers the central government to dismiss a state government on specific grounds. The central government was accused of acting in a partisan manner because it dismissed state governments on a flimsy and uncertain principle.

The Supreme Court set out to meet this challenge, and in the process defined secularism, religion and the role of the State in removing religious impediments to social and economic justice.[4] The set of judgements in the S. R. Bommai versus Union of India case are lengthy and complex, but we can isolate the following themes that are of interest to the argument at hand. First, secularism is part of the basic structure of the Constitution and, therefore, cannot be amended. The erstwhile state governments, controlled by the BJP, had deliberately violated this principle by subscribing to the campaign to demolish the mosque. Justice Sawant ruled that the ministries of the party could not be trusted to observe secularism, which was part of the basic structure as well as the soul of the Constitution.

Second, though this theme had been reiterated earlier, Justice Sawant ruled that secularism is derived from the cultural *principle* of tolerance and ensures the equality of religions. The cultural principle is referred to as *Sarva Dharma Sambhava*. His colleagues agreed with the notion that secularism is justified by the cultural ethos of the country. Justice Sawant ruled that the State is enjoined to accord equal treatment to all religions and religious sects and denominations. Third, the Court reiterated Nehru's opinion that no religion will be at risk in a secular India, because the government will not be aligned to religion. Justice P. B. Sawant, writing for himself, and Justice Kuldip Singh argued that whatever is the attitude of the State towards religion, religious sects and denominations, religion cannot be mixed with any secular activity of the State.

The honourable judge thereby separated the domain of the religious and the non-religious. Freedom and tolerance of religion can only extend to the pursuit of spiritual life. Secular matters have to remain within the domain of the State. The distinction between religion as faith and religion as politics that necessarily function in the private and the public sphere, respectively, remained unrecognised. Justice Sawant in the end passed the ruling that religious tolerance and equal treatment of all religious groups, and the protection of their life and property and places of worship, are an essential part of secularism enshrined in our Constitution. We have accepted the goal not only

[4] Much of the discussion of the Bommai case has been drawn from Jacobsohn, *The Wheel of Law*, 145–15; Sen, *Articles of Faith*.

because it is our sacred legacy but also as a creed of universal brotherhood and humanism.[5]

Fourth, Justice Ramaswamy ruled that there is an essential connection between secularism and democracy; the concept of the secular State is, therefore, essential for the working of democracy and the realisation of social and economic needs that are essential for material and moral prosperity and political justice. Justice Reddy in a parallel ruling stated that the essential basis of the Indian Constitution is equality of all citizens irrespective of the religion they subscribe to. The Indian State is (not expected) to owe loyalty to any one religion, it is neither religious nor irreligious because it gives equal freedom to all citizens. This is the essential characteristic of secularism writ large on all the provisions of the Indian Constitution. He spoke of positive secularism, that is, the State should ensure social and economic justice to all and remove religious impediments. There is, he argued, need to reform Hindu society and to dilute caste hierarchy.[6] In effect, religious practices could not be allowed to infringe the right to social and economic justice, and secularism provides a route to justice.

Although there was no clear consensus among the justices what secularism means, the concept was defined on the terrain of an overriding principle: *Sarva Dharma Sambhava*. In effect, the highest court of the land extended recognition to and legitimised a public doctrine based on neo-Vedanta which had become one of the creeds of the freedom struggle. This was defined as secularism. Strictly Hindu in origin, the elaboration and justification of the principle that all religions are equal, was identified as the governing principle of a plural society. The logic of secular modernity, namely that religion has no place in the public sphere, was put to rest. This was perhaps inevitable because the Court was deciding a case in which the religious right had used political Hinduism to evoke destructive political passions in the public sphere, where parties of ruling state governments owed allegiance to the majority religion, and where citizens had been subjected to brutality merely because of their membership of a religious community. The

---

[5] Ibid., xxxviii.
[6] Ibid.

politicisation of Hinduism since the 19th century had culminated in the destruction of the Babri Masjid. Political religion could no longer be ignored. If that was so, then it was preferable to follow the precept that all religious held equal status, reiterate the principle that majoritarianism was undesirable and affirm that the State should take care to regulate religious plurality. But, on the other hand, as suggested above, a doctrine intrinsic to Hinduism has been defined as the principle that adjudicates relations between different religious communities. Many of these communities do not subscribe to the notion of all paths to the divine as equal. The stamp of dominant religious understanding on the concept has been established and reiterated.

The Court and the Definition of Religion

On the one hand, the judiciary has defined secularism; on the other, it has clarified the nature of religion. The Supreme Court has carried on the colonial project of conceptualising religion. It has also carried on the nationalist project of refining Hinduism. Consider the Hindutva judgement, a series of seven rulings of the Supreme Court in December 1995. The issue at hand was the Representation of Peoples Act 1951, the RPA, which establishes the meaning of corrupt practices. The use of money and an appeal for votes by invoking religious animosity can subject candidates to serious legal penalties, including reversal of election wins. This case involved corruption charges against Ramesh Yeshwant Prabhoo, the mayor of Bombay, and his election agent Bal Thackeray.[7] They were accused of promoting enmity on religious grounds. The appellants challenged the constitutional validity of Article 123 (3) of the RPA, which prohibits election campaigning on the basis of religion. Another clause in the Act (3A) prohibits attempts to promote enmity on grounds of religion, race, community and language.

Justice J. S. Verma of the Supreme Court held that candidates cannot attack other religions or whip up personal animosities and irrational fears to secure electoral victories, and upheld the relevant

[7] Sen, *Article of Faith*, 22.

sections of the RPA. Justice J. S. Verma further ruled that under the guise of protecting one's own religion, culture or creed, groups and individuals cannot embark on personal attacks on others or whip up low instincts and fear among groups to secure electoral victories. Both the appellants were held guilty of corrupt practices. At the same time, the Court held that appeals for votes in the name of Hindutva is a legitimate course of action.

In the process, the Supreme Court engaged in a long disquisition on the nature of Hindutva, which it saw as synonymous with Hinduism. The honourable judges thus obscured the distinction between religion as faith and politicised religion as an ideology of the religious right. The Court proceeded to define Hinduism as a diverse set of practices rather than a coherent religion. Drawing upon scholarly works, the Court suggested that organised religion is characterised by one holy book, a church and one prophet. But Hinduism is different. Clearly, the shadows of Orientalism loomed large over the ruling of the Court.

Further, following Dr Radhakrishnan, the author of acclaimed works on Hinduism, the Court termed Hinduism as a way of life. The use of religious terminology by the Hindu right wing, ruled the Court, should not take away from the essential nature of the religion. Logically, therefore, the recourse to Hinduism by electoral candidates cannot be seen as a corrupt practice. This raises a problem of understanding; if candidates seeking votes appeal to Hinduism as a religion, the practice falls within the ambit of corrupt practices. But if they appeal to Hindutva as a way of life, this cannot be considered a corrupt practice. The onus is upon candidates; they have to establish the specific sort of Hinduism that has been used to appeal for votes. This definition of Hinduism remained as vague and as contested as secularism as tolerance.

Moreover, the conflation of secularism and the Hindu principle of *Sarva Dharma Sambhava* gives reason for worry. Should a multi-religious society be governed by principles that are overtly Hindu and that are not subscribed to by other religious communities? What is tolerance as *Sarva Dharma Sambhava* anyway? Bhikhu Parekh has outlined a theory of tolerance on the basis of the critique of this precise principle. Hindu pluralism is hierarchically structured but is also the basis of a new hierarchy, writes Parekh. Hindus were convinced that no religion exhausts the truth. It follows that other religions that claim perfection are flawed. The consequence is that, for Hindus, who claim superiority, other religions are to be tolerated, never accepted as equals.[8] The problem is that Islam and Christianity do not accept that all beliefs lead the way to the divine, and Buddhism and Jainism do not subscribe to any notion of God. Equating secularism with the principle of *Sarva Dharma Sambhava* lands us firmly into the domain of majority notions of what secularism means

It is time, therefore, to examine the principle of tolerance, both by reference to lived practices and as philosophy. This is what the succeeding section tries to do.

The Practices of Tolerance

During the course of a field visit to Tarn Taran, a district of Amritsar in the Punjab, our research team came across a rather spectacular phenomenon, a noisy fair organised around the *mazaar* of a Muslim *fakir* Baba Lakhanwala. A circular entrance in the exterior wall of a rough construction led to the inner sanctum. Here at a simple tomb lit by two oil lamps, Hindus and Sikhs genuflected before the *mazaar* of a Muslim saint. On the roof of the tomb flew a green flag encrusted with the sacred number 786. Outside the tomb, Sikh and Hindu women dressed in their bridal finery, carrying trays of offerings on their head, and accompanied by a band playing loud music, had lined up to pay homage to the Saint. 'Which *pind* [village] have you come from?', we were asked by a woman. 'Have you come to ask for a *mannat* or a boon'? 'Have you got what you asked for', we asked in turn. 'Yes', she said, 'Baba grants everyone his or her wishes, and every year we come here to thank him [and presumably ask for more]'. The story is simple and a fairly common one across Punjab. During his travels Guru Nanak Dev came across a goatherd, named Lakhan, and asked him for some food. Lakhan offered to the Guru some sweets cooked out

---

[8] Parekh, 'Some Reflections on the Hindu Theory of Tolerance', 6.

of goat milk. In return Guru Nanak Dev blessed Lakhan and granted him a boon: no one would return empty handed from his doorstep. Across the region, Lakhan is known as the giver who does not deny any one anything.

As our vehicle drove away from the fair, the thought crossed my mind: undivided Punjab must have looked like this. Hindus, Muslims and Sikhs worshipping together at the *mazaar* of a *fakir*, at the *dera* of a Guru and at the feet of a living Saint in accordance with the strong tradition of Sufism, which brought to the region a softer and less doctrinaire form of Islam. 'Saints of widespread renown occupy a very important place in the worship of the peasantry', stated Ibbetson's Report on the Punjab Census of 1881. 'They are generally Mahammedan, but are worshipped by Hindoos and Musalmans alike with the most absolute impartiality'.[9]

Punjab has developed and valued for centuries a long and glorious tradition of a composite culture, which has evolved from the teachings of Hindu and Muslim saints, Sikh Gurus and Sufi fakirs. Mystical hymns and prayers are sung at roadside shrines rather than at orthodox places of worship. Forming a common and invaluable heritage of all Punjabis, devotional lyrics have generated a distinct stream of poetry of Punjab, the Sufi *Kavya-Dhara*. This strain of poetry codifies a long and rich literary tradition. In the 12th and 13th centuries, Baba Farid, born in district Multan, wrote of the union of the self and of the divine. 'Oh Farid', he wrote, 'rent your silken veil and put on a rough woollen mantle, wear whatever clothes you must to meet the Beloved'.

This mystic poetical tradition was developed by Shah Hussain during the 16th century. But it was Bulleh Shah who contributed much to this distinct genre of poetry, weaving together the divine and rejection of the worldly, in the 18th century. How do I know who I am? I am not a believer in the mosque, not a pagan disciple of false rites, not the pure amidst the impure, not Moses and not the Pharoah.

---

[9] Census of British India. 1883. 'Appendix B: Extracts from Mr Ibbetson's Report on the Punjab Census. Noting Peculiarities of the Hindoo and Mahammedan Religions, As Practiced In That Province'. In *Punjab Report*, vol. III, x. London: Eyre and Spottiswoode for Her Majesty's Stationery Office.

Take away all markers of identity, the poet told us, and we will never know who we are. The dissolution of the self, central to Sufism, is essential for union with the beloved, who is the embodiment of the divine. But this desired union is fated to be left unrealised, recollect the poetic legends of Heer Ranjha, Sassi Pannu, Sohni Mahiwal and Mirza Sahiban. This subversive tradition, which mocks orthodoxy and defies separateness between human beings, and between human beings and God, introduced a destabilising note in religious orthodoxy and promoted inter-faith relations.

The tradition of inter-faith dialogue was furthered by other factors. In Punjab, the three religious groups—the Muslims, the Hindus, and the Sikhs—shared a common language as well as overlapping scripts, music, folk tales, historical memories, rituals of everyday life and forms of worship. Population distribution along an east–west axis gave a few opportunities to any one community to acquire a controlling position in the affairs of the region. No single group could dominate the region politically, economically or socially, nor was there a single over riding social system. Each group possessed its own social hierarchy.

From Unity to Fragmentation

Towards the end of the 19th century, shared traditions between Hindus and the Sikhs, on the one hand, and Muslims, on the other, were irremediably torn asunder. Harjot Singh Oberoi, writing on the remaking of the Khalsa in the Sikh community against the backdrop of the Indian army's assault on the Golden Temple, gave us the answer to the question why.[10] Oberoi mounted a sustained attack on the idea that religious communities in India were unitary and homogenous, and not plural and often divergent. He argued that it is just not possible to separate, or indeed distinguish groups that have lived together in a defined territorial area, along the lines of religion. Nor is it possible to speak of clear-cut religious categories such as Islam, Hinduism and Sikhism in Punjab, at least till the end of the 19th century. Sikhism permitted its adherents to belong to a number of groups, each of which

---

[10] Oberoi, 'From Punjab to "Khalistan"', 26–41.

had its own traditions: the Udasi, Nirmala, Khalsa, Nanakpanthi, Ram Raia, Baba Gurditta, Baba Jawahar Singh, Guru Bhag Singh, Nihand, Kalu Panthi, Ram Dasi, Nirankari, Kuka and Savaria. Many Sikhs shaved and cut their hair, and many did not observe the five external symbols of the faith adopted by the Khalsa Panth as markers of a distinct identity. A plurality of life styles, of rituals and heterogeneity of religious belief were freely allowed. The Sikh community simply did not possess an essentialised or pure form.

Across religious lines, Punjabis, suggested Oberoi, tended to experience life as members of a *zat* (caste) or a *biradari* (lineage) more, and as members of a discrete religious group less: What an individual did with his life, what were the values that guided him in this universe, and what the cultural equipment through which he interpreted daily experiences was, control over land, labour, patronage and the distribution of power was determined not so much by the framework of a single religious community but by what *biradari* or *zat* a person belonged to.[11] In turn, the membership of *zat* and *biradari* not only cut across religious divisions, it also brought members of various religions together in and through the practices of everyday life. In sum, Sikhs moved in and out of identities: village, cults, caste, lineage or tradition. There was no single source of authority, and multiple definitions of what it means to be a Sikh competed with each other.

Oberoi identified the main reasons for the drive to homogenise an otherwise plural Sikh identity, and cast it in the image of the Khalsa in the late 19th century. The primary cause was the powerful attempt of the Khalsas to impose their own doctrinal version on the community. The new discourse of identity, which was given the name of Tat Khalsa, or the 'pure Sikh', disowned plurality and enunciated a singular and orderly form of Sikhism. The Tat Khalsa was determined to tear Sikhs away from any moorings they may have had in what was seen as the amorphous sea of Hinduism … innovations were made in dress, language, the annual calendar and dietary taboos to provide Sikhs with a distinctive symbolic universe.[12] Popular practices were

[11] Oberoi, *The Construction of Religious Boundaries*, 418–419.
[12] Ibid., 345.

relegated to the realm of superstition, and Sikhs were presented with a single source of religious inspiration, the *Adi Granth*, the gurudwaras and the Gurmukhi script. Whereas the drive to negate other traditions was not new, it emanated from the attempts of the Khalsas to monopolise history, imaginations, traditions and visions of the world in the 18th century; what was new was the drive to dislodge other identities and to discourage practices that did not conform to the dictates of the Tat Khalsa.

With the beginning of intra-elite competition for urban professions and administrative jobs in the 1880s, the Sikh elite used this reinvented tradition to elbow out adversaries and profit from the opportunities provided by the British Raj. Even though this new religious identity did not mesh well with existing traditions that were polytheistic and covered a wide spectrum of practices, it came to command political imaginations simply because it proved lucrative. The drive to homogenise the Sikh identity was a response to the fact that other communities were also forging their own boundaries at roughly the same time. Arya Samaj, trying to purify Hinduism of all accretions, and creating a new identity for the Hindus, rejected religious groups that emerged later on the scene, such as Sikhs, as non-Hindu. The Aligarh Movement similarly constructed a new exclusive identity called Muslim. In sum, the definition and the conceptualisation of the sacred were the product of many strands of history, which coming together in the late 19th century constructed boundaries around religions, thereby negating shared practices and histories.

Oberoi identifies British rule and the colonial encounter as the major precipitant of the move towards Khalsa hegemony. The colonial state constructed ethnic categories to index and administer populations, extract revenue and govern populations. In the process, it created taxonomies that served to lump disparate Sikh traditions into one generic identity. For instance, the British decided that only the identity of the Khalsa was authentic to the Sikh tradition; other identities were either spurious or Hindu accretions. The impact of this and related colonial practices was indeed great: for instance, all Sikhs who entered the army had to undergo baptism and adopt the five sacred symbols even if they did not belong to the Khalsa tradition. Oberoi seems to suggest that in order to benefit from the opportunities provided by the colonial state, one had to belong to the right identity group within the Sikh community. This in a major way led to the homogenisation of otherwise plural identities, and to the consolidation of Khalsa identity within the Sikh community.

Roger Ballard in a parallel argument mounted an attack on Euro-centric explanations of religion. He suggested that all religious practices in Punjab, whether Sikhism, Hinduism or Islam, shared common beliefs, traditions and lived experiences. The 1881 census, for instance, revealed that a majority of *jat* or *biradari*'s (caste or kinship or in the words of British colonialists tribal groups) included Hindu, Sikh and Muslim members.[13] The upsurge of ethno-religious nationalism during the course of the 19th and 20th centuries resulted in an increasing degree of differentiation. As a result of the growing influence of religious reform movements, each religious community set out to delineate its boundaries as sharply and as unambiguously as possible.[14]

With the Arya Samaj, Singh Sabha Movement and Muslims in the late 19th century defining their religious groups in an exclusive manner, the community dimension of Punjabi religion gained salience, even as the spiritual and the experiential or lived aspects of religion waned. This led to religious polarisation, confrontation and definitions of 'insiders' and 'outsiders'. Once we break through contemporary reifications, wrote Ballard, it becomes quite clear that, since colonialism, each tradition reinvented the greater part of its theological and ideological position, as each formed itself into clearly bounded and essentialised community whose existence virtually all contemporary debate and discussion takes for granted.[15]

Historians generally agree that the colonial rule set off a chain of reactions in Punjab, on the one hand, religious reform to strengthen identities and establish cultural autonomy and, on the other, nationalism. Even as the frontier of each group was delineated, other religious

---

[13] Ballard, 'Panth, Kismet, Dharam to Quam', 9.
[14] Ibid., 24.
[15] Ibid., 26–27.

groups were alienated. Consequently, pluralism, the creed that not only Punjabis' but Indians across the country had valued, was seen as antithetical to the dynamics of identity.

The irony is that an underlying thread of togetherness held Punjabis of all persuasion together, till the bitter end when processes of differentiation and separation gained momentum in the 1940s. Despite the fact that the Muslims constituted about 53 per cent of the population, and that the state had a Muslim Chief Minister, the region did not support the Pakistan Resolution. The Unionist party, a coalition of large landlords from all confessional groups, hesitated to support the resolution till practically the very eve of Partition. Historians have still not been able to explain why the turnaround took place within the space of a year and why the Muslim community in Punjab began to support Partition.

When Partition came to Punjab, the process was gruesome and bloody. The region witnessed the kind of violence that is unparalleled in the history of South Asia. It is estimated that more than 500,000 people perished in the carnage that accompanied the Partition. Mohammad Waseem describes the partition of Punjab as one of the most violent processes of ethnic cleansing in recent history.[16] And Yunas Samad compares the Partition experience with the Rwanda case, and the breakup of Yugoslavia, that is, with two cases of ethnic cleansing and genocide.[17] Partition resulted in an almost total exchange of populations between the two parts of Punjab. The scale of migration touched about 10 million, with approximately 5.5 million Muslims fleeing from the eastern to the western part of Punjab, and 4.5 millions of Hindus and Sikhs fleeing in the opposite direction.

The Exception

However, in one part of Punjab, a small principality called Malerkotla defied the logic of the terror and bloodshed that accompanied the Partition. Except for a few members of the aristocracy, the Muslim

---

[16] Waseem, 'Partition, Migration and Assimilation', 20.
[17] Samad, 'Reflections on Partition', 43–46.

inhabitants of the town did not migrate to the newly formed country of Pakistan. The Muslim Nawab remained in the town.[18] This was in direct contrast to the rest of the region, for in 1947, practically all Muslims, who till then formed an overwhelming proportion of the population in Punjab, left all cities and all villages of the region. The only exceptions were two cities in Punjab: Kadian, the headquarters of the Ahmadiyya Muslim community which is banned in Pakistan and Malerkotla. Nor did Malerkotla witness any partition riots which were to scar memories of all three communities for decades after 1947. On the other hand, almost 200,000 Muslims fleeing from murderous mobs in other parts of India found a safe haven in the city. Sardar (Major) Balwant Singh, who was the Minister of Law and Order in the state in 1946, wrote that at the time of the Partition of India about 1 lac Muslims from other areas of Punjab took shelter in Malerkotla. Not a single killing took place in the whole state. All of them were safely sent to Pakistan, and Sardar Patel, the then Home Minister of India, on request, sent one battalion of Army to help the Nawab's army to send Muslims to the Pakistan border.[19]

The resources of the town were stretched thin with the presence of large numbers of refugees, though crowded and unhygienic conditions led to the outbreak of disease, and though families in Malerkotla began to suffer a paucity of food, every household contributed to provide for the refugees. In the period that followed the Partition of India, communal riots have periodically scarred the country, but in Malerkotla, not a single incident involving communal violence has occurred. The absence of communal violence during the Partition, and in the aftermath of the Partition, is a matter of great pride for the inhabitants of the city. This feature *defines* the people of Malerkotla as tolerant—a society in which communities belonging to different religious persuasions have found it possible to live together in peace and in harmony.

---

[18] The Nawab of Malerkotla Ahmed Ali Khan signed the Instrument of Accession with the Government of India in September 1947.

[19] Khan, *History of the Ruling Family of Sheikh Sadruddin*, Preface.

The Origins of Tolerance

Malerkotla has been ruled by a Muslim family, which traces its origins to Sadr-ud-Din known as Sheikh Sadr Jahan, a Sawani Afghan of Daraband in Khurasan.[20] A holy and pious man, and a disciple of Pir Rukn Alam, Sadr-ud-Din, planned to spend his life in seclusion and settled in Bhumsi, a place which lay on a tributary of the river Sutlej. One day, in 1450, Bahlol Khan Lodhi, the governor of Lahore and Sirhind, was passing by, and he decided to spend the night there. He was impressed by the piety and the personality of Hazrat Sadr-ud-Din. Lodhi promised that if and when he became the ruler of Delhi, he would give his daughter's hand in marriage to Hazrat Sadr-ud-Din. Lodhi took over the reins of the Delhi Sultanate in 1451 and became the first Afghan ruler of Delhi. Subsequently, his daughter Taj Murassa Begum married Sadr-ud-Din in 1454. Bahlol Lodhi also gave Sadr-ud-Din a tract of land containing 12 large and 56 small villages (including Maler) plus ₹3 lacs as dowry. The population of Bhumsi increased rapidly, and in 1466, Sadr-ud-Din founded the town of Maler, which in a short period of time became large enough to include Bhumsi. He subsequently married the daughter of the wealthy family of Bahram, the Bhatti chief of Kapurthala. In 1508, Sadr-ud-Din died at the age of 71, leaving behind three sons, Isa, Hasan and Musa from his first wife, and a daughter from his second wife. The Malerkotla family which ruled the state since then is descended from Isa.[21]

Maler remained the headquarters of the princely state, till Bayazid Khan the fifth descendent of Sadr-ud-Din founded Kotla in 1656. Kotla derived its name from the *kot* or the wall which was built around the town. Subsequently, the two towns were united by the building of the Moti Bazar in 1904–1905. In 1657, the ruler of Malerkotla was granted the title of Nawab by the Mughal Emperor Aurangzeb.

[20] The Nawabs of Malerkotla are of 'Kurd' descent who came originally from the province of 'Sherwan' north of Persia and after settling for a time in Afghanistan near Ghazni came to India and settled at Maler, the old capital of the state in 1442.

[21] *Punjab State Gazetteers*, 1908, vol. XVA *Malerkotla State*, 1904, Lahore: The Civil and Military Gazette Press, 702.

Originally, the descendants of Sadr-ud-Din, the Nawabs, held positions of trust under the Lodhi and the Mughal emperors. As the Mughal Empire began to decay, they gradually became independent. Sadr-ud-Din was not only the founder of Malerkotla, but he was also a powerful spiritual leader. At the symbolic centre of Malerkotla lies the *mazaar* of Sheikh Sadr-ud-Din or Sheikh Haidar, as he came to be known. From the 15th century onwards, on every Thursday, a fair is held at the shrine. Hindus, Muslims and Sikhs jointly offer money, jewellery and grain in the form of cooked rice to the shrine. On the first Thursday of every month, the fair takes on larger proportions, and thousands of people from outside the town come to pay homage at the shrine. On occasion of accession to the throne, and on Id, the royal family makes offerings of horses, robes and money. The shrine is managed by the descendants of the Saint. The interesting part of the story is that hundreds of Hindus and Sikhs flock to the *mazaar*. The author of the *Malerkotla Gazetteer* of 1904 was puzzled by this: 'It is strange that these fairs are mostly attended by Hindus though Sadr-ud-Din was a Muslim Saint'.[22]

Ethnographers may well be similarly intrigued by the variety of practices seen at the *Dargah*. Whereas Hindus and Sikhs touch their foreheads before the shrine, Muslims do not. Hindus and Sikhs behave exactly as they would in their own houses of worship. In large part, this multi-confessional community has been inspired by the tradition of Sufi culture in Malerkotla since the time of Sheikh Haider. This is a town in which Sufi tombs coexist with temple bells hanging in the front of a mosque. When the keeper of the shrine raises his hands in Islamic prayer, discernible on his wrist is the spiritual Hindu tattoo, Om.

Pilgrims to the shrine have unbounded faith in the generosity of Sheikh Haider. Town dwellers believe that Malerkotla escaped the horrors of communal riots because it had been blessed by him and continues to be so blessed. The shrine represents not only a shared physical space for all religious communities, but it also stands for the

---

[22] Ibid.

flexibility of identities that Punjab was known for till the end of the 19th century. Town dwellers also believe that they are blessed by the 10th Sikh Guru, Guru Gobind Singh. The story runs thus. A descendant of Sadr-ud-Din, Nawab Sher Mohammed Khan, was a loyal vassal of Emperor Aurangzeb, who helped the Mughal armies in the battle of Chamkaur Sahib against the army of Guru Gobind Singh, the 10th Guru of the Sikhs. But he opposed the inhuman treatment that was meted out to the two sons of the Guru, Zorawar Singh and Fateh Singh, by the governor of Sirhind. Sher Mohammed Khan, a close relative of the Chakaldar Wazir Khan, lodged a vehement protest against the inhuman act of bricking alive the two sons of the Guru. The Nawab argued passionately that crimes against children were against the glorious tenets of Koran and Islam, and that history would not forgive those who sought to murder children. Reportedly, at this stage, Wazir Khan thought of freeing the Sahibzadas, but Sucha Nand, a diwan or the court official of the Nawab, cautioned that the sons of Guru Gobind Singh would in the course of time become 'deadly snakes' and poison Muslim rulers. It was much better, suggested Sucha Nand, that they be put to death. Wazir Khan acquiesced and ordered that the Sahibzadas should be tortured and bricked alive. The Nawab of Malerkotla walked out of the court in protest.

Sher Mohammed Khan subsequently wrote a protest note to Emperor Aurangzeb. He stated,

> The humble and devoted petitioner … begs to lay his humble appeal before your most Gracious majesty and hopes from Your Imperial majesty's unfathomable kindness and illimitable magnanimity that the August person of the Shadow of God … be pleased to bestow his compassion and forgiveness on the young sons of Guru Gobind Singh the 10th Guru of the Sikh nation.[23]

It would be quite compatible with justice, the letter went on to state, if the Emperor wished to inflict punishment on the Sikh nation, but it would in no way

---

[23] Ibid.

[B]e consistent with the principles of sovereignty and supreme power to wreak the vengeance of the misdeeds of the whole nation on two innocent children who, on account of their tender age are quite innocent and unable to take a stand against the powerful Viceroy. This sort of action obviously appears to be absolutely against the dictates of Islam and the laws propounded by the founder of Islam ... and ... the enactment of such atrocious Act would perpetually remain, an ugly blot on the face of Your Majesty's renowned justice and righteousness. It may be considered that the mode of inflicting the punishment and torture as contemplated by the Viceroy of Sirhind can be no means be considered compatible with the principles of Supreme rule, equity and justice.[24]

Guru Gobind Singh recognised that Sher Khan's protest was motivated by the finest principles of righteous conduct or *dharma*. After profusely thanking the Nawab of Malerkotla, the Guru blessed him with a Hukamnama and a Kirpan, which are among the prized possessions of the Malerkotla house. Guru Gobind Singh also promised that the Muslim community in Malerkotla would be safe for times to come. It is interesting to note that whereas the Sikhs under Banda Bahadur attacked and ravaged the territories of Muslim rulers of Punjab, they did not attack the town of Malerkotla and Rai Kot, because of the blessings of the Guru. According to a documentary aired on the television channel *Discovery*, when Muslims fleeing from murderous Hindu and Sikh mobs during the Partition riots crossed the boundaries of the town, their pursuers were halted in their tracks by a white horse which patrolled the borders of Malerkotla. The white horse is the steed of Guru Gobind Singh, the protector of the Muslims.

The last of the descendants of Nawab Sher Mohammed Khan, Nawab Iftikhar Ali Khan, died a few years ago. On the occasion of the tercentenary celebrations of the birth of the Khalsa, the late Nawab's wife Sajida Begum sent greetings to the Sikh community. The act symbolically reminded younger people of the Sikh community that the Sahibzadas had sacrificed their life for the protection of their religion. She asked the Sikhs to remember the great sacrifices of the

[24] Ibid., xii–xiii.

young Sahibzadas and abstain from any act which might deprive them of the blessings of Guru Gobind Singh.

If the first strand of tolerance was woven by the spiritual inclinations of the rulers that is Sufism, oral histories which speak of the benediction given by the Guru compose the second strand. The third strand which wove into the fabric was the nature of princely rule. The Nawabs practised tolerance. For instance, the Nawab ruled that no cow will be slaughtered within the precincts of Malerkotla. Till today, the inhabitants of the city do not consume pork or beef. It is of considerable significance that the rule of the Nawab was marked by generosity and kindness to all his subjects, *irrespective* of their religious affiliations. Each of the 22 rulers offered high posts to Hindus and Sikhs, and bestowed privileges and property on members of the two minority communities.

Oral histories, shared forms of worship in the *mazaar* and respect for tradition have instilled a perceptible sense of belonging among those who made the town their home. The hold of these traditions cannot be underestimated, because they serve as a referral for the making of a political community. As our repeated visits to Malerkotla showed us, the citizens of the town showed exemplary democratic leanings. They possessed a strong sense of ownership of a collective public life; they simply see themselves as shareholders in the public sphere. Pride in their unique historical tradition of tolerance and fellowship or *bhaichara*, which withstood the partition of Punjab, is accompanied by a deep-rooted commitment to ward off collectively any threat to this tradition.

For instance, the destruction of the Babri Masjid by the Hindutva brigade, and subsequent communal riots through the country, agitated young people, both Hindu and Muslim. At that point of time, elders from all communities came together and counselled restraint. The role of the elders in upholding tradition appears to be tremendously significant in the collective life of the town. They continue to remind inhabitants that they share equal responsibility for upholding the traditions of the political community that have been constituted by the oral tradition, symbols and festive occasions. In Malerkotla, the notion of citizenship involves obligations to a shared public life. This commitment goes beyond the possession of fundamental rights, holding the political status of a citizen, and as the rightful recipient of the privileges accorded by the ruling class.

In 1947, Punjab was compelled to pick itself up from the shattering experiences of massive communal violence, and the Partition which practically destroyed the region, dust off the debris of inter-group hatred, and proceed to reconstruct collective life. Malerkotla resisted the two-nation theory that had been constructed during the colonial period, a notion that narrowly defined who the citizen is and which religious community is entitled to a state of its own. Town dwellers were thereby enabled to battle narrowly defined notions of a nation in search of its own state, and resist being sucked up in the horrors of the Partition. This is because the inhabitants of the town disdain to pursue their own projects and their own notions of the good, and let others be. In this town, people have refused to remain confined to identities that in other parts of the country are valorised and affirmed through the imposition of structured narratives. The inhabitants of Malerkotla have refused to remain barred behind symbolic or even concrete walls of self-constructed ghettos. And they have refused to commit themselves to an uncritical celebration of distinctive, unique, but separate identities. On the contrary, people pride themselves on the spirit of what they call 'bhaichara' or fellow feeling. These shared sentiments have allowed them to cross figurative boundaries of communities and come together in all kinds of shared projects.

The personalised rule of Nawabs has supported this tradition of inter-faith harmony. Now that the Nawabi tradition has come to an end, and competitive electoral politics has come to dominate the town, now that communal organisations have entered and consolidated their position in Malerkotla, can the inheritance survive? The question is a troubling one. The important question that we should consider is that not only the rulers but citizens have adopted tolerance towards others who live in the same space. In the process, they have protected pluralism. Tolerance comes out as an unambiguous good in the transition from empirical to normative pluralism.

Why Tolerate?

It is perhaps indicative of the *geist* of our disenchanted times that the absence of communal tension between Hindus and Muslims in Malerkotla forms a research agenda in itself. The project of civil coexistence in the town offers a model that is worthy of emulation. Here the tolerance of other religious communities is not born out of inertness, indifference or deliberate, distancing from others. The virtue is actively fostered in and through the practices of everyday life. Everyday practices find voice in common spaces such as the political, the social, the festive and the sacred, and have resulted in the creation of a political community, which is concerned with the common good in two ways. The inhabitants are intent on protecting the legacy of the past, and they are equally determined to safeguard harmony in the future. It is this double focus of the community that makes Malerkotla such an interesting case for our project on living together in civility.

Sadly enough doubts remain. Will the practices of tolerance survive the passing of princely modes of politics? We do not know, but we suspect that tolerance, as a property of pre-modern societies, might not be able to endure the malaise of modernity, with its atomism, its acquisitive instincts, its competitiveness and its self-serving, instrumental rationality. So we are compelled to ask: Is tolerance difficult to sustain when the political and the social context as well as the social contract changes, as it must? It has been observed by the celebrated anthropologist Ernest Gellner that culturally plural societies worked well in the past, but genuine cultural pluralism ceases to be viable under current conditions.[25] We might, even as we learn from Malerkotla, have to essay another supportive argument for tolerance.

The lesson we learn from actually existing tolerant societies is that the principle cannot be a once and for all affair in a plural society and one characterised by majorities and minorities. The tradition is in need of reinvention, refashioning and restoration, particularly when factors inimical to the convention (electoral competition, communal ideologies, market competition) relentlessly intrude upon the

[25] Gellner, *Nations and Nationalisms*, 55.

self-understanding of the political community. Modernity brings with it its own pathologies: individualism, competition, homogenisation of identities and, above all, the idea of the nation as a primary unit of political life. Consider our own country where the making of nationalism and subsequently the two-nation theory wrought havoc on populations that had till then lived together. By the turn of the 20th century, riots between Hindus and Muslims had become an enduring feature of the body politic, and people were willing to kill and die in the cause of cow protection or music before the mosque. Recollect Bhisham Sahni's powerfully evocative play *Tamas* on precisely these times and themes. When political passions are ignited by such acts, it is difficult to appeal to the perpetrators of violence on grounds of common humanity or an oral tradition of toleration. It is also impossible to hold before them the Constitution as a mirror that reflects unconstitutional behaviour. We will have to look elsewhere for a more robust answer to the question: How do people who subscribe to different belief systems come to live together in some degree of civility?

We could begin by looking at the political theory of tolerance through another lens. Notably, when people do not engage with each other or live in harmony, we do not require tolerance. The principle is not a product of social indifference towards, or lack of knowledge about others. In any case, in modern market economies and electoral systems, it is difficult to believe that any group can be so insulated from the multiple transactions of a society that others remain unknown or the unknowable. Who our children go to school with, who we meet in our professional capacities, who our friends are, which religious persuasion the candidate who asks for our vote belongs to, what are the codes that govern the project of living together—secularism or theocracy—have deep implications for the way we live our lives. It is precisely because our paths, our careers, our lives impact others, as much as others' lives impact us, that the concept of tolerance becomes of dominating importance. The moment we come into close touch with people who are not like us, the imperative that we should tolerate their conceptions of the good becomes even more pressing. We practice intolerance in such societies at great risk to our collective futures. In other words, tolerance acquires moral significance when we *are* in a position to make judgements about the non-desirability of certain practices, and yet we accept these practices simply because we accept the *right* of people to engage in these practices. How do we understand toleration?

Toleration and the Philosophical Virtue of Doubt

The concept of tolerance flows from a certain conception of what we owe others, how we perceive the moral standing of people who are like us and people who are not like us, and how we organise our own relationship with others. In liberal theory, we respect other points of view because we believe that persons have good reasons for subscribing to certain notions of the good, that they are entitled to these beliefs and that this is valid irrespective of our own approval or disapproval, or sympathy or lack of sympathy for these values. It follows that the concept makes sense only when we live among people who do not speak, in many ways, quite the same language as we do. Tolerance is, therefore, of utmost importance for a plural, but a divided society where people find it difficult to live with each other. It is, of course, a given that there are certain things we should not tolerate, child abuse, or caste discrimination, or coercion and cruelty. The principle falls within the boundaries of what is democratically desirable.

It is, however, incontrovertible that liberal theory comes unstuck at the precise moment when liberals are confronted with illiberal cultures. Why should we tolerate illiberal cultures which do not tolerate us, and which are heedless of the rights of their own members such as women? Tolerance comes into play and acquires relevance only when we are confronted with the intolerable, but why should we tolerate the intolerable? Conversely, what is the point of tolerating only those beliefs which sit well with our own considered convictions? And if we cannot tolerate the intolerable, to what extent can toleration be considered a good?

Tolerance is on trial today in a world dominated by extreme and palpable intolerance towards racial, sexual, religious and ethnic minorities and refugees. At some point of time, not so far ago, liberals believed that we should tolerate others because people have good reasons for their beliefs. Today, we see the infliction of massive violence on religious and ethnic minorities, take the Rohingyas in Myanmar, and intolerance towards refugees and alternative sexualities for no reason other than prejudice, rumours and our willingness to buy into hearsay. Our confidence that democratic liberal theory can order an inherently violent world has taken a hard knock. The other side of intolerance is violence, and violence negates the standing of human beings as people who count, and count equally. Intolerance leads to violence because the target group has been typed in perverse ways. It thus erases the fundamental obligations we owe to other persons, that of treating them in ways that are distinctively human.

Suppose we were to take a metaphorical step back, hesitate from foregrounding the 'I' (as an embodiment of sage judgement) and reflect on the possibility that our knowledge of what should be tolerated is seriously flawed. Would we be quite as hasty in judging others as unworthy of respect and therefore as less than human—something that, buffeted by hate-filled political discourses in social media and popular opinion, we seem to do? My suggestion is that the philosophical virtue of doubt in our capacity to know the truth can, perchance, articulate an ethics of toleration and of respect as constitutive of the social order.

The story of epistemic deficits begins, as most ethical narratives in political theory do, with the philosopher Socrates. In Plato's *Apology*, the philosopher defends himself against what to Athenians appeared a serious charge, that he spread discontent because he encouraged and facilitated questions, discussion and challenges to prevailing wisdom. His friend Chaerephon, recounted Socrates, asked the Oracle at Delphi whether anyone was wiser than the philosopher. The Pythian prophetess replied in the negative. Socrates confessed that he was taken aback, because he knew that he was not the epitome of wisdom. He set out to prove the Oracle wrong by discovering a man wiser than him. But when he began to speak with men who had formidable reputations for wisdom, he realised that he had an advantage over them. Whereas he himself knew that he did not have complete knowledge, so-called wise men did not even recognise the limits of their wisdom.

'Well', he concluded, 'although I do not suppose that either of us knows anything really beautiful and good, I am better off than he is, for he knows nothing and thinks that he knows; I neither know nor think that I know'.[26]

This, let me hasten to add, does not make Socrates tolerant of other points of view, he tended to regard ignorance with contempt. But his defence allows us to understand that all of us suffer from an epistemological deficit and that our knowledge is necessarily incomplete. Before we rush to participate in the mythologies of hate, the typing of other communities as 'inferior', as the 'enemy', and in short, the 'other', we ought to pause, consider and rethink. We might refrain from hasty actions that diminish other people and ourselves because we are in doubt about the state of our own knowledge.

The Socratic notion of wisdom helps us to understand that the truly wise recognise that boundaries are set to knowledge. The implication is that we ought to subject our opinions and prejudices to rigorous scrutiny before we participate in the mythologies of hate, typing other communities as inferior, as the enemy, or indeed as the 'other' with whom we can have no truck or transaction. To return to the example given above, it is shameful how the Rohingya community has been stereotyped as Islamist terrorists by its own country, Myanmar, and by neighbouring countries like India. We can and we should be able to share the pain of people hounded and hunted by the army, but only if we stop and wonder whether our responses to stories churned out by an irresponsible media are wise and prudent.

Doubt in our own capacity to know the truth and nothing but the truth is not always a negative quality. In the Indian epic Mahabharata, Yudhishthira, the eldest of the five brothers who wronged by their kinsmen fight a just war to reclaim their rights, is a Hamlet-like figure. Ever moral, ever obsessed with what is right, ever steeped in doubt, Yudhishthira is wracked by moral dilemmas, or so it appears. But he is also *Dharamraj*, the keeper of *dharma* or the normative order. His reflections on the delicate balance between *dharma* and *satya*, the

---

[26] Plato, *Apology*, 202.

truth, provide some of epic's most compelling instances of dialogue with the self.

The same philosophy of doubt overpowers Yudhishthira's brother, the great warrior Arjuna, on the battlefield. Is it proper to wage war against kinsmen when the outcome will be nothing but death and destruction? It takes nothing less than divine intervention to convince him. A righteous human being must uphold the normative order, even by war, if necessary. At precisely this point of the story, doubt assails the reader or the hearer of the epic. When two values of equal import, non-violence and protection of the normative order conflict, which one should the doer choose to resolve the dilemma?

Dilemmas, wrote the philosopher Bimal Matilal, are like paradoxes, and genuine paradoxes are seldom solved.

> They are generally speaking, resolved or dissolved. Those philoso-phers and logicians, who have tried over the centuries to solve the well-known logical and semantical paradoxes, have more often than not created new problems elsewhere in the conceptual apparatus, which exposes the non-existence of a universally accepted solution. Can moral dilemmas be put into the same category as unsolvable paradoxes?

Theologians, ethicists and 'strong-minded moral philosophers', he goes on to argue, have often been reluctant to admit the reality of moral dilemmas. If there can be genuine unresolvable moral dilemmas in a moral system, then it would be good as courting defeat in any attempt to formulate rational moral theories.[27] But we are, suggests the philosopher, fated to inhabit a world of irresolvable dilemmas.

Matilal illustrates his argument with a story found in the great Indian epic the Mahabharata. A hermit named Kaushika had vowed always to tell the truth because he desired above all to go to heaven and thus break the endless cycle of rebirth. One day as he was sitting near a cross road, he saw a group of traveller's rush by in a desperate attempt to escape a gang of bandits. When they passed the hermit,

---

[27] Matilal, 'Moral Dilemmas', 1–19.

the travellers requested the he should withhold information on which direction they had gone from the bandits. The bandits seemed to know that Kaushika was committed to telling the truth, and naturally asked which direction their quarry had fled. Kaushika, bound by his vow, directed them to the road the benighted travellers had gone; the bandits rushed after the group, killed members and looted their belongings. And Kaushika did not ascend to heaven. His duty to tell the truth had violated his obligation to save innocent lives.

The Mahabharata, suggests Matilal, is shot through with the meta-concept of *dharma*, which can be interpreted as righteous conduct or a normative order. There is, however, no definitive meaning assigned to *dharma* and the concept is ambiguous and elusive. Not surprisingly, we discover dilemmas within the structure of *dharma ethics*. These are not culturally specific, Matilal hastens to add; they are universal and can be effectively used to illustrate arguments in moral philosophy. Moral dilemmas arise when the agent is committed to two or more moral obligations, but circumstances are such that an obligation to do *x* cannot be fulfilled without violating an obligation to do *y*. Dilemmas present irreconcilable options, and the actual choice among them becomes either irrational, or is based upon grounds other than moral.

This is contrary to the system of Kantian ethics. For Kant, objective practical rules should form a harmonious whole and a consistent system, much like a system of true beliefs. The system presumes that two mutually opposing rules cannot be necessary at the same time. Therefore, if it is a duty to act according to one of them, it is not only a duty but contrary to duty to act according to the other. Moral conflicts cannot be genuine; there can only be conflict between genuine duty and a ground of duty. In Kantian ethics, truth telling gets the highest priority, as does keeping of promises. This is equally true in the Indian systems of ethics that extols truth telling as *satya rakhsa* (protection of the truth). No cultural relativism can be found here. But when two equally strong obligations—that of truth telling and that of saving lives—conflict,[28] keeping of a promise cannot be an unconditional

[28] Ibid., 8–9.

obligation. In such situations, we have to make a choice between different sorts of options that might minimise harm.

The implication is that we bear moral responsibility for the choices we make. For instance, suggests Matilal, Kaushika could have told the bandits that though he knew which way the travellers had gone, he would not share this information, or simply kept quiet. But he interpreted his commitment to the truth and nothing but the truth unthinkingly and unimaginatively, and innocent lives were lost. We learn from Matilal that the dilemmas we find ourselves in might well prove intractable, but there is no reason why we cannot negotiate them with some degree of resourcefulness and ingenuity. We have to think deeply before we adopt a course of action, we have to enter into a debate with ourselves and we have to understand the significance of doubting our own state of knowledge.

The advantage of the philosophical virtue of doubt is that it forces a rethink, forces us to know that we do not know enough, forces us to sometimes retract, and if we proceed, proceed cautiously, particularly if valuable human lives are at stake. Arjuna knows that war against injustice that has wrecked the normative order is unavoidable; he opts for it, but with great reservations. And after the war is over, the five brothers recognise the futility of violence. Interestingly, the concept of non-violence takes powerful hold of Indian mentalities in the period following the compilation of the Mahabharata.

Another story from the epic spotlights the dilemma between *dharma* and non-violence towards living beings very well. An upper-caste sage wandered from place to place, searching for wisdom, and ultimately sat at the feet of a low-caste butcher amidst carcasses of animals in a slaughterhouse, and learnt how to balance righteous conduct with tolerance and non-violence. Vrinda Dalmia suggests that the sage Kaushika's transformation began when he shamefully confronted his moral fall (his gaze had shrivelled a crow to cinders because its cawing had disturbed his meditation) and linked it with a cognitive limitation. He realised that whereas he might not know, or only know imperfectly, there can be others, even those who are on the margins of society, who might know more than him. The acknowledgement of imperfectability can lead to a conversation in which both recognise each other as bearers of wisdom.[29] We learn tolerance towards other points of view because we simply do not know enough.

Gandhian Perspectives on Toleration

A compelling argument for toleration and for non-violence, along the same line of argument, was made by Gandhi. Gandhi's defence of tolerance and of non-violence is anchored, what to him, is an epistemic deficit. Discovery of the truth, which Gandhi identified with God, is an essential precondition for leading lives that are worthwhile. The problem is that persons can never come to know what this truth is. I, he wrote, have been striving to serve the truth and have the courage to jump from the Himalayas for its sake. But, he added, I know I am still very far from that truth. 'As I advance towards it, I perceive my weakness ever more clearly and the knowledge makes me humble'.[30]

Evoking the parable of the seven blind men who had only limited knowledge about the elephant they were asked to describe through touch, Gandhi suggests that different sorts of truths can only approximate the ultimate truth, like different leaves on the same tree. This does not mean that we stop searching for the truth, because our ontological status is connected to our knowledge of the truth. But we are seekers not finders; therefore, we can never be confident that we have discovered the truth. Gandhi, in effect, tells us that the one ultimate truth is manifested in the shape of many truths, but each of these truths is but an incomplete version of the ultimate truth.[31]

Notably, the implications of Gandhi's insistence that each of us cannot possibly know the truth and that all that we can know is a partial truth are far reaching. If persons have the moral capacity to know the truth, but not the entire truth, then no one person or group can claim superiority over others, because their truth is the ultimate truth, and other truths are false or travesties of the real thing. Therefore,

[29] Dalmia, 'Care Ethics and Epistemic Justice', 121.
[30] Gandhi, 'What Is Truth', 474.
[31] Gandhi, 'Letter to Mrs R. Armstrong and Mrs P.R. Howard', 111.

we realise that just as our (partial) truth is dear to us, others (equally partial) truths are bound to be dear to them. There is simply no point in comparing world views in grading them, or in pronouncing one conception of the good as superior to the other. If we had attained the full vision of the truth he was to write,

> We would no longer be mere seekers, but become one with God, for truth is God. But being only seekers, we prosecute our quest and are conscious of our imperfection. And if we are imperfect ourselves, religion as conceived by us must also be imperfect … [and] is subject to a process of evolution and reinterpretation.… And if all faiths outlined by men are imperfect, the question of comparative merit does not arise.[32]

But where do we begin to look for this ultimate truth? Any search must begin from somewhere, lead in some direction and towards some end. Even if we never reach the end, at least the path to that end should be in sight. Truth, argued Gandhi, can be found in great religions because each of these religions shares a commitment to the same moral core: respecting the dignity of persons, and understanding the best life as one that moves beyond hatred or necessity, and one that aims at non-violence and morality. The rules of morality that are contained in the world's greatest religions wrote Gandhi, are largely the same … if morality is destroyed, religion which is built on it comes crashing down.[33] If this proposition holds, then all the principal religions are equally valid and deserving of respect. Gandhi himself was what he was—a great moral leader and a giver of remedies for the maladies of the human condition, because he drew inspiration from a variety of sources. His philosophy is indebted to four great spiritual and moral traditions: Hinduism, Jainism, Buddhism and Christianity. Gandhian philosophy is constituted as much by the Bhagavad Gita as it is by the Sermon from the Mount. And he drew inspiration as much from Tolstoy and John Ruskin as much as he drew inspiration from Vivekananda and other spiritual leaders in India.

---

[32] Gandhi, *From Yeravada Mandir*, 55.
[33] Gandhi, 'Ethical Religion-V', 313.

Parekh suggests that Gandhi's notion of non-violence is conceptually located in a 'novel epistemological argument' that violence rests on false epistemological foundations.[34] Prior to Gandhi, however, Socrates and then John Locke, as we have seen, espoused tolerance on these grounds. Gandhi's theory of tolerance and proscription of violence was elaborated in the same context of violence between religious communities as Locke's. Religious violence had become the norm in India during the second decade of the 20th century. He wished to negate this violence for three reasons, of which one reason was pragmatic and the other two embedded in his philosophy. First, conflict between religious communities made the task of forging a mass movement impossible—a way out of this pointless violence had to be found. This he found in the precept of equality of all religions or *Sarva Dharma Sambhava*. Second, the employment of violence in the pursuit of goals dictated by 'this' or 'that' religion—went against his deeply held conviction that no religion can ever provide a reason for or legitimatise violence. Third, the partial nature of our knowledge or truth proscribes violence. It is only when one agent believes that his or her truth is the final truth, and that other truths are false, and that he or she practices violence. The conviction that we possess the truth and others do not leads to arrogance, intolerance and violence.

But the moment we realise that all of us can know but the partial truth, we learn to respect others as well as modify our own pretensions. This recognition curbs instincts that impel a person to intolerance and helps us to accept other convictions and beliefs as worthy of respect. Otherwise, animosity, hate, distrust and violence become the defining features of a body politic. We are consequently embroiled in the politics of suspicion. Tolerance, on the other hand, prevents humanity from sliding into religious bigotry, racism, chauvinism, discrimination, casteism and communalism.

The nature of Gandhi's truth might prove relevant for today's world, because the one urgent political task is to bring individuals who are suspicious of each other together, encourage them to speak to

---

[34] Parekh, *Colonialism, Tradition and Reform*, 173.

each other and keep the conversation going. We only engage people when we recognise them as equal partners in a dialogue. And we do so because they might know what we do not know. Let us, therefore, begin the search for the truth together. We might come to see others who we formerly regarded as inferior or lacking in knowledge as equals because they possess knowledge of the truth.

I am by no means suggesting that the spirit or the ethos of tolerance will help us to sort out all kinds of ethnic conflict. Tolerance is a social principle that is best realised within a democratic state, a state committed to the equality of its people as well as all religious and ethnic groups. Conversely laws, regulations and prohibitions are simply not enough. When persons are subjected to intolerance because they belong to 'this' or 'that' ethnic group, other people ought to be agitated and disturbed. This may not happen unless toleration is incorporated into social values through arguments and struggles for non-violence, and more importantly secularism as a principle of the democratic state. The task is difficult. But howsoever rocky the allegorical road to tolerance may be, we need to painstakingly construct it through argument, struggle and dialogue. The future of our common humanity is, after all, at stake.

This can only be resolved when we understand that we must engage with others in society and institute thereby a conversation. Unless we take care to create a climate of civility in the country, we will be irrevocably trapped in the never-ending cycle of communal tensions that erupt into conflict at the veritable drop of a hat. Our lives will become, as the English theorist Thomas Hobbes described the state of nature, 'nasty brutish and short', with no assurance of life itself, let alone the assurance that we will be able to enjoy divine music, experience exciting sport, read intense literature, watch imaginative films, engage in exhilarating conversations, indulge in warm social interactions, as well as all the activities that make for a life worth living. Civility, it has been argued earlier, can only be built up and maintained, nurtured and cherished when we begin to see others who are like us and not like us as worthy of dignity, as worthy of being engaged with. A great many unnecessary conflicts can be ironed out only if we come together.

And we have to come together because as Gandhi wrote we are born into a world that has been creatively fashioned by the mental and the manual labours of not only the members of our own community, but also those of other communities. Notably, the world that shapes our moral personalities is not only our country, or our society, but humanity. We would not be what we are without the contributions of other human beings to the making of our world. Therefore, we *owe* humanity; we owe a debt of gratitude to many people both proximate and distant, simply because they have contributed to the vitality of our institutions, to the constitution of social values that informs our choices and to the satisfaction of our material needs. We inhabit a world that has been created by shared labour and we learn to respect each other as bearers of labour.

Our respect for others is, therefore, based on the mutual recognition of dependence. For Gandhi, we are born debtors in the world to which we owe a debt, and we are dependent on others right from birth. Man becomes man only by recognising his dependence on others.[35] We owe the living, as much as we owe earlier generations for what they have contributed to the best that we have today. These are enormous contributions, and we cannot repay them all, but in repaying what we can, we show we are part of a world that is interdependent over time and space.

This is a relational notion of the world; we cannot be fulfilled beings without the other. The other is an integral part of who I am. Not only is the construction of divisions between human beings, or the forging of notions of 'us' and 'them', highly arbitrary, but also this construction is completely unnecessary. This becomes clear the moment we realise our dependence on others when we begin to make moral choices that are needed to live fulfilled lives. This becomes clear the moment we realise that the relationship between human beings is not one of exteriority but of deep interiority.

This does not mean that we leave our own community for an abstract entity called society, but that we inhabit a number of

[35] Cited in Brown, 'Gandhi and Human Rights', 91.

overlapping communities, within the political community forged by democracy. Again we learn this from Gandhi. Despite the fact that Gandhi forged and 'led' the freedom struggle against British colonialism, he refused to be bound by narrow notions of 'us' versus 'them'. So long as man remains selfish, stated Gandhi, and does not care for the happiness of others, he is no better than an animal and perhaps worse. His superiority to the animal is seen only when we find him caring for his family. He is still more human, that is, much higher than the animal, when he extends his concept of the family to include his country or community as well. He climbs still higher in the scale when he comes to regard the human race as his family.[36] Families, communities, nations and humanity are not exclusive entities. The harm done to oneself or one's family cannot bring about the good of the nation. Similarly, one cannot benefit the nation by acting against the world at large.[37]

As mentioned earlier, Gandhi taught us that our ability to live lives worth living depend not only on the languages given by our community but also on the languages we learn from other cultural communities and people, because we jointly inhabit a universe.

It follows that if our imaginations, our conceptual resources and our energies are constricted by the rules of only our community, or if we have access to only *one* set of cultural traditions, those we inherit as members of a community, we are diminished as human beings. We are so diminished because our capacity to broaden our perceptions and deepen our value systems is constricted. Simply put, containment within narrow cognitive and evaluative resources subtracts from the essential human capacity to learn from many languages and many cultures.

This recognition carries a significant implication for our defence of pluralism, which we began this argument with. A plurality of values enables us to be aware of other possibilities of the human condition lived with others, those other who are like us and not like

[36] Gandhi, 'Ethical Religions', 330–331.
[37] Gandhi, 'Dharma and Self Purification', 81.

us. In short, we can reasonably assume that when persons design their lives, they take their cue from themselves as well as other human beings, whether these human beings belong to their immediate community, to other communities, to the national community, the regional community or to the global community of cultural and intellectual production and reproduction. If this is so, then we are inexorably led beyond the paradigm of the national community to embrace a regional, if not an international community of belonging. We correspondingly assume that our projects can neither be formulated nor revised without entering into a conversation with other human beings. This would mean that neither individuals nor their proximate community constitute the *only* source of cognition and evaluation. Human beings derive their conceptions of how to make their own histories from a mélange of ideas, projects and cultural contexts, all of which are mediated by their reason. It follows that the making of intelligent and fulfilled lives demands that a plurality of values be respected and encouraged.

A diversity of cultures provides the best context for the quintessential human capacity to formulate and rethink projects. These simply enable persons to make their own histories. If this recognition helps us to connect the domain of empirical pluralism and normative pluralism, it also allows to us acknowledge that plural societies are far better as context for human beings and their activities than the relatively monochromatic societies that communal elements who seek to construct a purely Hindu society believe. Unless we talk to others who hold different points of view and familiarise ourselves with other perspectives, other horizons of understanding and other evaluations, we cannot possess informed judgement about any issue or matter. In fact, our own judgements may even degenerate into mere opinions and thoughtless assertions. But uniformed thought possesses neither cognitive nor moral status. We, of course, initiate deliberation by putting forth our own perspectives and that is both natural and desirable.

Through the process of dialogue, we, however, discover slowly, but surely, areas of commonality with other members of the discursive community—areas that we were unaware of earlier. If these points of view prove complementary to ours, they will enrich and supplement our position. If they prove contrary to our own, they may compel us to rethink our position and perhaps accept that other arguments are much better than ours. Alternatively, if we believe that other positions are flawed, we try to reason with and persuade the holders of these views. We, in sum, cannot formulate or evaluate our own projects unless we approach the issue from as many vantage points as possible, and unless we can be persuaded that 'this' and not 'that' vantage point is the most desirable.

Therefore, even though people may enter the discursive forum from radically divergent positions, the exchange of ideas can be so enriching and persuasive that the discursive community is able to generate some kind of consensus, howsoever provisional, on the most vital aspects of collective and individual existence. Correspondingly, participants realise that what we call impartiality is not a 'view from nowhere' but a matter of viewing the world from the perspective of other people. What is important is that through sustained interaction, we may find ourselves making the move from a purely 'self-regarding' to an 'other-regarding' perspective.

There is more to dialogue than mere fine-tuning of our own per-spectives, opinions and beliefs. Even as we establish our readiness to listen respectfully to other ideas of what is true and just, we establish that we respect others as free and equal partners in deliberation. Dialogue, therefore, validates the standing of others as people who have something worthwhile to contribute to the elaboration of an idea or a worldview. The process just recognises the other person as some-one who matters. And this by itself contributes to the ironing out of senseless conflicts that arise out of the lack of recognition. Moreover, if we discuss all dimensions of issues relating to the truth in a principled manner, we may be able to winnow out and defend desirable ideas and destroy undesirable ideas more effectively than not discussing them would. Correspondingly, if we cannot generate consensus on a contested norm, we move towards the forging of a new norm. We do this because our collective deliberations have shown us that the norm under discussion just does not command shared allegiance. It, therefore, needs to be drastically revised or even jettisoned. Arguably, dialogue appears particularly appropriate for plural societies, which are marked not only by a variety of perspectives, belief systems and values, but also stamped by deep disagreements on the basic norms of a polity, as well as on which belief system is acceptable. In these contexts, it is secularism as well as tolerance that helps us negotiate our way through the thickets of a complex society.

CHAPTER 8

Wrapping Up

Unhappily there is hatred today in India and strong aversions, for the past pursues us and the present does not differ from it.[1]

In the opening chapter, I had suggested that we need to make a transition from empirical to normative pluralism or respect for different communities, for at least three reasons. The first reason is instrumental insofar as individuals can be harmed if their constitutive community is harmed in different but equally hurtful ways. The second reason relates to what human beings dream of, aspire to and accomplish. None of this is possible unless the individual has secure access to his or her constitutive community. It is this community that gives us the primary language that enables us to make sense of the world. Third, a society in which pluralism is respected adds to our comprehension of what being human means.

Secularism bridges the empirical proposition that our society is plural and the normative proposition that pluralism is a good. Today when the status of secularism in the country is in danger of being dislodged from political imaginations and political life, it is time to re-inscribe and revalue the concept. This is what this work has tried to do: to bring out the significance of secularism and that of tolerance

[1] Nehru, *The Discovery of India*, 564.

to our collective life. The argument is located within the wider notion of pluralism. There is no moment like the present to take up a job that is worth doing, even in negative circumstances.

Brutus, in the immortal play *The Tragedy of Julius Caesar* written by William Shakespeare, says:

> There is a tide in the affairs of men. Which, taken at the flood, leads on to fortune; Omitted, all the voyage of their life Is bound in shallows and in miseries. On such a full sea we are now afloat, And we must take the current when it serves, Or lose our ventures.[2]

Indians must recognise that it is time to take a decision. We can harness the tide and turn the country towards the project of living together in civility or we can shrug our shoulders and accept that we are bound by a malignant fate to repeat again and again the horrors that resulted in the Partition of the country. We have to learn from history. Perhaps we can do that best when we read the production of novelists and short story writers who have captured the horror of the long moment of Partition in evocative detail. In a short story on the Partition of India, Upendra Ashk has described the dread of the moment of Partition chillingly:

> When Lehna Singh reached Islamabad, he found himself in the middle of a violent riot. People of one religion were busy slaughtering people of another religion with the same mechanical efficiency with which his machines chop grass. Sardar Lehna Singh also pulled out his kirpan and was determined to prove that he was a man by killing the first Muslim who came his way.[3]

Note that the bloodlust generated by communal violence did not drive him to just kill any person, but a person belonging to another community, who had been in mythology and history typed as enemy. This is what rabid and competitive nationalism did to the country. This is what Partition meant for India.

---

[2] Shakespeare, 'The Tragedy of Julius Caesar', 641.
[3] Ashk, 'The Fodder Cutting Machine', 30.

More than seven decades after Partition, we really have to ask ourselves: Do we really want to live in a bare and stark society marked by informal apartheid? Or do we earnestly desire to inhabit a social order that fosters warm relationships based on civility and mutual respect? The first kind of society will drastically constrain our minds and hearts, our sensibilities and our perspectives. The second sort will enable the unleashing of creative imaginations and allow us to become fuller human beings, at ease with ourselves and with others in a plural society. The first sort of social order will encourage the democratic project of mutual engagement with other citizens, the second will develop nothing but suspicion and fear of others, and loss of confidence in our own ability to wend our way through the world supported by people like us, and not like us. If we wish to block the tide of animosity and awfulness that has swept the country in the past few years, we have no option to ask the question: What kind of a society have we become? What should strive towards? Is it possible to live a good life unless we inhabit a good society where other people respect us, and where we reciprocate by extending to them civility?

We have to, in other words, recognise the malaise of Indian society. The recognition causes us discomfort, but we can no longer believe that only the institutionalisation of formal democracy will help us to extend mutual respect, ensure dignity and pre-empt violence. The contradictions of Indian democracy are stark, and somewhat ugly. Amidst all the fanfare that attends the rituals of elections, Indians routinely practise gender and caste discrimination that spills over into violence. Our religious minorities are subjected to incredibly abusive hate speech and vicious acts. Our belief that democratic dialogue is the only way to resolve problems has been shattered. The conviction that our democracy has no room for violence has been belied.

And this presents a dismal scenario. Violence leads to harm, results in the untimely death of innocent bystanders, generates fear and resentment among others and sweeps up the perpetrator, the victim and innocent bystanders in a vicious spiral of merciless destruction and impairment. There is little that is noble about violence. 'Each new morn', laments Macduff of war in Shakespeare's *Macbeth*, 'New widows howl, new orphans cry, new sorrows Strike heaven in the face that it resounds'.[4] Routine and reiterative violence appears to be an anomaly in democratic theory. And yet in India's democracy, groups buffeted by the strong desire to stamp the body politic with their own intolerable agenda of discrimination give cause for 'new sorrows' that strike heaven in the face.

This is the paradox. Democracy and violence are, or at least should be, strangers to each other—ships that pass in the night with nary a nod to each other, the unknown and perhaps the unknowable. They should not be inhabiting the same conceptual and political universe, for the logic of each concept runs in in different directions. Democracy enables citizens to come together across boundaries of class and ethnicity. The right to freedom of association, which is an essential precondition for the existence of a vibrant civil society brimming over with discussion, debate and contestation, is highly conducive to the formation of dense networks of social associations. These associations may be philanthropic, or passionately concerned about the state of civil liberties in the country, focused on the quality of national governance, or on local matters such as the dismal performance of neighbourhood schools, fan clubs that lapse into delirium the moment superstars in films, or in soccer, or in cricket are mentioned, or reading societies that solemnly and laboriously work out what a particular author or her work signifies. It matters little what specific objective associational life promotes, the simple pleasure of sociability, monitoring the state or keeping watch on uncivil groups in civil society. It is enough that an energetic civil society connects people who would have been otherwise locked into their own little worlds of isolation, sometimes permanently so.

Acts of violence, on the other hand, systematically and irrevocably separate, divide and segregate individuals and groups. These groups might have, till then, lived in some civility if not perfect harmony and neighbourliness. Violence positions them as combatants in a great divide. With a rapid flick of its long-forked tongue, the serpent of violence poisons the environment, seeds an atmosphere of suspicion and terror, relentlessly casts a miasma of hate and doubt over communities

---

[4] Shakespeare, 'The Tragedy of *Macbeth*', 993.

and societies, and destroys every hope that people sealed into circles of apprehension and fear may even consider initiating a conversation with others.

This is exactly what took place in Muzaffarnagar in India in early September 2013 when neighbour turned viciously on neighbour. 'They dismembered our people and raped our women', said Shoib of right-wing element. He was the inhabitant of a refugee camp for those who had managed to escape violence. Among the rioters were faces known to Shoib—faces of individuals whose family festivals he had routinely taken part in.[5] Similar stories of how people who had lived together as neighbours and co-workers for decades were transformed into vicious marauding mobs thirsting for their neighbour's blood have come to us from Bosnia, Kosovo, Sudan, from the struggle for the independence of Bangladesh and from the Partition of India. The lesson is clear: between a group that is intent on, say, ethnic cleansing and the target group, there can be no truck or transaction, let alone dialogue. The momentum of violence, that of sundering relationships, runs counter to that of democracy, which brings otherwise solitary people together in shared networks of associational life.

There are other deep differences between democracy and violence. Democracy enables people to route their aspirations, demands and expectations of the State through peaceful methods such as public gatherings, demonstrations, petitions, lobbying, campaigns, social networks, political movements, political theatrics and the media. Violence erupts outside these prescribed and institutionalised channels in public spaces, in cobbled streets and the sidewalks of our cities and villages. Democracy secures the legitimacy of the State and of the holders of political power, whereas violence disputes the democratic credentials of elites to rule.

This is not to argue that democracy and violence occupy the same political space. This metaphorical space has been rendered vacant because democracy has waylaid its own presupposition—that of equality. When institutions of the democratic State foster injustice, when the holders of State power are silent even as innocent citizens are slaughtered merely because of their food habits, when the interests of the minority are betrayed and the interests of the majority are supported overtly or covertly, and when the people who are subjected to injustice are anonymous and faceless both for the State and for civil society, the space that should have been filled in with democratic contestation, social movements, campaigns, protest petitions, marches, demonstrations and strikes, is emptied out, into this space step in the merchants of violence.

Violence, we have learnt, is part of the human condition; it hovers on the margins of social, political and economic relations, waiting to subvert civility. The political trick is to make it stay on the margins and prevent it from occupying the space of democratic politics. And this is possible, for violence is a political phenomenon and, therefore, has to be dealt with politically. The political negotiation of violence demands innovation, creativity, imagination and determination, but it can be done, and it has to be done. Otherwise, violence between religious communities will continue to occupy the same space as democracy. And society will continue to pay heavy costs for the waylaying of the basic principles of equality.

Democracy and Recognition

These principles are normally waylaid because of the gap between the basic norms of political democracy, that is, equality and social and economic inequalities. Indisputably, democracy has enabled large numbers of people to understand the power of the franchise, enter the public arena of politics and, to some degree, influence the political discourse. Thereby, political equality has been realised. Admittedly, the realisation of political equality is no small matter; it is of enormous importance because it is one way of facilitating demands for redistribution of power and resources by the poor. Political equality enables and facilitates challenges to the system by those who have been marginalised. It is this aspect of democracy that offers hope and a fair degree of political excitement. We simply do not know how configurations of power will be challenged, how they will be adapted and what the new balance of power will be in the near future.

Yet, despite the achievements of formal democracy, we should also recognise that political equality can be deeply compromised if people experience multiple disadvantages in the economic and the social domain. Or even if political equality enables people to make claims for power and resources, to what extent do these demands, or even the grant of resources, translate into concrete gains for ordinary beings? Despite rhetorical flourishes, policy pronouncements and enactments of large numbers of laws on social policy, huge numbers of our people continue to live in dire want. This compromises democracy because political democracy and social/economic democracy are not distant or even first cousins, *they are constitutive of democracy itself.* Democratic equality cannot reduce domination if there are huge imbalances between the political system and the distribution of wealth. For no matter how equal my vote may be, I will continue to feel deeply unequal if my neighbour possesses more resources, more power and more privilege than me. The State has to lessen this gap, in full knowledge that equality is a relational category and, therefore, a handful of grain here and a handful of grain there will not resolve the problem. The life chances of citizens ought to be roughly equal so that they can take advantage of the opportunities that are on offer.

Economic inequality is, however, not the only problem that stalks the promises of political democracy. Equally significant is the issue of social discrimination based on caste or religion. Let us focus on religious discrimination and sort of inequality that arises in a plural society when some groups form a demographic majority and others fall into the category of a minority. Notably, not all minorities are politically significant for majoritarian agendas; only those who are associated in history and mythologies of hate, with events such as rulers in medieval India, and communal riots and Partition in modern India as the Muslim community is.

At first glance, there is cause for perplexity. The Muslim minority in contemporary India can hardly be held responsible for the rule of the Mughal dynasty in medieval India. Nor can citizens of contemporary India be held accountable for communal riots that scarred the body politic and society irremediably in the past. This is as futile as holding the Hindu majority responsible for the assassination of Mahatma Gandhi. But majoritarian agendas are not in the business of rational or democratic thinking. They are in the business of accumulating power through the demonisation of another community that has been stereotyped in perverse ways. Members of the minority community, mainly Muslim but also Christian, attacked for engineering conversions and thus depleting the numbers of Hindus, suffer from what we can call a lack of respect.

Increasingly, we recognise that economic redistribution alone is not the solution to social discrimination. This becomes clear the moment we pose a specific question of egalitarian theories *equality for what?* To put it bluntly, is there any connection between the redistribution of material resources and (a) extension of respect to the beneficiary, on the one hand, and (b) development of self-respect in the beneficiary, on the other? We have to admit that it is not easy to establish a relationship between tangible things such as material resources—income, shelter, education and health care—and the cultivation of sentiments such as self-respect, self-esteem and a sense of self-worth. But presumably the deeper logic that underlines and penetrates philosophies and policies that seek to realise equality is targeted towards the inculcation of precisely these sentiments. After all, the provision of basic needs happens to be a prerequisite for human flourishing or for expanding the realm of choices. If we go further, the redistribution of resources is necessary to neutralise oppressive structures. Access to resources that meet basic needs allows individuals to realise their humanity in its fullness. This is the *maximal* take on redistribution. *Minimally*, the argument holds that if I do not have to beg for my daily food or clothing, if I am not dependent on the charity of others for the satisfaction of my daily wants and if I can provide for my own social reproduction as well as that of my family, I can be fairly sure that I will not be subjected to humiliation every day or every hour of the day. Most defenders of equality desire that individuals should be protected against the kind of humiliation that will necessarily occur, when they are dependent on others for the satisfaction of their basic requirements to live a decent life. They would not be committed to egalitarianism otherwise.

The link between redistribution (of material resources) and what has come to be known as recognition (development of feelings of self-respect) has, however, proved more tenuous than originally conceived of by these supporters. For one, not only is recognition an elusive concept inasmuch as it belongs to the realm of human prejudice, attitude and notions of group identity, but it is also a matter that is not so easily commanded by politics. Politics can, to put it differently, negotiate the distribution of scarce resources. The matter requires vision, courage and commitment, but as history has shown us, it can be done. How does politics negotiate recognition? How does it lay down parameters of what human beings owe each other by virtue of being human? Too many troubling factors cast their dark shadow on this precise issue—aspects that relate to individual and group psychology, all of which do not lend themselves easily to political negotiation or intervention.

And yet recognition is vital to human beings, for it determines how they think of themselves and how they relate to others. There is more. A good life is dependent on being held in regard by others, as seen by others as someone who possesses worth. Essentially, therefore, the concept of recognition is located in the overlap between the individual and the community. We achieve the recognition of ourselves as people who matter, when others show us through their actions and their behaviour that we matter. Conversely, the potential for moral injury arises from forms of life based on sociability. Human beings are vulnerable because their self-awareness is dependent on the approval or the disapproval of other human beings. Expectedly, the proposition that the constitution of the self is dependent on its being recognised by other selves shifts our focus away from the individualist notion that the self is autonomous to the idea that the self is a relational entity. Selfhood is, in other words, located in the overlapping processes of identity formation.

'Human integrity', suggests the German philosopher Axel Honneth, modifying the Hegelian concept of recognition through employment of the ideas of George Herbert Mead, 'owes its existence, at a deep level, to the patterns of approval and recognition'.[6] The only

---

[6] Honneth, *The Struggle for Recognition*, 131.

way in which individuals are constituted as persons—as being with certain positive traits and abilities—is by learning to refer to themselves from the perspective of an approving or encouraging other. In this way, the prospect of basic self-confidence is inherent in the experience of love, the prospect of self-respect in the experience of legal recognition and, finally, the prospect of self-esteem is found in experiences of solidarity. Correspondingly, since the self-image of individuals is based upon experiences of recognition, disrespect carries with it its own form of injury. That is why, suggests Honneth, individuals describe experiences of non-recognition as insult or humiliation. The consequences of disrespect or humiliation are serious: 'psychological death' of those whose bodily integrity has been violated, 'social death' for victims of slavery and 'scars' for those whose cultures have been denigrated.

Theories of recognition in sum help us to understand that it may not be enough to grant individuals access to material resources through redistribution, but it is equally important to recognise them in the sense of validating their self-image, for when an individual is subjected to disrespect in his or her daily dealings in the public or in the private sphere, or when he or she is subjected to humiliation, the consequences can be serious—the spectre of demoralised, diminished and degraded beings, on the one hand, and struggles for respect or dignity, on the other.

Consequently, we can identify two types of discrete/overlapping conflicts in the world today: struggles over socio-economic resources and struggles over the revaluation of identities. But where we can negotiate economic and political marginalisation through the distribution of tangible resources, how do we deal with issues of cultural marginalisation, which require the revaluation of devalued identities? Will the first negotiation help us to negotiate the second problem? It is doubtful. All this, as we can see, stacks up serious problems when it comes to the politics and policies of equality and mutual respect. We have to shift the ground of our approach to equality in order to secure respect for all religious communities.

One minor point before we proceed. We tend to assume in our daily lives that respect has to do with human properties that we admire, whether they may be talent, skills, exceptional abilities or, indeed, loyalty and integrity in friends. And this is true to some extent. We respect Pandit Jasraj because he has mastered the intricate art of Hindustani classical music. We respect Virat Kohli because he is a skilled cricket player. And we respect social activists because they are committed to justice for the powerless and because they have, with great courage, expanded the political agenda in the country.

In normative political theory, however, respect is a generalised concept insofar as it has to do with the need to regard each person, no matter how ordinary she or he may be, as being of value. It is premised upon the notion of human worth. The extension of respect, it is important to note, need not be positive; it need not extend to intentional action. We, after all, do not have to go up to persons we know or do not know and tell them that we respect or admire them. It is enough if we refrain from actions that humiliate other human beings. Respect for other persons is generally practised through restraint and control over hateful or hurting speech and actions.

But we also need a legal framework and a State that is committed to the protection of the dignity of minority communities that are at risk in a majoritarian India. To put the point across plainly, institutions and practices of formal democracy find it difficult to breach the ramparts of economic and social inequality. But the practice of treating unequal constituencies equally results in the reproduction of inequality. Democracy has to be supported by additional institutions and practices to realise its own promises. One of these practices is the redistribution of resources to the disadvantaged in society, so that they can participate in the multiple transactions of society from a plane of equality. After all, a hungry or a homeless individual cannot be equal to others who do not suffer from these shortfalls in well-being.

The redistribution of resources is not impossible. All that is required is the political will to do so, to understand that democracy is severely compromised if people in their daily lives are condemned to eke out a bare existence, or if they are trapped in the cycle of never-ending poverty. There are, however, other forms of inequality that need to be tackled—the denial of respect or the demonisation of the minorities. How do democratic states manage to secure respect for people who are vulnerable, because the group of which they are members has been treated as lesser citizens of India?

The leaders of the freedom struggle recognised the problem early in the 20th century. Along with redistributive justice and affirmative action, another plan of action to secure equality or at least non-discrimination against religious minorities was set in place; this was the doctrine of secularism. Because secularism has developed in India as equality of all religions, the freedom to be religious or non-religious, and the non-alignment of the state with one religion, its natural home is democracy. It is, as suggested earlier, best conceived of as a companion concept of democracy. The necessary preconditions of secularism are, therefore, a constitutional commitment to the generic principle of equality, and State neutrality towards all religions particularly minority systems of belief.

The corresponding point is that majorities, even if they have been elected, cannot pass laws that violate the basic principles of democracy, freedom, rights or equality that are granted in the fundamental rights chapter of the Constitution. For instance, the legislature can hardly rule that only members of the majority community will be allowed to vote. This is proscribed by constitutional provisions and by the presuppositions of democracy. Liberal constitutionalists have always been wary of the power of 'brute majorities', and therefore fundamental rights are normally taken off the anvil. These rights are non-negotiable, and if there is need to amend them, the procedure of amendment requires special procedures. The power of arbitrary majorities is restricted in every democracy by constitutional provisions and judicial fiats. The argument becomes stronger when it comes to vulnerable minorities.

There is a second case in which the power of the majority should be restricted in plural but unequal societies like India. The case relates to special protections accorded to the right of religious minorities. Whereas all Indian citizens have the right to freedom of religion, the minority community is given the right to preserve and protect its language, script and culture, and along with other citizens establish educational institutions. Minorities possess universal as well as special rights that protect them against the tyranny of majorities. The procedure is fair and democratic when we recollect the implications of the phrase 'permanent minorities'. Electoral majorities and minorities are flexible terms. If a party loses in one election, it can be elected to power in the next round, provided that the processes that govern elections are fair. But religious minorities are permanent minorities. Permanent minorities are not only defined by numbers or more precisely the lack thereof, but also they are not likely to find place in the cultural self-representation of a nation, and they are likely to be under-represented in institutions of decision making such as legislatures. This is the case in today's India. The Muslim minority has the lowest representation in the Parliament constituted after the 2014 elections since Independence. The BJP and its allies did not put forth the name of a single Muslim candidate to represent the sizeable Muslim community in the Uttar Pradesh assembly elections of 2017. This guarantees that the interests of Muslims, who constitute 19 per cent of the population, are not represented at all in the state assembly. The marginalisation of the Muslim community is not mere happenstance; it is the product of a deliberate choice to marginalise a politically significant minority.

The BJP represented itself as the only party that could protect and further the interests of the majority community. The majority was ironically presented as under siege, contrary to the pro-minority stance of the socialist Samajwadi Party and the Dalit-based Bahujan Samaj Party. The sizeable majority ironically continues to be projected at risk from a minority. It works because Uttar Pradesh has a substantial Muslim population, and the cynical manipulation of the majority community could consolidate resentment and angst against Muslims that belong to one of the poorest groups in the country. The Gujarat model, which has succeeded in completely dividing the Hindus and the Muslim, has been deployed effectively in UP in 2017, even if it did not work in subsequent elections in Punjab, Goa and Manipur in 2017 and 2018 and in Karnataka in May 2018.

The trouble is that the litany of the grievances of the majority community that incongruously appears to be at risk from the minority has acquired considerable power to shape perceptions and ideologies. The trouble is that a majority of Indians are unmoved by scenes of brutality against Muslims in the public domain. The connection forged by the cadres of the Hindutva brigade between Muslim citizens of India and the perennial enemy Pakistan should have occasioned scepticism and even mirth. The impact of this toxic rhetoric has, however, been disquieting. It excavates age-old prejudices and legitimises the marginalisation of the Muslim community. Almost 16 per cent of our own people have been rendered irrelevant. The fault lines in our society have been further deepened by leaders who should have tried to paper them over and ensure justice for all.

The marginalisation of the Muslim community is crucial because it rips the overlap between democracy, secularism and toleration. In a democracy, all citizens have the right to voice, that is the right to participate in debates in the public sphere, and the right to be represented in decision-making bodies through electoral means. Unfortunately, we cannot be sure that the interests of a minority that has been subjected to vilification, will be adequately submitted in the legislative assembly by representatives belonging to the majority community. We also cannot be assured that members of the minority community will be given enough space in the public sphere to express their views. Though representatives who are elected on the base of geographically delineated constituencies are expected to proxy for all voters, including those who did not vote for them, in communally charged situations the representation of minorities by a member of a majority group is debatable, and most probably negligible.

Lack of representation in decision-making bodies is worrying because every morning, newspapers tell us that the culture, religion and practices of minority groups, particularly the Muslims, have been targeted in perverse ways by mobs subscribing to the ideology of the Hindu right. And the Muslim minority has no one to speak for it in the Parliament and state legislatures. On the other hand, the ideology of Hindutva has drawn enough supporters to speak against them. Vulnerability is exacerbated if minorities are pushed to the margins of society through threats, intimidation, and violence. It is not surprising that members of a minority community are likely to be socially marginalised, politically insignificant in terms of the politics of 'voice' as distinct from the 'vote', humiliated, dismissed and subjected to intense disrespect in and through the practices of everyday life. This compromises democracy because some citizens do not possess full rights, just because they belong to a community that has been maligned and denigrated.

In a society dominated by the self-arrogated spokespersons of the majority Hindu community, minorities are at risk in two ways. One, their culture has been and continues to be subjected to vicious stereotyping. Cultures, whether based on religion or language, are important for human beings, because it is from here that we learn the first language that allows us to make sense of the world. Individuals are diminished because their cultural community is diminished in tangible and intangible ways. This results in fear and insecurity. Two, if individuals are diminished in the public eye, they can easily come to harm. All human beings have rights simply because they are human, and we need no other justification for the recognition that people have rights. But if individual citizens are denied rights simply because their community is cast in destructive modes, their rights are violated. Our fellow citizens might have committed no crime, done anyone an injury, broken the law, or acted in a manner that is considered disorderly. And yet they are harmed only because they are members of a community that has been disparaged in language and in action. Therefore, protection for the religious community is an essential precondition for protection of individual citizens. Minority rights are not an exception to the democratic principle, they are a condition for the fulfilment of democracy, notably equality, freedom, and justice.

To conclude, though there is a strong link between social and economic vulnerability, but there is an equally strong link between social and economic deprivation, and cultural vulnerability rooted in practices of disrespect, disregard and non-recognition. Cultural disrespect is the product of the marginalisation of a community through lack of representation, exclusion from the symbolic construction of society, and subjection to deprecating and humiliating images. Cultural disrespect means that lives, liberties, and properties are at perennial risk. People who are subjected to disrespect cease to matter. They have been rendered irrelevant.

The leaders of the freedom struggle had recognised this precise aspect of Indian society in 1928 in the Motilal Nehru Constitutional Draft. They were motivated by three considerations, one minorities should not fear that in an independent India, which is sociologically dominated by a religious majority, their cultures and their religion will be vulnerable to attacks. Two, cultures are important for individuals for many reasons, and if cultures are diminished individuals are harmed. Three, no one should be harmed only because he or she belongs to a group that has been vilified and subjected to disrespect by a majority group.

The eruption of massive communal violence during the Partition of India, caused expected reverberations in the Constituent Assembly. Mahavir Tyagi, the Congress member from the United Province in the Constituent Assembly, suggested that any consideration on minority rights should be postponed until Pakistan's stand on minorities becomes clear. However, Dr Ambedkar, the chairman of the drafting committee of the Congress, made it clear that the rights of minorities are absolute rights. These do not depend on what other parties might like to do to minorities within its jurisdiction. I think, said Dr Ambedkar, the rights indicated in the draft are rights which every minority irrespective of any other consideration is entitled to claim.[7] He added that unless minorities have rights, they might be subjected to considerable injustice at the hands of a majority. This is what we have to remember.

There is more to a good and just society than just redistribution of goods. A good society does not harm a person's self-respect by subjecting her or his community to discriminatory remarks. This gravely damages the self-esteem of the members. Consider how devalued we feel when we are told that our culture is of little or no value, and that our group should integrate with a dominant tradition or assimilate.

[7] *Constituent Assembly Debates*, 1989, Official Reports, vol. 3, Delhi Lok Sabha Secretariat, 507–508.

Cast in the mould of cultural nationalism, majoritarianism calls for the erasure of all specific identities, and demands the constitution of a culturally homogenous nation. There is cause for concern for cultural nationalism has been associated in history with Fascism and Nazism. And there is cause for concern because this form of nationalism is the product of particularly vicious notions of ethno-nationalism. Secularism and the social principle of toleration are meant to guard against these very situations.

Those scholars who attack secularism in India as based on European notions of the separation of religion and politics in the public sphere, have not perhaps, come to grips with Indian history. The Indian version of secularism codes the historical legacy of post-Independence India; the salience of religious identities, the politicisation of religion in the public sphere, the fragile line between religion as personal faith and religion as politics, and plurality of religious identities and belief systems. Secularism guaranteed the existence of a public sphere where religious identities not only lived cheeky by jowl with each other, but with also secular or non-religious value systems.

Democracy and Secularism

The concept of secularism has however been overburdened by numerous tasks, from reform of religion to nation-building. The overburdening is a product of our tormented history of religious conflict, but in the process secularism itself might collapse. The absence of the term secularism in today's political discourse in India provides enough testimony to the fragile nature of the concept. It is time to take stock of secularism within the context of democracy, and see what perhaps a reworked concept of secularism would look like. How can we recover secularism in and for a plural society that is wracked with anxieties about its own pretensions to democracy, and about the many injustices that have led to violence, and disregard for the human condition? This is what the argument in this essay seeks to emphasise.

The argument tries to strengthen secularism by locating the concept in democracy. If the basic aim of secularism as it has historically developed in India is to secure equality of all religious denominations, *the concept of secularism* is derived from the principle of equality. In fact, let me suggest that secularism gains meaning and substance only when we see it as legitimate from the perspective of democracy and its core principle of equality. Logically there is no reason why a society should be committed to secularism, unless it is committed beforehand to the concept of equality. A prior commitment to the principle of equality is a *condition* for equality of all religious groups. In effect unless a polity subscribes to the principle of equality, there is nothing that compels it to subscribe to secularism, nothing unless equality has been codified as the organising principle of the polity.

The only solution to this inequality is that majorities cannot be allowed to ride roughshod over the rights of the minorities. The minorities should be given special protection against the kind of brute force that majorities are prone to exert. This is fundamental to liberal democracy, and that is why liberal democrats control majority opinion by laying down constitutional principles, particularly fundamental rights, that trump every rule that is predetermined by the majority. If this is so, then the grant of minority rights vide article 29 and article 30 of the fundamental rights chapter of the constitution is perfectly legitimate, simply because it protects minorities against majority opinions and actions that violate of individual rights. Minority rights are accordingly not an infringement of secularism as equality of all religions; they concretise the principle of equality of all persons *irrespective* of what a majority believes at a particular point in time.

For these reasons, concept of secularism can, justifiably, be interpreted as a companion concept of democracy. Both democracy and secularism are constitutive of a just state, a state that ensures equality of status between individuals, as well as between religious communities. Democracy takes care of the first avatar of justice, the equal right of all individuals to certain goods. Secularism secures the second avatar of justice, that religious groups are not disadvantaged for arbitrary and irrelevant reasons, and that these groups have equal moral standing in society. Tolerance is a social principle that helps people understand that other human beings are entitled to be treated with dignity and their respect. Tolerance, is grammatically speaking, an unfortunate term, because it carries the implication that we must endure persons even if we do not particularly care for their opinions, beliefs and practices. The use of the term can sound patronising. However, the concept of tolerance as we have seen is normative, because it is tied up with the freedom to religion, freedom of speech, and dignity of the human body. If individuals are stripped of the right to express their opinions, hold belief systems, or the right to their practices, they are diminished. And if we, convinced of the rightness of our cause, diminish other people, we diminish ourselves in our own eyes.

Tolerance is important because the political norm of secularism alone may not be able to guard the rights of minorities to equal status. We see with a considerable amount of discomfort, how quickly the norm of secularism has been subverted and even tossed aside by the religious right the moment it came to power. It is disconcerting to see how norms, which were once thought of as the constitutive principles of a democratic state, prove dispensable once a party gets a majority in the lower house of Parliament. It is even more disturbing when the highest court in the land pronounces judgements that are deeply inimical of equality. In the 1995 Hindutva judgement. Justice Verma reiterated the definition of Hinduism first given by the Court in the 1966 case of Sastri Yagnapurushdasji versus Muldas Bhundardas or the Satsangi case. According to the earlier decision of the Court, Hinduism is an inclusive religion. Justice Verma conflating Hinduism as a religion, and Hindutva the ideology of the religious right, and inclusiveness and toleration, ruled that the latter was a way of life and could not be equated with narrow fundamentalist religious bigotry. He went further and ruled that both terms depict the way of life of the Indian people, and not only the religious community of Hindus. The word Hindutva is used and understood as a synonym for Indianisation, or the development of a uniform culture by the obliteration of differences between all cultures coexisting in the country. Therefore, these terms did not violate the provisions of the Representation of Peoples Act. He concluded that it would be unfortunate if despite the liberal and tolerant features of Hinduism recognised in earlier judicial decisions these terms are used by people to gain unfair advantage.[8] By

---

[8] Sen, *Articles of Faith*, 22–24.

identifying Hinduism and the ideology of the religious right and by identifying Indians with Hindus, the Court gave the freedom to majority political groups to mobilise constituencies in the name of religion. Notably parties that represent minorities are not given similar freedom.

It is not entirely clear whether Hinduism is tolerant of other religions or whether it seeks to include religions within its fold. The leaders of the mainstream freedom struggle argued that tolerance was a part of Hindu ethics. Hinduism was an open-ended religion, a collation of different belief systems whether they had emerged as a challenge to dominant metaphysical conceptions of the self, or come in from the outside. Swami Vivekananda spoke of Hinduism as a tolerant religion, which accepts all religions as true. Dr Radhakrishnan argued in his Upton lectures at Oxford in 1926 argued that Hinduism is not a form of thought but a way of life. The theist and the atheist, the skeptic and the agnostic are all Hindus if they accept the Hindu system of culture and life. This understanding has powerfully influenced the Supreme Court when it rules on the nature of Hinduism. In 1966 in the Yagnapurushdasji case Chief Justice P. B Gajendragadkar drawing from Radhakrishnan's conceptualisation of Hinduism, suggested that the religion does not satisfy any of the requirements of a narrow conception of religion. Hinduism is a way of life, and nothing more.[9]

This sort of reading becomes problematic in a multi-religious society where different groups hold their own unique concept of religion and of God. When the Supreme Court defines Hinduism as a way of life, as tolerant, and as exclusivist, it overlooks the fact that this conception of toleration is primarily Hindu. Other religions, for instance, the first of the Ten Commandments of Christianity forbids believers to worship any other God besides the God of the faith. Buddhists and Jains, as suggested above, do not believe in God. These conceptions take a hard knock when Hinduism with its mixture of the formless divine, and numerous idols that embody the culture and belief systems of the region, different practices that contradict each other, and different ways of worship is held to be a superior and indeed a supra-religion that can organise numerous religious communities

---

[9] Ibid.

on principles that are intrinsic to the majority religion. Tolerance is significant even important but to make it relevant for a plural society, to see it as supportive of secularism, we have to abstract the concept from its Hindu moorings. We have to secularise both secularism and toleration.

Six points might be in order before concluding the argument. One, secularism per se has little to do with inequality or injustice within religious groups. These fall within the provenance of democracy. Secularism is concerned about a weak form of equality, or non-discrimination between religious groups. The norm ensures that the state should not be aligned to one group that for this reason acquires dominance. Two, secularism is part of the democratic imaginary and is not a stand-alone concept. Three in the social world secularism will succeed in achieving its objectives if people comprehend the significance of tolerance both for themselves and for their relationship with others. Four though secularism has been presented as the binary opposite of religion, or in India communalism, it is the binary opposite of theocratic states bring together religious and political power in one set of hands, mainly the civilian executive, or the army. Five, the challenge to secularism has not come from personal faith or religion, but from religious groups that struggle for power or against power and domination. Six, the challenge is to democracy because denial of secularism catapults issues about the rights and privileges of citizenship and throws into sharp relief the intersections between religion and other concerns such as lack of voice, inadequate distribution of goods, and recognition of the distinctiveness of groups.

Finally, the coexistence between religious identity and democratic politics is not easy. There is, arguably, a fundamental discrepancy between religious and secular languages. Religion gives to believers 'thick' or comprehensive conceptions of the good that help them to make sense of the world, order their lives, and relate to others. This is the basis of religious assertions in the public sphere. The concept of secularism is, in comparison, 'thin' insofar as it establishes procedures that indicate what the place of religion in the public domain is, and what the relationship between different groups should be. I am not suggesting that secularism is not a good; merely that secularism does not tell people how to lead their lives or what to strive for. The principle of secularism contributes to the construction of a normative structure where people can pursue their faith or any other substantive conception of the good unburdened by discrimination, and where the state does not discriminate between different religious groups. The two languages pertain to different sorts of goods and are in many cases difficult to translate. But that is the nature of democratic political life, irresolvable dilemmas that can only be negotiated through the deployment of imagination and creativity in thinking and practice. Let us remember and take heart from Jawaharlal Nehru's words in the *Discovery of India*. He quotes the chorus from the Bacchae of Euripides, translated by Gilbert Murray. 'What else is wisdom? What of man's endeavour/ Or God's high grace, so lovely and so great? To stand from fear set free, to breathe and wait; To hold a hand uplifted over Hate; and shall not Loveliness be loved for ever?'[10]

[10] Nehru, *The Discovery of India*, 33.

References

Agarwal, Poonam. 2017, 28 September. 'The Dadri Truth: A Personal Grudge Twisted into a Communal Killing'. Available at: https://www.thequint.com/news/india/was-the-dadri-lynching-really-a-murder-based-on-a-personal-grudge (accessed on 26 May 2018).

Ansari, Iqbal. 1996. *Readings on Minorities: Perspectives and Documents*, vol. 1, xvi. Delhi: Institute of Objective Studies.

Ashk, Upendra. 1994. 'The Fodder Cutting Machine'. In *Stories about the Partition of India*, edited by Ashok Bhalla, vol. 3, 29–33. Delhi: Indus.

Badrinath, Chaturvedi. 2006. *The Mahabharata: An Inquiry into the Human Condition*. Hyderabad: Orient Longman.

Ballard, Roger. 1999. 'Panth, Kismet, Dharam to Quam: Continuity and Change in Four Dimensions of Punjabi Religion'. In *Punjabi Identity in A Global Context*, edited by Pritam Singh and Shinder Singh Thanddi, 7–37. New Delhi: Oxford University Press.

Benes, E. 1942, January. 'The Organisation of Postwar Europe'. *Foreign Affairs* 20 (1): 226–242.

Berger, Peter L. 1990 (1967). *The Sacred Canopy: Elements of a Sociological Theory of Religion*. New York, NY: Anchor Books.

———. 1999. *The Desecularisation of the World: Resurgent Religion and World Politics*. Washington, DC: William B. Eerdmans Publishing Company.

Bhargava, Rajeev. 1998. 'What Is Secularism For?' In *Secularism and Its Critics*, edited by R. Bhargava, 486–542. New Delhi: Oxford University Press.

———. 2010. 'The Distinctiveness of Indian Secularism'. In *Indian Political Thought: A Reader*, edited by Aakash Singh Rathore and Silika Mohapatra, 99–120. Oxon: Routledge.

Bhasin, Agrima. 2014. 'Surviving'. *The Hindu*, Sunday Magazine, 12 January, 1.

Bilgrami, Aheel. 1998. 'Secularism, Nationalism, and Modernity'. In *Secularism and Its Critics*, edited by R. Bhargava. New Delhi: Oxford University Press.

Breman, Jan. 2004. *The Making and the Unmaking of a Working Class*. New Delhi: Oxford University Press.

Brown, Judith. 2000. 'Gandhi and Human Rights: In Search of True Humanity'. In *Gandhi, Freedom, and Self-Rule*, edited by Anthony Parel, 87–101. New Delhi: Vistaar.

Canetti, Elias. 1984. *Crowds and Power*. New York, NY: Farrar, Straus and Giroux.

Casanova, Jose. 1994. *Public Religions in the Modern World*. Chicago, IL: University of Chicago Press.

Chandhoke, Neera. 1999. *Beyond Secularism: The Rights of Religious Minorities*. New Delhi: Oxford University Press.

Chandhoke, Neera, Praveen Priyadarshi, Silky Tyagi, and Neha Khanna. 2007, 27 October. 'The Displaced of Ahmedabad'. *Economic & Political Weekly* 42 (43): 10–14.

Chatterjee, Partha. 1998. 'Secularism and Tolerance'. In *Secularism and Its Critics*, edited by R. Bhargava, 380–417. New Delhi: Oxford University Press.

Constituent Assembly Debates, Official Reports, vol. 3. Delhi: Lok Sabha Secretariat.

Coomaraswamy, Ananda. 2000. 'Preface'. In *Perception of the Vedas* (Indira Gandhi Centre for the Arts), edited by Vidya Nivas Misra. New Delhi: Manohar.

Dalmia, Vasudha. 2007. 'Introduction'. In *The Oxford India Hinduism Reader*, edited by Vasudha Dalmia and Heinrich von Steitencron, 1–28. New Delhi: Oxford University Press.

Dalmia, Vasudha, and Heinrich von Stietencron. 1995. 'Introduction'. In *Representing Hinduism: The Construction of Religious Traditions and National Identity*, edited by Vasudha Dalmia and Heinrich von Stietencron, 17–34. New Delhi: SAGE Publications.

Dalmia, Vrinda. 2014. 'Care Ethics and Epistemic Justice: Some Insights from the Mahabharata'. In *Mahabharata Now: Narration, Aesthetics, Ethics*, edited by Arindam Chakrabati and Sibaji Bandyopadhyay, 115–131. New Delhi: Routledge.

Deshpande, Sharad. 2015. 'Introduction: Modern Indian Philosophy from Colonialism to Cosmopolitanism'. In *Philosophy in Colonial India*. New Delhi: Springer; Simla: Indian Institute of Advanced Studies.

Doshi, Harish. 1974. *Traditional Neighbourhood in a Modern City*. New Delhi: Abhinav Publications.

Erikson, Erik H. 1969. *Gandhi's Truth: On the Origins of Militant Nonviolence*. New York, NY: W.W. Norton and Company.

Gandhi, M. K. 1932. *From Yeravada Mandir*. Ahmedabad: Navjivan Press.

———. 1935. *Young India, 1927–28*. Madras: S. Ganesan.

———. 1961. 'Ethical Religion—VII (16–2–1907)'. In *The Collected Works of Mahatma Gandhi*, vol. VI, 330–332. New Delhi: The Publications Division, Ministry of Information and Broadcasting.

———. 1961. 'Ethical Religion—V (2–2–1907)'. In *The Collected Works of Mahatma Gandhi*, vol. VI, 312–313. New Delhi: The Publications Division, Ministry of Information and Broadcasting.

———. 1966. 'What Is Truth? (20–11–1921)'. In *The Collected Works of Mahatma Gandhi*, vol. XXI, 472–475. Ahmedabad: Navjivan Trust.

———. 1969. 'Letter to Mrs R. Armstrong and Mrs P.R. Howard (9–7–1926)'. In *The Collected Works of Mahatma Gandhi*, vol. XXXI, 111. New Delhi: The Publications Division, Ministry of Information and Broadcasting.

Gandhi, M. K. 1971. 'Speech on Fundamental Rights, Karachi Congress, The Collected Works of Mahatma Gandhi, vol. XLV, Delhi, Government of India, The Publications Division, 372–374.

———. 1986. 'Dharma and Self Purification (14 August 1932)'. In *The Moral and Political Writings of Mahatma Gandhi*, edited by Raghavan Iyer, vol. II. New Delhi: Oxford University Press.

———. 1971. 'Speech on Fundamental Rights (31 March 1931)'. In *The Collected Works of Mahatma Gandhi*, vol. XLV. New Delhi: The Publications Division, Ministry of Information and Broadcasting.

Gellner, Ernest. 1983. *Nations and Nationalisms.* Oxford: Basil Blackwell.

Ghosh, Aurobindo. 2011. 'The Renaissance in India'. In *Indian Philosophy in English*, edited by Nalini Bhushan and Jay Garfield, 39–65. New York, NY: Oxford University Press.

Gillion, Kenneth L. 1969. *Ahmedabad: A Study in Indian Urban History.* Canberra: Australian National University Press.

Gokhale, Pradeep. 2015. *Lokaya/Carvaka: A Philosophical Enquiry*, 1–48. New Delhi: Oxford University Press.

Gopal, Ram. *Lokmanya Tilak.* Bombay: Asia Publishing House.

Gopal, S. 1980, ed. *Jawaharlal Nehru: An Anthology.* New Delhi: Oxford University Press, 330.

———. 1988, November. 'Nehru and Minorities'. Special issue, *Economic & Political Weekly* 23 (45–47): 2463–2465.

Habermas, Jurgen. 2006. 'Religion in the Public Sphere'. *European Journal of Philosophy* 14 (1): 1–25.

Haider, Najaf. 2005. 'A "Holi Riot" of 1714: Versions from Ahmedabad and Delhi'. In *Living Together Separately: Cultural India in History and Practice*, edited by Mushirul Hasan and Asim Roy, 127–144. New Delhi: Oxford University Press.

Halbfass, Wilhelm. 1988. *India and Europe: An Essay in Understanding.* Albany, NY: State University of New York.

Hegel, G. W. F. 1952. *The Philosophy of Right.* Translated and with notes by T. M. Knox, edited by Robert Maynard Hutchins. Great Books of the Western World series. Chicago, IL: University of Chicago Press.

Heimsath, Charles. 1964. *Indian Nationalism and Hindu Social Reform.* Princeton, NJ: Princeton University Press.

Holmstorm, Mark. 1984. *Industry and Inequality: The Social Anthropology of Indian Labour.* Cambridge: Cambridge University Press.

Holyoake, George Jacob. 1854. 'Secularism: The Practical Philosophy of the People'. Source: Cowen Tracts, 3. Available at: http//www.jstorr.org/stable/60201761, accessed on 1 December 2018.

Honneth, Axel. 1995. *The Struggle for Recognition: The Moral Grammar of Social Conflicts.* Translated by Joel Anderson. Cambridge: Polity Press.

Jacobsohn, Gary. 2003. *The Wheel of Law: India's Secularism in Comparative and Constitutional Context.* New Delhi: Oxford University Press.

Kakar, Sudhir. 1995. *Colors of Violence*. New Delhi: Viking Press.

Khan, Nawab Iftikhar Ali. 2000. *History of the Ruling Family of Sheikh Sadruddin: Sadar-I-Jahan of Malerkotla*. Edited by R. K. Ghai. Patiala: Punjab University Press.

Kumar, Priya. 2008. *Secularism; The Ethics of Coexistence in Indian Literature and Film*. Ranikhet: Permanent Black.

Kumar, Ravinder, and Hari Dev Sharma, eds. 1995. *Selected Works of Motilal Nehru*, vol. 6. Published under the auspices of the Nehru Memorial Museum and Library. New Delhi: Vikas Publishing.

Locke, John. 1968 (1689). *A Letter Concerning Toleration*, 67. Oxford: Clarendon Press.

———. 1997. 'An Essay Concerning Toleration'. In *Locke: Political Essays*, edited by Mark Goldie, 134–59. Cambridge Texts in the History of Political Philosophy. Cambridge: Cambridge University Press.

Madan, T. N. 1998. 'Secularism in Its Place'. In *Secularism and Its Critics*, edited by R. Bhargava. New Delhi: Oxford University Press.

———. 2003. 'The Case of India'. *Daedalus* 132 (3): 62–66.

———. 2003. 'Hinduism: An Introductory Essay'. In *The Hinduism Omnibus*, edited by Nirad C. Chaudhuri, Madeleine Biardeau, D. F. Pocock, and T. N. Madan, xi–xxxvi. New Delhi: Oxford University Press.

Matilal, Bimal Krishna. 2005. *Epistemology, Logic, and Grammar in Indian Philosophical Analysis*, 2nd ed. Edited by Jonardon Ganeri. New Delhi: Oxford University Press.

———. 2014. 'Moral Dilemmas: Insights from Indian Epics'. In *Moral Dilemmas in the Mahabharata*, edited by Bimal K. Matilal, 1–19. Simla: Indian Institute of Advanced Studies; New Delhi: Motilal Banarsidass Publishers.

Mohanty, J. N. 2000. *Classical Indian Philosophy*, 1–5. New Delhi: Oxford University Press.

Mukherjee, S. N. 1968. *Sir William Jones: A Study in Eighteenth-Century British Attitudes to India*. Cambridge: Cambridge University Press.

Munshi, K. M. 1967. *Indian Constitutional Documents*, vol. 1—Pilgrimage to Freedom. Delhi: Bharatiya Vidya Bhavan.

Nandy, Ashish. 1998. *An Anti-Secularist Manifesto*. New Delhi: Oxford University Press.

Needham, Anuradha Dingwaney, and Rajeshwari Sundar Rajan, eds. 2007. *The Crisis of Secularism in India*. Ranikhet: Permanent Black.

Nehru, Jawaharlal. 1946. *The Discovery of India*, 541–47. Calcutta: The Signet Press.

———. 1976. 'Notes on Minorities'. In *Nehru: Selected Works*, edited by S. Gopal, vol. 4. New Delhi: Jawaharlal Nehru Memorial Fund and Sangam Books.

———. 1980. 'A Secular State'. In *Jawaharlal Nehru: An Anthology*, edited by S. Gopal. New Delhi: Oxford University Press.

———. 'A Common Cultural Inheritance'. In *Selected Works of Jawaharlal Nehru*, 2nd series, vol. 5, 24–26. New Delhi: Oxford University Press.

Oberoi, Harjot Singh. 1987. 'From Punjab to "Khalistan": Territoriality and Metacommentary'. *Pacific Affairs* 60 (Spring): 26–41.

———. 1994. *The Construction of Religious Boundaries: Culture, Identity and Diversity in the Sikh Tradition*. New Delhi: Oxford University Press.

Pamuk, Orhan. 2004. *Snow*, translated from Turkish by Maureen Freely. New York: Alfred N. Knopf.

Pandey, Gyanendra. 2006. *The Construction of Communalism in North India*. New Delhi: Oxford University Press.

Parekh, Bhikhu. 1999. *Colonialism, Tradition and Reform: An Analysis of Gandhi's Political Discourse*. New Delhi: SAGE Publications.

———. 2003. 'Some Reflections on the Hindu Theory of Tolerance', 1–11. Available at: http://www.india-seminar.com/2003/521/521bhikhu parekh. htm

Plato. 1996. *Apology*, 200–12. Edited by Mortimer J. Adler. Great Books of the Western World series. Chicago, IL: Encyclopedia Britannica.

Ramanujan, A. K. 1990. 'Is There an Indian Way of Thinking? An Informal Essay'. In *India through Hindu Categories*, edited by McCim Marriott, 41–58. New Delhi: SAGE Publications.

Ray Chaudhary, Anasua Basu. 2007, 24 February. 'Sabarmati: Creating a New Divide'. *Economic & Political Weekly* 42 (08): 698–699.

Raychaudhuri, Siddhartha. 2001. 'Colonialism, Indigenous Elites and the Transformation of Cities in the Non-Western World: Ahmedabad (Western India) 1890–1947'. *Modern Asian Studies* 35 (3): 677–726.

Roy, Rammohun. 1816. 'Translation of *An Abridgement of the Vedant or the Resolution of All the Vedas; the Most Celebrated and Revered Work of Brahmanical Theology; Establishing the Unity of the Supreme Being; and That He Alone Is the Object of Propitiation and Worship*'. In *The English Works of Raja Rammohun Roy, 1982*, edited by J. C. Ghosh, vol. I. New Delhi: Cosmo Publications.

Samad, Yunus. 1997. 'Reflections on Partition: Pakistan's Perspective'. *International Journal of Punjab Studies* 4 (1): 43–46.

Schama, Simon. 1989. *Citizens: A Chronicle of the French Revolution*. London: Penguin.

Schlegal, Friedrich. 1849. 'On the Language and Wisdom of the Indians'. In *The Aesthetic and Miscellaneous Works of Frederick von Schlegel*, translated and edited by E. J. Millington, 425–526.

Sen, Amartya. 'Secularism and Its Discontents'. In *Secularism and Its Critics*, edited by R. Bhargava, 454–487. New Delhi: Oxford University Press.

Sen, Ronojoy. 2010. *Articles of Faith, Religion, Secularism, and the Indian Supreme Court*. New Delhi: Oxford University Press.

Shah, Ghanshyam. 1970, January. 'Communal Riots in Gujarat: Report of a Preliminary Investigation'. *Economic & Political Weekly* 5 (3–5): 187–200.

Shakespeare, William. 1994 (1599). 'The Tragedy of Julius Caesar'. In *The Oxford Shakespeare*, edited by Stanley Wells and Gary Taylor, 599–641. Oxford: Oxford University Press.

Shakespeare, William. 1994 (1601). 'The Tragedy of Hamlet Prince of Denmark'. In *The Oxford Shakespeare*, edited by Stanley Wills and Gary Taylor. Oxford: Oxford University Press.

Smith, Adam. 1996. *An Inquiry into the Nature and Causes of the Wealth of Nations*. edited by Mortimer J. Adler. Great Books of the Western World series, vol. 36. Chicago, IL: Encyclopedia Britannica.

Smith, W. C. 1963. *The Meaning and End of Religion: A New Approach to the Religious Traditions of Mankind*. New York, NY: Macmillan.

Sri Aurobindo. 1959. *The Foundations of Indian Culture*. Pondicherry: Sri Aurobindo Ashram.

Stietencron, Heinrich. 2007. 'Religious Configuration in Medieval India and the Modern Concept of Hinduism'. In *The Oxford India Hinduism Reader*, edited by Vasudha Dalmia and Heinrich Stietencron, 50–89. New Delhi: Oxford University Press.

Swami Vivekananda. 1907. 'Addresses at the Parliament of Religion'. In *The Complete Works of Swami Vivekananda*, Mayavati Memorial ed., vol. 1. Calcutta: Advaita Ashram.

Thapar, Romila. 1989. 'Imagined Religious Communities? Ancient History and the Modern Search for a Hindu Identity'. *Modern Asian Studies* 3 (2): 209–231.

———. 1999. 'Syndicated Hinduism'. In *Hinduism Reconsidered*, edited by Gunther-Dietz Sontheimer and Hermann Kulke, 54–81. New Delhi: Manohar.

The Mahabharata of Krishna-Dwaipayana Vyasa. Translated by Kisari Mohan Ganguly, vol. VIII, Santi Parva, Part I. Delhi: Munshiram Manoharlal Publishers.

The Telegraph. 2016. 'SC: Religion Bigger Poll Evil Than Caste', *The Telegraph*, 26 October 2016, http://www.telegraphindia.in, accessed on 1 December 2018.

Vanaik, Achin. 1997. *Communalism Contested: Religion, Modernity and Secularisation*. New Delhi: Vistaar.

Waseem, Mohammd. 1999. 'Partition, Migration and Assimilation: A Comparative Study of Pakistan Punjab'. In *Region and Partition: Bengal, Punjab and the Partition of the Subcontinent*, edited by Ian Copland and Gurharpal Singh, 203–227. New York: Oxford University Press.

Yagnik, Achyut, and Suchitra Sheth. 2005. *The Shaping of Modern Gujarat: Plurality, Hindutva and Beyond*. New Delhi: Penguin.

Index

About the Author

Neera Chandhoke held a professorship in the Department of Political Science, University of Delhi. She has been a visiting fellow at the Centre for the Study of Law and Governance, Jawaharlal Nehru University, New Delhi, India; Justitia Amplificata, Goethe University, Frankfurt, Germany; Centre for Ethics and Global Politics, Luiss University, Rome, Italy; and Centre for Civil Society, London School of Economics and Political Science, London, United Kingdom. She was awarded the Gaetano Mosca Fellowship at the University of Turin, Torino, Italy. She has been a Jawaharlal Nehru National Fellow, and a fellow at the Centre for Contemporary Studies, Nehru Memorial Museum and Library, Teen Murti Bhawan, New Delhi. She has published on civil society—*Democracy and Revolutionary Politics*; *Contested Secessions: Self-Determination, Democracy and Kashmir*; *Beyond Secularism: The Rights of Religious Minorities* and *State and Civil Society: Explorations in Political Theory*—and is a regular contributor to academic journals and newspapers. Her interests include reading particularly detective novels, listening to music and watching films.